WORLD LITERATURE
IN TRANSLATION

A Jew

MEÏR GOLDSCHMIDT

Translated with an Afterword by
KENNETH H. OBER

GARLAND PUBLISHING, INC.
NEW YORK & LONDON 1990

Library of Congress Cataloging-in-Publication Data

Goldschmidt, Meïr, 1819–1887.
    [Jøde. English]
    A Jew/Meïr Goldschmidt; translated by Kenneth H. Ober.
        p. cm.—(Garland library of world literature in translation;
v. 7)
    Translation of: En Jøde.
    ISBN 0-8240-2993-3
    I. Title. II. Series.
PT8129.G5J613   1989
839.8'136—dc20 89-16882

Book and cover design by
Renata Gomes

Printed on acid-free, 250-year-life paper
Manufactured in the United States of America

»Og Fjendskab vil jeg sætte imellem Dig og Kvinden og imellem Din Æt og hendes Æt. Den skal knuse Dit hoved, og Du skal saare dens Hæl.«

1ste Mose Bog, 3die Kap., 15de Vers.

"I will put enmity between you and the woman, and between your seed and her seed; he shall bruise your head, and you shall bruise his heel."

Genesis 3:15

This translation was made from the second edition, which was revised by the author and which appeared in 1852. The footnotes are those of the author. Translator's comments are enclosed in square brackets.

Part One

Chapter 1

"WHAT IS THAT NOISE, I wonder?" said Philip Bendixen softly, cautiously pushing the shutters out and opening the window to the early summer morning. He saw several townspeople hurrying down the street, and waved at the closest one, but the latter did not notice him, and he did not dare to call out for fear of disturbing his sleeping wife. "I think I hear a drum," he said and closed the window, "I wonder what it can be?"

Carefully he stole out into the shop, where his clerk Benjamin, half asleep although dressed, was shoving the heavy iron crossbar from the front door.

"Don't stand there asleep, *hamor*!"[1] said Philip Bendixen in a muffled, angry voice; "Run over to my brother-in-law and see if you can find out what's going on in town."

Benjamin tried to hurry, and in his haste the iron bar fell over as he put it down.

"*Krieg die mise Meschunno!* May all the bad luck in the world happen!" Philip burst out; "If that's not a racket to make for my poor wife! God of Israel, help her . . . Hear that, now she's calling! You waked her up, *ohs*!"[2]

"What's wrong with your wife?" asked Benjamin.

"I don't know from one minute to the next when I'll have to send for the midwife!" said Philip, furious over Benjamin's calmness; "Now do you understand, *beheimo*?"[3]

In an instant the shutters were taken down and the door was opened, and Benjamin dashed off to the brother-in-law, who lived diagonally opposite.

---

[1] Fool.

[2] Carrion, evil person.

[3] Blockhead.

A little later the brother-in-law came over with his wife. He went cheerily with her into the front room where Philip's wife had taken her place at the breakfast table. "Ah, how is Madam?" he said, addressing Jette; "May it please Madam to be strong today. We don't have time for any foolishness; the Spaniards are deserting. Madam might be scared by the shots, although nobody wants to do her any harm."

"*Schema Yisroel!*[4] She's getting pains!" cried the sister as she dashed to the door to call the maid.

Philip pulled Isak Bamberger out the door with him. "How careless of you to talk like that and scare her!" he said reprovingly.

"Careless?" said Isak; "Doesn't she know me well enough to know that I don't want to scare her? . . . Just listen to them beating drums and shooting! Wasn't it after all best that she was prepared for it?"

Loud drumbeats resounded on the street, so that the windows rattled; after the drummers marched the militia, whose teeth were chattering in competition with the windows. Isolated cannon shots boomed out—it was uncertain where; confused shouts crisscrossed each other from the neighboring houses.

But through all this noise there was a sudden scream from the bedroom. Isak Bamberger's face became very serious, and without saying a word he went over to his own house. Philip Bendixen in his terror ran first to the door to the bedroom, but turned around and fled out into the courtyard. While his spirit was in the house, his body moved of its own volition. He ran into the stall to the cows and began to fill their troughs with feed; then he dashed out to the pump and filled a pail; but every time he pumped it full he poured it out in the gutter.

At last the top half of the kitchen door opened, and the midwife appeared in the opening. She waved and called, "A son, Mr. Bendixen! A son! Congratulations!"

---

[4] "Hear, Israel!" A cry of fright.

Philip sprang away from the pump. "A son!" he cried as he put his hand to his head, "*Adonoi Elohenu! Gebenscht sei Dein Nome!*[5] A son! A son!"

With his cheeks wet with tears he ran in after the midwife. "Let me come in and kiss my son and his mother!"

"Oh sure! No, you go out and pump some more," said the midwife, slamming the door.

"I will be patient," he said, "I won't rush things. God has presented me with a son! I am father to a son!"

He hurried out into the shop. "My wife has had a son!" he cried, embracing Benjamin and kissing him.

"*Mazol tov!*"[6] said Benjamin.

"*Jeschar-koach, Rabbi Benjomin,*[7] *jeschar-koach!*" cried Philip in his ineffable happiness.

"Listen, Benjamin," he said after a moment, "It's best that you run right over and report this to Rabbi Jokuf; he'll have to be *mohel.*[8] Also report to Simon Nasche and the other Jews in town that my wife has had a son. Where is my brother-in-law? That's right, he went home. Run over to him and say that he's welcome to come back. . . . Wait a minute, Benjamin!" he shouted as the latter was already out the door; "There, take a pound of coffee and a couple of pounds of sugar and a little rice and grits and this money and take it to old Marthe. Tell her that it's so that she can have a happy day on account of my son's birth. . . . My son! Oh, I have a son!"

Almost as quickly as this had taken place in the house, the militia was delivered of its terror. It had been out to see the Spaniards happily and well board the English ships, and it could have been a question as to who was now happier, the Spaniards or the militia in the little Funen town.

Now the Jews were in for it. Because they had not joined the militant mob, they were called cowards to whom love of the fatherland and civic-mindedness were utterly alien. Several

---

[5] "Lord, our God! blessed be Thy name!"

[6] "Congratulations."

[7] (Literally: "May your strength increase.") "Thanks, Mr. Benjamin."

[8] Can perhaps be translated by "act as godfather."

small groups stopped on their way to the tavern for a moment in front of individual Jews' houses and made their great contempt known through energetic shouts.

"*Kemech,*[9] when you come to think of it, are funny people," said Isak Bamberger when one such small group had sent its greeting in to Philip, as he looked after them with an ironic eye; "They won't put up with Jews serving with them in the army when there is peace, and as soon as there is war, they curse the Jews out because they don't serve. I think I'll go over and curse out my watchdog because it always stays at home."

"Who cares about that? Let them yell!" answered Philip Bendixen as he listened outside his wife's room.

•   •   •

Eight days later, the little family was assembled around the new mother's bed, and the congratulators gathered to celebrate the little boy's reception into the Jewish community. Everybody naturally poured out his admiration of the boy's healthy and lively appearance. Old Rabbi Jokuf placed on the cradle a *horro*— a gold coin in which was incised a Hebrew blessing that protected the child against evil eyes—as he solemnly said, "May he be as strong as Judah and as blessed with riches as Asser."

Isak drank a glass of wine and cried, "Yes, that's all very well, but I still insist that it was not a reasonable time to celebrate a birth. If the lad were at least a Christian, then the uproar during which he was born might mean that he was to become a great hero. But as a Jew it will only give him double the aversion to all war and strife; he will definitely be so cowardly that even Jews will call him cowardly."

Everybody laughed except the mother; for women by nature have a chivalrous turn of mind and prefer to give birth to heroes. She said, "Now, now, Isak! If the boy grows up under your eye and looks at your big saber every day, then maybe he won't be that scared."

---

[9] (Coarse flour.) Christians.

"Agreed!" cried the uncle, "I will bring him up! First let him suck, since that I cannot do, and then let him come to me for schooling."

It is best that we right here make the readers more closely acquainted with this uncle, who took on himself an Aristotle's role with the Funen Philip's son. He was—what is rarely the case among Jews—a tall and very strong man. In town they told the story about him that once when two farmers started a fight in his shop he picked them up, one in each arm, knocked their heads together a few times, and then threw them out. Although he was hated as a Jew and envied as a rich man, he still always inspired respect in the other townspeople whenever they saw his powerful figure among them, and the grey sparkling eyes—half whimsical, half challenging—regarded them. His hair was already beginning to turn grey—he was something over fifty. In his youth in Germany, his native land, he had served in the war against the French, and after various adventures and vicissitudes had come to Denmark, where he settled down and married. His wife brought him no dowry, and various misfortunes plunged him into extreme poverty. Afterward he used to tell with a certain pride that one whole winter he had supported himself and his wife with a capital of two rix-dollars, which he converted into goods with which he "went to the country." One Friday evening he came home, found his house burned down, his wife sick, and his only child dead. Calmly he observed his Sabbath, buried his child on Sunday, and set forth again with his capital, in a bundle of scarves, under his arm. Now he lived in a big house and was a rich man; but he never failed to remark, at the sight of a two-rix-dollar bill, that his big house had had its origins in such a bill, and from that presumably came the almost superstitious reverence he cherished for rix-dollar bills.

Philip Bendixen, the young father, was a quiet and peaceable man. Servants, who most frequently give the surest information concerning their masters' character, were of the opinion that he was only bad when he became angry, for he was very slow to regain his good temper. In his bachelor days there had been a rumor that he was living too roisterously and transgressing the

7

rituals, but it was a doubtful and obscure rumor, and in any case it was certain that after his betrothal he had returned to religion with redoubled fervor and bitterly reproached those who neglected it.

Late in the evening after the boisterous day of congratulations Philip Bendixen stepped into the little bedroom. His wife was sleeping peacefully behind the white hangings; the Jewish matron who had volunteered to sit with her had collapsed in her chair in a light sleep; the red-cheeked child slumbered in its cradle, and the night lamp cast its dim light on its pillow.

Philip took in his cosy bliss with a long look; his heart swelled, and he covered his head and prayed: "Almighty Father! Ruler of the world! I thank you for giving me a son to recite *kaddish*[10] over my grave. If it is Your will, let it happen soon! If it please You, take all happiness from my head and bestow it on my son. I will bow down in the dust and bless Your name, if only he is happy!"

Such a blessing was pronounced over the cradle of the child who is the hero in this story.

---

[10] Requiem.

Chapter 2

AS THE CHILD GREW UP, his father pronounced another blessing over his son:

"He shall not go to school. He shall not suffer *risches*[1] from the other boys and learn mischief. When he gets old enough I myself will teach him what a Jew needs to know; then I will send him to Copenhagen."

No one was happier over this decision than the uncle; as a result of it he would be able to occupy himself with the child to his heart's content. He would often run over and take the boy from his mother and carry him home. Then he would go to a side room and shut himself in with the child, so that one might have thought that he was practicing some sort of magic. If one had spied on Isak Bamberger, one would perhaps have been confirmed in this belief, seeing his strange motions. First he hopped around on the floor with the boy in his arms and hooted in his ear, trumpeted, drummed, and imitated a horse's neighing, a cow's lowing, and a dog's barking. When the child then laughed aloud and scratched him in the face, he would sit down and ride him on his knee with such violence that Jacob, after a fruitless attempt to find it enjoyable, would burst out crying. Then the uncle would take him hard by the ear, stare fiercely at him until he stopped crying, and say, "I'll teach you to be scared, boy!" He would persist in staring him in the eye and making faces until both broke into roars of laughter, then would spring up again, dance around, and press the child so affectionately and violently to his breast that it would again cry and want to go home. "Do be quiet, Jacob!" said Isak disheartened, "and I'll tell you stories. Don't tell them at home that I hurt you! All right?"—"No," sobbed the

---

[1] Malice toward Jews, persecution of Jews.

9

boy.—"Good comrade, as little as you are!" cried the uncle; "Listen to this!" And then he told about soldiers and about cavalrymen and about foreign lands, or Bible stories about Jewish heroes, so that the child at a later time did not remember having learned these legends, but almost imagined having been born with them.

The father often said, when he saw Isak running off with the child, "You have the boy with you too much, Isak! He'll end up not knowing who his father really is."

"I can always be just as good a father to him as you can!" answered Isak. "The boy will become smart, being with me," continued the uncle, "just see what an intelligent face he already has."

"Do you really think he got that with you?" asked Jette roguishly.

"If he hasn't been out in town to steal it!" cried the uncle. "Where else is he supposed to have gotten it from?—He can already say his *krischmo*[2] by heart—who has taught him that? And now I'll teach him to *bensch* from the table."[3]

"Oh, yes, Isak!" said the father, "You keep him only till he is six; then it is my duty as a father to teach him what he as a Jew should learn."

"You both teach him too much; you talk too intelligently with him," said the mother anxiously. "The boy needs to talk sensibly in his own way among other children and run and play in the fresh air."

The child looked at its mother as if it understood her, as if she had discovered the right medicine for the greedy void that was making its cheeks pale.

The uncle cried, "Tomorrow without fail I'll walk with him a good distance down the highway!"

---

[2] The Jews' creed (Schema Yisroel), recited in all the day's prayers. Here the evening prayer is meant.

[3] To say a prayer of thanks after the meal.

Chapter 3

YOU LUCKY PEOPLE, who can say, "That was a childhood playmate of mine!" Do you really know what this single word means? Doesn't it speak of green meadows where you ran and played in childish gaiety, or of the little courtyard where you gathered with the neighbor's boys and fought and cried—how you would like to cry like that again!—or of the dark parlor where you were supposed to play nice and quietly because Grandfather was sleeping in the next room, where you did play quietly, too, until the joy soared and you forgot Grandfather and the whole world—then suddenly there stood the old man kindly threatening in the door and asked, "Just let me sleep a quarter of an hour yet." Or of the thousands of pranks you later perpetrated as schoolboys: of the greengrocer's oranges which were stacked in a pyramid in the window, and which to his great amazement rolled down because you pressed on the window? Of the cellar woman's cat to which you tied a couple of balloons, so that she had to chase it as if it were her canary? . . . Doesn't it speak of the little girl for whom you both wanted to pick flowers, and for whose sake you became enemies—you yourselves didn't know why.

It was that time when you received the first filing down in order later to fit into the active game called the world. It was that time when the intellect was being prepared to put forth and bear life's blossoms—friendship and love—but also when you all were being molded in the same form, so that your characters present almost the same uniformity as your dress.

Jacob grew up alone. He had no playmates; for the other Jewish families in the town had no children of his age, and the Christian children would abuse him when they saw him. Although his name was Jacob, they called him Moses, and when he approached, they made signs with their hands under their chins as if to ridicule his beard. Generally it happened, when he played with them, that they gradually made him the object of their games, shouted "kike," and poked at him. When it became too much for him, he would walk away from them and from a distance longingly watch their games. In spite of everything he would have so liked to be together with them. This persecution had begun so early that it had never occurred to him to search for the reason for it; it was no more the object of his wonderment than was the fact that he had been born and was alive—he had after all been born with it; he believed that was the way it should be.

Once his maternal uncle came from another town for a visit and brought his little son along. The boy in a friendly fashion went up to Jacob, who recoiled shyly, but when the boy persisted in his friendly attitude and approached more closely, Jacob, his big brown eyes stiffly fixed on him, asked, "Why aren't you calling me 'kike'?"

All those present were taken aback by this unexpected outburst.

"They have made *risches* with the poor boy," the uncle finally said.

The father went over and took his son's head in his hands and kissed him with trembling lips. But Uncle Isak cried out, "Who called you kike, Jacob?"

"That's what the boys down at the beach always say," answered Jacob.

The next day Uncle Isak went with him down to the beach; but when the boys saw the tall man, they were naturally silent. Isak Bamberger nevertheless could not control himself, but ran over and seized a boy, whom he hurled into the middle of the gang. When Jacob saw this, it was suddenly clear to him why his father had kissed him the day before, and why Uncle Isak had come with him. In a single quick flash the memory of the insult he had endured pierced the child's soul. Like a freed tiger he threw himself on one of the boys, knocked him down, and hung onto him in a fury. His uncle, who thought it was an ordinary fight, shouted his approval, but when he saw blood flowing from the other boy, he rushed over and pulled his nephew away. Seeing Jacob's deathly pale cheeks, blue lips, and clenched teeth, his eyes seemingly glazed, and his hands full of hair from the boy's head, he thought his nephew had become ill. He had him put to bed and sent for a doctor. The child slept for several hours and awoke then as if from a fainting spell, apparently without any recollection of what had happened.

But Isak Bamberger had to appear before the municipal authorities on account of the children he had injured when he threw one into the midst of the others. He had to pay a good number of his precious banknotes to get the matter settled amicably with the parents, and in order to avoid similar unpleasantnesses in the future it was decided that Philip Bendixen's property that went down to the beach should be enclosed by a high board fence.

Then Jacob would sit here for many an hour, by the board fence separated from the entire rest of the world, with only the broad strait with its few sailboats spread out for the eye. Solitary and still, he wandered among flowers and trees and contemplated the proud sea, when it smilingly bathed in the sun or darkly and threateningly rolled toward the shore.

There in his solitude he created for himself a whole world, in which there were no other persons than those he knew, and among whom the principal role was played by the one who occupied him the most—himself. When he was scolded or was hurt he took refuge here and told himself of another state in which things went better for him. These little episodes little by little expanded into coherent fantasies, in which each new event he experienced gave rise to a new chapter. But the most important in all this always remained the memory of the boys at the beach, his longing for them and his animosity toward them. When one of them had met him on the street and greeted him in a friendly way, he went down into the garden and enumerated for himself all the good things he would give this boy. He would tell himself a story about how this boy was in danger and how he then would dash up and rescue him, and how the rescued boy would show his gratitude by climbing over the board fence into the garden every day, in mortal peril, and playing with him.

But when—what happened most often—one of the boys from the beach met Jacob and, relying on the uncle's absence, repeated the slurs while dashing by him, he would go down into the garden and tell himself:

"Then I set fire to the grainfields by catching jackals and tying torches to them. They searched for me, but every time they came, I put them to flight. But then once I was sleeping and they found me and tied me up. And then they put me in their temple between the two pillars holding it up, and they thought they had me secure, and ran around me yelling, 'Kike! Jew, can you eat pork and cream, too!' But then I grasped the pillars and lifted them with a powerful arm, so that the whole building fell, over them and over me as well." . . . A cold shiver ran down his back, he closed his eyes, he felt the sinking and the collapse every time he, by way of various beginnings, came to this part. Then he would be close to tears from the pain of having had to kill them.

Chapter 4

THESE FANTASIES DEVELOPED and became too strong for the boy; they were spirits he had conjured up and did not understand how to control. They lay like mists in his head until he approached the place where their home and birthplace were; then they came alive and beat their wings and took possession of the child. He suffered from them; they caused his head to swim and his nerves to tremble, and nevertheless they had a secret allure that, as often as he could be alone, drew him to the solitary place in the garden.

Once as he was sitting there with his eyes convulsively closed and fear trickling through every vein, his father came strolling up. That day there were no people in the shop and no work in the house for the industrious man, and he called to his son, "What are you doing there, Jacob?"

Jacob started up and replied, "Nothing."

"It's high time that you were learning something proper," said Philip. "Your uncle preaches your ears full of stories—come along, and we'll begin on *ol'phbeis*".[1]

An instinct told Jacob that in his father's company he would find the best protection against the frightful fantasies, and he happily clasped his father's hand.

"I haven't yet given you your *arbakanfos*,[2] either, although you are going on seven," continued his father, shaking his head over his negligence. "We must hurry, Jacob! From now on you

---

[1] The Hebrew alphabet.

[2] A rectangular piece of cloth with a hole in the middle for putting on over the shoulders. In each corner are braided threads, *tsitsis*. It is the sign of the Jews' pure religion and pure pact with God.

should know that you are a Jew and should get acquainted with your religion."

"Yes, father," said Jacob, secretly proud of the maturity bestowed on him.

The father now continued daily and with great zeal to instruct his son, and Jacob used all his time to fix in his mind what he learned, for when he fastened his thoughts on this, the fantasies had no power. He revived like a plant that has been watered, and his cheeks became red again. But his mother often scolded and said that the child was being overtaxed.

"Certainly not, no," interrupted his father once; "He likes to do it himself. Besides, he knows what I have promised him if he is diligent."

With these words he looked over at Jacob as if there were a great secret between them.

"Well, what have I promised you, Jacob?" asked his father. "Don't you remember what I promised you if you knew *Schemonesreh*?[3] Don't you remember that? What do we have on Monday?"

"Purim!" cried Jacob. "Will we go in disguise then, father?"

"No, but you'll go with me to *schul*[4] then, and hear the *megilla*[5] and be permitted to beat Homon."

"Who is that, father? Why should I beat him?"

"Don't you know him? He was the one who wanted to kill all the Jews in a single night; but our Lord was with the Jews, and Homon was himself hanged. See this device here: when you pull on the string, the hammer falls down and hits Homon's name. Every time his name is read out in the *megilla*, you pull on the string and beat him."

"I'd rather beat the real Homon, father."

"He's dead, my boy" said the father laughing with pleasure at his son's zeal. "You're supposed to beat his name when we grownups read it out."

"No, I don't want to," said Jacob.

---

[3] The eighteen prayers.

[4] The synagogue.

[5] The story of Esther and Haman.

"Why don't you want to, Jacob? Don't you want to beat Homon, who wanted to kill the Jews?"

"No, I don't want to!" shouted the boy again, beginning to cry.

"All right, you won't have to; you shouldn't cry because of that," said his father, patting him. "But study hard anyway, and at *Pesach*[6] you will sit beside me and read the *Haggadah*[7], and then I'll tell you everything that's in it."

"Oh, tell me right now," pleaded Jacob, drying his eyes.

"No, you only talk about that at *Pesach* time."

"How long is it till *Pesach*, father?"

"Four weeks; study hard and be good till that time."

The eagerly awaited Passover celebration then arrived, as could be sensed several days in advance from the preparations. A ship brought a well-sealed box from Copenhagen; it was carefully placed in a remote corner in the loft to avoid contact with anything impure, for it contained *matzos*, unleavened bread. All the house's glassware was placed in water for three days, the copper and iron ware were purified by fire, and on the last day before the holiday the entire house was cleaned and all the *chometsdicke* vessels[8] were set aside and the *jomtovdicke* vessels[9] were taken out of the hiding-places where they had stood the whole year.

Toward evening, when the first star appeared in the sky, the father wandered through the house with a quill in one hand and a wooden vessel in the other, to sweep up all the leftovers of *chometz* he could find and in this way to make certain of the purity of the house. Crumbs of leavened bread had been put down by the housewife for him to find; but under the sofa she had hidden a large crock of butter, since she would later have to prepare food for the domestic help.

---

[6] Passover.

[7] The book about the Exodus from Egypt.

[8] *Chomets*, anything leavened; all vessels that are not usable in the Passover feast because they cannot be purified from leavening, such as porcelain, wooden utensils, etc.

[9] Ceremonially pure.

After the father, quietly praying, had swept up the crumbs and was leaving the room, Jacob, who had attentively followed him, said, "Father! Mother has hidden a crock of butter under the sofa."

"Hush, boy," cried his father, going to the door, "I'm not supposed to know that, or else I have to take it along and burn it."

"But, father," said Jacob, "then you're doing like the customs officer when you give him money."

"For God's sake, boy! Your mouth can get me into trouble," said his father anxiously as he went out the door.

The next day, *Eref Pesach*, passed in reverent preparation for the feast. The father fasted on behalf of his son, for on that day the Lord's angel had slain the Egyptians' first-born and spared the Jews'. "Today and for a few years more I'll fast for you," his father affectionately said to Jacob. "When you are thirteen you'll pay your debt to our Lord yourself."

The other members of the family dared not eat leavened things; but unleavened bread they did not dare to taste, either, before it was consecrated, when night came on and the stars came out in the sky.

When it got dark, Isak Bamberger and his wife came over—for they had no children to have the feast for—and everybody went into the main room where the Passover table was set, radiant with candles.

A seat of honor covered with cushions was set up for the head of the house; on the table, covered with a dazzling white napkin, stood the *Seder* vessel—a large dish with *matzos*, sweet and bitter herbs, and the bone of a lamb; a bottle of sweet raisin wine was set before each place.

The father took his place in the seat of honor, dressed in a smock, the fine linen garment which the bride presents to the bridegroom on their wedding day, and he wears, besides on Passover feasts, only on *Yom Kippur*, the great day of atonement, and when he is laid in his coffin.

After a fervent thanksgiving to the Lord who has given the Passover feast, the bread, wine, and herbs were blessed. Two large pieces of the Passover bread, *afikomon*, were put away in the seat of honor in order later to be distributed among those present as amulets against dangers on sea and on land.[10]

Then the *Haggadah*, the book about the slavery in Egypt and the liberation, was read aloud by the head of the house for the small, devout congregation. At the enumeration of Egypt's plagues, each dipped his little finger in the wine and sprinkled a drop on the floor for each plague.

When he had read of the deliverance, Philip paused and gave Benjamin a signal: amidst a profound silence, the latter rose and opened all the doors in the house. The head of the house poured a glass of wine and broke a piece of the unleavened bread and placed both at his side, as if he expected one more guest.

Benjamin returned and sat down, and suddenly they all joined in a fervent prayer: that God would send his deliverance and happiness to the people who at that moment over the whole world opened their doors for His grace.

Everybody sat bent over the book, without raising his eyes, as if not to see what at that moment came in the door.

When the prayer was ended, the doors were shut, and the wine and the bread were removed to a side table to stand overnight, so that during the entire festival night the house could be prepared hospitably to receive *Elio Novi*, the prophet Elijah, him who is to come and announce the Messiah.[11]

Now the house was filled with grace and sanctified to receive God's messenger, and now the master of the house cast a cheery glance at the assemblage and extended his hand to beat time to the song:

---

[10] But it is permitted to sneak these pieces of bread from the head of the house, and when he then is to distribute them and can not find them, he must ransom the *afikomon* with a present.

[11] Cf. Malachi: IV, 5, "Behold, I will send you Elijah the prophet before the great and terrible day of the Lord comes."

Adir hu! jivne beshro bekorov!
Bimhero!
Bimhero!
Bejomenu! bekorov!
El bene!
El bene!
Bene beshro bekorov![12]

The joy mounted and became almost wild; they were singing Danish, German, and Hebrew indiscriminately; each gave God the most affectionate appellations:

Sweet God! Great God! Blessed God! Gebenschte God!
Reicher Gott! Starker Gott! Gewaltiger Gott!
Nun bau Dein Tempel schier!
Und also bau!
Und also schier!
And build Your temple schier!—schier!—jo schier![13]
El *bene! etc.*

Higher and higher swirled the exultation; the adults sang with tears in their eyes, and the child beat time on the table with a glass in one hand and a bottle in the other and wept with joy so that the clear tears rolled down his cheeks.

The frugal meal was brought in—for on this evening, in contrast to the other festivals, simple dishes are eaten, because the forefathers on this evening, dressed for a journey, in fear held the last, quickly prepared meal in the land of Egypt—and people entertained themselves by recalling all the wonderful deeds with which at that time God had stood by the Jews. With intense colors the father depicted the Jews' slavery and afflictions, which went so far that the king's henchmen came and took their male children and killed them so that the Jews would not become too

---

[12] Great is God! Soon he will build up the temple!
Soon may it happen!
Soon may it happen!
In our days may it be built!
Build up your house!
Build up your house!
Build the temple in our days!

[13] "Schier": quickly, soon; "jo schier": yes, soon.

numerous and rise up against their oppressors; but, he said, it was just this atrocity that became the Jews' salvation, in that Moses thereby came to Pharaoh's court and was brought up to be a military commander and a lawgiver.

The evil King Pharaoh already sensed at an early stage what potential was in Moses, and was plagued by ominous dreams about him, and without God's help the child would have been killed. For the king called together his dream-interpreters and took counsel with them, and they advised him to put the child to the test by having two vessels brought, one with gold and one with coals; if the child reached for the gold, it was a bad sign, and it should die; but if it reached for the fire, then it was harmless, and the dream meant nothing. When the vessels were brought, Moses was already reaching for the gold, but God's angel caught his hand and conducted it to the fire. The boy then picked up a coal and when it burned his tender fingers, he stuck his hand in his mouth, as children will, and that is why Moses did not talk well.

"And," said the uncle smiling, "that is why Moses' entire people became clever, and ever after reached for the gold instead of the coals."

"That may very well be," answered Philip laughing.

It had gotten late, and after saying grace everybody went to bed.

When Jacob got into bed he felt no fear for the fantasies that sometimes still would come in the dark and visit him. He had acquired an object other than the boys to think about and to yearn for; that was the beloved being they called God. He said to himself, as he snuggled under the covers, "Now I will no longer do any harm to the boys; when they deserve it, the God of the Jews will do it."

The next evening of the festival his father told the story of Joseph and his brothers, particularly about the journey to Egypt and the efforts the brothers made to get Benjamin ransomed. When it seemed that it wouldn't succeed without compulsion, related his father, and since Judah feared that he wouldn't bring Benjamin back to his old father, he decided to show Joseph what sort of people he was dealing with. Two of them, Simeon and Levi, had after all waged war against a king on account of their sister, had taken his city and killed all the males. Judah said to Naphtali, "Run over quickly and count how many marketplaces (places of assembly) there are in this city." Naphtali ran and came back quickly and said, "There are twelve marketplaces and in each marketplace there are many men." "Good," said Judah, "I will kill the men in three of the marketplaces. You others each take a marketplace and clear it." Thereupon he uttered a cry, the war cry of the sons of Jacob, and it was so powerful that the earth shook and the king fell down off his throne. Then Joseph's son Manasseh stepped over to Judah and laid his hand on his shoulder. Judah hastily turned around and said, astonished and joyful, "That hand's strength is of my father's house!" And to Manasseh's father, Joseph, he said, "You are no Egyptian, but you are one of us; you must be Joseph, whom we believed dead!" And then Joseph made himself known.

"There are no such giant warriors any more among the Jews," said Philip sadly; "For that reason we are oppressed, you see."

"Oh, yes, there are, too—Uncle Isak!" cried Jacob.

"Do you really think so, you little rascal?" said his uncle, flattered. "No, no; but it was also only in those times that such roars were tolerated; nowadays you would get trouble from the king if you yelled so loudly."

"It was really odd that Judah could yell so loudly that the king fell down off his throne," remarked Jacob.

"In my day," said Isak, turning confidentially to Philip, "while I was still in Germany, the Frenchmen yelled so loudly that their *melech*[14] fell down and broke his neck."

"Yes, at that time there were *mackos Mizraim*[15] over the great!" said Philip.

"Yes, and then they were so friendly, even to us Jews, and called us patriotic."

"What was that you said, Uncle?" asked Jacob.

"It was nothing, my boy, it was something we Germans were fighting over with the French."

---

[14] King.

[15] The plagues of Egypt.

"Oh, Uncle, tell something about the French, like you usually do. Tell the story about how they caught you and thought you were a girl. You have often promised me that!"

"Not this evening, my boy; on *yomtovim*[16] you don't talk about such things; but now I'll tell you why the Jews in Gnesen don't wear *kittels* on *Yom Kippur*."[17]

"What is a *kittel*, Uncle?"

"It's a kind of linen coat, like your father has on this evening.—You see, the Jews in Gnesen for a long time had no peace in their houses. Every night something would come walking in the door, now at one's house, now at another's, and the next day there was always somebody sick in the house where it had happened. Then the rabbi ordered them all to put up new *mezuzos*[18] because the old ones had become *posul*,[19] and that helped. A short time after that it was *Yom Kippur*, and at that moment when *Maskir neschommos*[20] was being recited, there was a great crush in the synagogue. There was a swarm coming in the door, and the congregation was finally close to suffocating, while one could not recognize the other, since they were all wearing the *kittel* and the *thallis* over their head as well; for the dead are as you know buried in their *kittels* and *thallisim*. Then the rabbi forced his way to the *Aron hakodesh*,[21] picked up the holy parchment roll and extended it out toward the congregation, calling out, 'In the name of the almighty God! All those who belong here, take your *kittels* off!' They did, and all of a sudden there was room; but since that time the Gnesen Jews to this very day stand there on *Yom Kippur* without *kittels*."

"I wonder if there really are such supernatural things?" asked Jette shyly.

---

[16] The High Holy Days.

[17] The great festival of atonement.

[18] A kind of talisman which is fastened to the doorpost.

[19] Spoiled, impure.

[20] Requiem over all the congregation's dead.

[21] The tabernacle.

"Of course there are!" cried Isak Bamberger eagerly. "Wasn't I myself on the point of buying a horse from the devil?"

"Oh, tell us, Uncle!" begged the boy.

Uncle Isak did not at all need to be urged, since the doubting expression on Jette's face was invitation enough, and he began:

"What I see with my own eyes nobody can talk me out of. And as surely as I want to see my little Rebecca again—may she rest in peace!—that surely it is that I saw what I'm now going to tell. Before the outbreak of the war, when I was still a youngster of twenty, big and strong as I am still, and not afraid of anything, I bought horses for a French horse trader who was located in Frankfurt. One Thursday afternoon—I remember that afternoon as if it were yesterday—I rode up to a tavern lying about 15 miles the other side of Sachsenhausen. I was supposed to be home the same evening, but there were a number of people in the tavern who offered me horses, and it was almost dark before I had finished the business. When I started to ride off, they asked me rather to wait till the next morning, in order not to ride in the dark through the little wood that was on my way. 'Do you think I'm afraid?' I asked, annoyed. 'Whether or not you are afraid, Mr. Isak,' said the proprietor, 'it still couldn't hurt anything to be cautious.' 'Oh, I don't care if the devil himself comes to me in the woods!' I called out, had my horse brought to the door, and rode off. But now I can't deny that I secretly regretted my last words, and actually I regretted them the same moment I uttered them. A man should be humble and not challenge God. When I entered the woods, I would have liked to turn back; but I was ashamed and said to myself, 'Shame, Isak! Don't you have a good horse and an able fist? No fear!' If I had depended on God instead of my horse and my hand, and prayed a *Schema Jisroel*, what happened later surely would not have happened. Well, I rode on, and with the strange feeling I had, I can't deny that I was happy to hear brisk hoofbeats behind me and thus could expect to get a traveling companion. I reined my horse in until the stranger came alongside. He said good evening in a friendly way, I did the same, and we were soon chatting warmly. By chance I happen to tell him that I am a horsetrader, and the stranger asks me if I might want to buy his horse. 'Right on the highway?' I ask smiling, 'you really have to look at a horse's teeth before you buy it.'—'You're welcome to do that immediately; a good horsetrader mustn't put off a deal. Just look at my horse's teeth, Isak Bamberger!'—I was surprised that the stranger knew my name, but without thinking any more about it, I bend down over the saddle pommel and open the horse's mouth. *Adonoi Elohenu!* There spewed a blazing fire out of the horse's throat! Without uttering a word I drove the spurs into my horse and raced off, all the way to Sachsenhausen."

"That could maybe after all be explained naturally?" suggested Jette.

"How, then?" asked Isak Bamberger.

"For example, by assuming that your eyes had deceived you," said Jette with a roguish smile.

But Isak wrinkled his brow and said, "You know, Jette, that you can say whatever you like to me, but do remember that I swore it was the truth by my daughter, my little Rebecca, who was burned to death."

"There are incomprehensible things in nature," Philip began now to speak with quiet earnestness. "And isn't already every leaf that comes out on the tree an incomprehensible matter, although we see it so often that it seems quite simple to us? But the *Thoro*[22] itself teaches that there are dark secrets which it is not good to explore. Didn't Moses transform his staff into a serpent and dust into living insects? But even if *he* did that with God's direct help, how then could his enemies, the Egyptian wise men, do the same? And the truth of this must not be doubted, for it is written in the *Thoro*. There are still supposed to be people who can perform such feats. Don't the Jews in Lemberg every Friday evening still say an odd *berocho*[23] on account of such a feat?"

"What was that?" asked Jette.

Jacob scarcely dared to breathe.

"There lived in Lemberg," Philip began, "a rabbi who, as *kemech* says, knew more than his Lord's Prayer. Since he didn't

---

[22] Torah, Law of Moses.

[23] Prayer, blessing.

have the means to keep a servant, he shaped a person out of clay, and by putting a piece of parchment with certain holy words under this person's tongue he made it come to life, and it worked for him six days of the week. Every Friday evening he took out the parchment with the holy words, and the clay lay there dead until he had said *avdolo*[24] and put the parchment back under the tongue. But one Friday evening the rabbi had remained out in the town longer than usual, and when they lit the Sabbath candles in the synagogue the clay man became uncontrollable. He broke into the synagogue and killed people with one single blow of his hard arms, and he certainly would have killed everybody if the rabbi had not come up just in the nick of time and taken the holy words out of his mouth. So he died again, and in accordance with the congregation's fervent prayers, the rabbi didn't bring him back to life ever again. But the Lemberger Jews still say an odd prayer in thanks because they were that time saved from misfortune."

"There most certainly are dark and mysterious things," Philip went on after a pause. "Aren't we a mystery to ourselves? But the devout Jew need not be afraid of anything. If my rest is mysteriously disturbed at night, I can be certain that it is a warning sign that our Lord permits the dead to give me that my *mezuzos* are *posul*. If I take my *tephilin*[25] with me, I can without worrying go over land and sea and sleep in the homes of *goyim*. The Lord, the God of Israel, is with His children. See, my son, we are only a weak and downtrodden people, and what has all the same happened to our enemies and those who have lorded it over us? Emperor Titus, who burned the temple, was slain by his own brother. Antiochus Epiphanes, the Syrian, wanted to compel the Jews to sacrifice to his gods—the plagues of Egypt on them— what happened to him? Wasn't he forced while still living to see his flesh consumed by worms? And now recently the King of Prussia, Friedrich Wilhelm III? Although he knew that Jews

---

[24] The blessing with which the Sabbath ends.

[25] Cases containing a written narrative of the Exodus from Egypt, and which every morning are bound with leather straps around the head and left arm, while blessings are recited.

dare not dig up their cemeteries, seven years ago, in 1806, he ordered that they all be dug up before the end of October. Before the end of October, Napoleon had taken all Prussia, so that the king himself scarcely had a cemetery. And finally the mighty Napoleon himself? As long as he was Turk among Turks, Jew among Jews, and Christian among Christians, he prospered and the Lord was with him in battles. But a couple of years ago when he called together the rabbis from all corners of the earth to reform the Jewish religion and change that in which every jot must be immovable as long as the world stands, what happens? In Russia his entire army freezes to death, and let's see how long he still holds out now that the God of Zion has turned away from him."

"But Napoleon is surely a great hero, greater than both Joab and Abisai," remarked Jacob eagerly.

"Oh, what is difficult about sitting still and shooting people down with big cannons!" said Philip. "That is, after all, done only with the help of abilities that the good God has given him. No, the Jew Eleazar was greater! He was also a warrior; but he sacrificed himself and stabbed the elephant to death to kill the evil king who desecrated the temple, although he himself had to die when the animal fell. My son, when calamity comes over the children of Israel, our Lord sends warriors, and everyone seeks to hold himself in readiness in case God perhaps chooses him. *Bensch* every morning your *zizis*[26] that you may be pleasing to God."

"*Kemech* here talk about one who resembles Eleazar," remarked the uncle. "They call him Hvitfeldt, I think. He was blown up for the sake of his people."

"He was also a great hero," said Philip, bowing his head as if in reverence. "Sacrifice and humility are greater heroism than victory in thousands of battles," he added, in accordance with the Jewish custom of extracting a moral from every conversation.

"*Rebbosai, wir wollen benschen,*"[27] exclaimed the master of the house after a pause, and following this formula, with which

---

[26] A kind of talisman (see previous note); "bensche"—to bless, recite a prayer over.

[27] "Gentlemen, we will thank God for the food."

the cantor opens the prayer of thanks when three or more Jews eat together, the father, the uncle, and Benjamin, along with little Jacob, covered their heads and recited the thanksgiving, after which everybody went to bed.

The quiet community in whose midst Jacob lived slept securely and serenely after the evening's stories, but for the child these did not die away as quickly as they were recited; the mysterious power which they contained, or which he found in them, were left fermenting in his soul. Many nights thereafter he dreamed of terrifying figures—the terrible judge who sat on dizzying heights and held the threatening lightning bolt, ready to hurl it down toward poor frightened people; horses of fire pursuing his uncle; white-clad figures swarming in frightful mysterious throngs; but in the midst of the terror that made his hair rise on end, he seemed, to his reassurance, to hear his mother's gentle voice whisper, "Perhaps it can be explained naturally!"

Chapter 5

JUST WHAT IS THERE TO TELL about the years of childhood? The life of the child is a receiving, for there exist only conditions and occurrences; its history is the report of events in its surroundings. But it is from these occurrences and conditions that the child's soul absorbs its nourishment, just as the tender shoot from soil, water, and air prepares the blossoms to come. Are these blossoms to be lovely and refreshing with their aroma, or are they to be sinister and overpowering? Are they to be plucked by joyous human hands or to wither forlorn on their stem? Yes, for plants this is immutably predestined by nature, and the poisonous hemlock sways on its stalk just as happily and innocently as the delight-bringing violet. The human being on the other hand—it must itself create its blossoms; philosophers call that human freedom. Good heavens! Do I then create my blood myself, with its mysterious sympathies and antipathies, with its calm seas and its wild waves? Do I myself select the earth, the air, and the light from which my life's roots absorb their nourishment? . . .

Jacob grew up protected by loving hands, and all the same so very alone. He went around like a deer in a fenced-in garden, staring with his brown eyes out into the wide nature—it may indeed well be said, like one of the forest animals; for no matter how loving the persons surrounding him were, in many respects, in all the childish relations, there was still no language possible between him and them; they were like fence palings surrounding his little sanctuary and denoting its limits.

This solitude brought about an event that was of decisive influence on his entire future.

It was mild spring weather. The sun shone, on the roof sparrows twittered, the cat lay on the cellar door, sunning itself and squinting through half-closed eyes at the lively birds. Around the big pile of gravel and stone fragments lying, since time immemorial, in the middle of the street, had gathered a large band of boys; with paper helmets on their heads and wooden swords in their hands they were mightily storming the awesome fortress, which was equally mightily defending itself. Shrill war cries, howls of pain, and laughter resounded in a medley. Through the blinds Jacob peeked out at all this splendor; he looked at the large numbers of heartfelt beatings being dealt out, like the thirsty wanderer on a hot summer day looks at the distant sea.

Several times he rushed from the window down into the garden to begin a similar game, but each time he came back downcast, for he had found himself just as alone in the garden as in the living room.

Suddenly a happy thought flashed through his head, and the plan was just as quickly carried out. There outside lay the splendid cat; Jacob took possession of it, placed it up on a table in the garden—which was to represent the fortress—and he himself was the assaulting army. So that the cat would not run away, he tied it to the table (a praiseworthy precaution toward a garrison commander). Violent skirmishes were now delivered daily, in which blood flowed, if not precisely in streams, from Jacob's hands and face. After a certain time's practice, the cat became so accustomed to the game that as soon as it saw the table it sprang up miaowing, seeming belligerently to challenge its adversary.

But finally Jacob found that for one thing, it wasn't fair in that the cat was far better armed than he, and that for another thing, the whole war was unnatural in that nobody fell on the side of either the attackers or the attacked. Perhaps mixed in this was also a secret grudge against the cat over the fact that he always had to be the one to sue for peace, and although he was bleeding everywhere, he had to propitiate the cat with a good meal to boot, something which incidentally usually is incumbent upon the defeated power at the conclusion of peace. So much is certain, that Jacob did not rest until his uncle had given him a small dagger, a war souvenir, and armed with it he renewed the war. The cat undoubtedly remarked, like Hector of old, that its adversary, in some way or other, had come into the possession of an invincible weapon, but nonetheless it did not give way and fought to the last drop of blood.

Philip Bendixen arrived at precisely the moment his son was for the last time burying the dagger in his enemy's breast, and he burst out, "But what are you doing, my son?" The shocked Jacob replied, completely confused, "I wanted to see what was inside the cat." The surprised father stood silent for a long time, and then he said gravely, "My son, I see in this a sign from heaven. At an early age, I intended you to study, but I had already halfway given that up in favor of having you help me with my business. But now I know that you are destined to be a doctor like *der Rambam*[1] who was also by nature impelled to dismember animals and plants in order to acquire wisdom."

"Who was *der Rambam?*" asked Jacob, prepared to hear a story and glad that the slain cat was forgotten.

"*Der Rambam* was a great doctor among the Jews in Spain. So untiringly did he search for wisdom that after hearing that an even greater doctor lived in another country, he sent a message to him asking to be taken on as his apprentice. But the other doctor was afraid that somebody would learn his secret knowledge, and replied, No. Then *der Rambam* disguised himself as a servant and in that way he succeeded in being engaged by the doctor to wait on him, carry his instruments, and other such services. Once the doctor was called to a sick person who had a worm in his brain and he took *der Rambam* along to hold the patient during the painful operation. When the brain was bared, the doctor extended the forceps to grasp the worm, but then suddenly *der Rambam* held his arm back, saying, 'Great master! Wouldn't you rather place a green leaf outside the brain? The worm will follow its natural instinct and voluntarily crawl out on the leaf, whereas it will resist and perhaps kill the patient if you grasp it with the forceps.' The doctor turned amazed to *der Rambam* and cried, 'Truly, if you are not the devil, then you are *der Rambam!*' 'I am not the devil, but *der Rambam*,' said the wise man, humbly bowing. 'No, no!' cried the old doctor, 'It befits me

---

[1] Acronym for the man's name: Rabbi Mosche Ben Maimon (Maimonides).

to kneel before you, who are superior.'—My son, become as great a wise man as *der Rambam*, and just as humble as he."

After many consultations and discussions with his mother and his uncle, it was decided that right after his *barmitzvo*[2] Jacob would be sent to Copenhagen to study. His further upbringing and regular training in religion would be the responsibility of Philip's brother Marcus, who lived in the capital.

"And now," said his father, "we will get to work in earnest on the *Gemoro*, so that when you get to Copenhagen, they can satisfy themselves that we out in the country are not illiterate, either."

"Jacob, my boy," he went on, taking out one of the large volumes, "prepare yourself to approach with reverence that treasury of wisdom which the great scholars of the past have preserved there. There is no branch of human knowledge they have not investigated, and everywhere you will find traces of these studies, even though their expression is often obscure and for the layman cloaked, so to say, in riddles."

And now began the study of the old rabbis' ingenious, sophistic, hair-splitting interpretations of the Law, interwoven with interesting stories, legends, and anecdotes, which relieved the exhausting work and gave it allurement.

But if in this way work in this time of redoubled effort was coupled with enjoyment, then every enjoyment was also coupled with learning.

He was strolling with his father outside of the town. On a meadow sheep were grazing with their lambs, and Jacob rushed in among them in tumultuous joy, in order just once to play with creatures his own size.

"Jacob, come here, I want to ask you about something," his father called with a friendly smile, as if he had hit upon a pleasant surprise for his son.

Jacob resignedly came over and took his father's hand.

"Can you answer me this question?" Philip began. "All people eat lamb, but few eat pork. Jews don't eat it, neither do

---

[2] The solemn admission into the community of adults, a kind of confirmation.

Mohammedans and Hindus, and even among Christians only the poor class eats pork frequently. Further: a sheep brings forth only one—at the most, two—lambs, while a sow brings forth six, seven, even as many as nine pigs. So there are born by far more swine than lambs, and by far fewer are eaten, and there are still more sheep in the world than swine. Can you explain this riddle?"

Jacob racked his brain to find a reasonable explanation for this striking circumstance, but it was impossible.

Finally his father released him from his impatience. "See, my son, this is a new proof for the correctness of the Jewish religion. The dear God does not give his *masol*[3] to that which according to his Law to the Jews is *tereipho*[4]; in spite of all its fecundity, it can not thrive."

And now his father got involved in the sphere of interpretations and similes of the Law, and the son listened attentively to him until they arrived at home.

Thus Jacob steeped himself in his people's mysterious erudition. The world in which his spirit moved shaped itself for him as a series of quiet cells in Solomon's temple where holy men with long white beards sat and prayed; it often seemed to him that he was standing in the long, low temple building with small windows, but with rich golden ornamentations twisting in strange knots and dark fairy-tale figures; from the temple's court he heard the throng of believers mumbling prayers around the priest of the sacrifice and the God of Zion softly speaking to them.

But through all this sometimes resounded a lively alien melody—it was his mother's songs when she, as often happened, walked up and down with him in the twilight. When the moon cast its faint beams in through the window at him and her sitting alone on the sofa, she would rise and take him by the hand and sing in her soft voice the songs she had learned in her youth, in the theater and among her girl friends, and it was as if she were entertaining herself with memories through these

[3] Blessing.

[4] Unclean.

melodies. They were for Jacob tones from another land and another race; blond locks and blue eyes bobbed up from these waves of sound, looking at him in such an alien way and yet it was as if there was a mysterious familiarity between them and him. A melancholy yearning seized him, but the insurmountable board fence stood in the way. And when his mother then with a clear and joyous voice sang one of those clear melodies in which the rhythms dance and jingle like women's feet with golden spurs on their dainty heels, rise and sink like a maiden's bosom, and the fair-eyed figures intertwined with each other like the tones, it was as if the immense deprivation of all childish joy matured the child's soul in an unnatural way; for him it was unconscious, not as if he were looking ahead in life with longing—and vain longing—but as if he were looking back on a completed, barren, and joyless life; privation and pain overflowed his heart, and the child burst violently into tears.

"Why are you crying, Jacob?" asked his mother in astonishment.

"Because the song you were singing was so sad," sobbed the boy.

It was inexplicable to his mother, but a mother's solicitude extends farther than her experience, and an anxious presentiment stole into her breast as she thought of the fact that her only child was to go out into the world.

Chapter 6

THESE MELODIES REPLACED THE FANTASIES, only they did not live except when his mother sang. Then the strange figures appeared, always in the same form, frolicking in the air around him and his mother, playing in the corners and under the ceiling, delighting and frightening him; now they sprang mockingly out the window and disappeared, now they drew sorrowfully nearer and died on his mother's lips.

It was a long time before Jacob could listen so calmly that he discovered words in the tones; only when he had learned by heart the intelligible, tangible words did the ethereal shapes acquire flesh and blood and lose their magical power. Then he wanted to learn these words himself to be able later to conjure up the frolicking pictures, and his mother gladly recited for him everything that she knew herself. But when Jacob demanded more and more, she searched out old books, relics from her youth, and gave them to her son and taught him to read in them.

In this way she also became his teacher, without herself noticing it, and she taught him what he never forgot; she bestowed on him the most beautiful gift he brought with him from his parental home out into the world—a mother tongue as pure and clear as it rang through the rhythms of the poets.

His father was visibly displeased when Jacob began to translate the *Gemoro* into Danish instead of German; but when his mother came to his assistance and said, "Do you want to make the boy into a rabbi? Is he not to be able to speak the language the Christians speak, when he's supposed to go out among them?" he gave in.

The books which Jacob in this way got possession of— comedies, collections of drinking songs, travel descriptions, and the like—had been stored unheeded. From some the rats had eaten large pieces, others had been more or less used for wrapping paper; some were missing a beginning, others a conclusion, most were missing both parts; but for Jacob these deficiencies served only to increase the suspense and the mysterious presentiment of the life beyond the board fence where, he thought, the continuation was to be found.

While these various studies were going on, time proceeded as monotonously as the rotation of the heavenly bodies which produces days. The new moon brought the great days of rest; they made up the year's mileposts; exceedingly seldom an epochmaking comet appeared on the family life's horizon. That was one of the itinerant Poles, one of those strange guests who suddenly appeared in town without anyone knowing where they came from, and after a short stay, disappeared without anyone knowing where they went. But what a celebration it was, when the *balbos*[1] of the house brought home a Pole he had bought in the synagogue!

There were many grounds for joy over such a guest's arrival. In the first place, they had a *minyan*[2] for the synagogue. The number of Jews in the town was only small, and when one became annoyed with another, he generally took revenge on all the others together by not going to the synagogue. When a Pole came, it was at once a whole man's reinforcement, and the cantankerous ones were ashamed in the presence of so holy a man and came to the synagogue. The only time a Pole was not needed was *Yom Kippur*, the great day of atonement, for on that day one Jew forgives the other any affront that has been inflicted, and even mortal enemies extend their hands to each other and say "*Scholom*," peace, and forgive each other as they want God on this day to forgive them—but the next day for the most part the quarrel begins all over again.

---

[1] "Bal ha bajis"—head of the house, paterfamilias.

[2] There must be ten adult Jews present to constitute a congregation (*minyan*) in the synagogue. If fewer are assembled, they may indeed pray, but not as a group, and the Torah must not be read, or any of the religious ceremonies carried out, just as in parliaments they may deliberate, but not vote, when a certain number of members are not present.

Moreover, hospitality is a cherished and holy duty. It is a *mitzvo*, a deed pleasing to God, to refresh the traveler, to treat him to the best the house has to offer, and make him its master. Now that the Enlightenment is in the ascendant and people like to put on a good appearance before the Christians, without, however, completely breaking with God, they don't fight over the Pole in the synagogue to which he first betakes himself, don't lead him in triumph through the streets to their home, don't give him their best slippers to put on—after having provided him with stockings—but rather make do with paying for him in a Jewish restaurant—restaurant! You upas tree, in whose proximity hospitality is poisoned and dies!

But at that time, and in that town, where Jews were still cowed enough to feel that they were nothing but Jews, where they did not find themselves called upon to compete about anything other than who was the most Jewish, the old-fashioned hospitality still flourished, and a Pole literally sold himself at auction: he went home with the one who offered him the most travel money in return for living in his house.

Now, it may well be true that the Poles were not always exactly the most agreeable guests for a neat housewife, and not always the most modest ones, either. Thus it happened once that Philip Bendixen had as a guest a Pole who greatly liked sour-cooked fish. When Philip had eaten his portion and showed signs of asking for more, the Pole took the dish and handed it to Jette with the words, "My dear Jette! Save this for me for supper." But such things were gladly tolerated, for the greater the inconvenience caused by the guest, the greater the favor that God found in the hospitality involved; and besides, such a Pole was an inexhaustible source of witticisms and stories. These witticisms depend mostly on the peculiar intonation with which they are uttered, or on plays on words, the rendering of which would require a whole lexicon. For instance, a story is told of a Pole who was to fight a duel, which we must preface with the remark that the Danish and German word for "rule"—"Regel"—in Hebrew means "foot," whereas Hebrew "rosh" means "head." A Pole, so runs the story, had been challenged and the agreement reached that the two adversaries should fight with swords.

When the Pole got his rapier in his hand, he began to slash away at his opponent, caring about neither tierce nor quarte, which he most likely did not even know by name. The seconds dashed between them and said, "*Aber, Herr Ephraim, das is ja gar nicht nach der Regel.*" "*Wie?*" cried the raging Pole, "*Regel? Ich schloge nischt nach der Regel, ich schloge nach dem Rosch!*"

They were real festival evenings, such Friday evenings, when a Pole enlivened the course of the story-telling, and the one had a story ready at hand as soon as the other was finished. If it was taken for granted that such a story was familiar to the adults, and it was particularly addressed to the child, it would do the adults good to hear it one more time. And it really did do them good. Although everyone could himself tell the same story, he nevertheless listened to it with rapt attention, as if it were quite new to him; it was not the bare material one heard in the usually religious tales—it was the spirit of God one recognized, always new and interesting, even in the old familiar raiment.

It was on such an evening that Jacob got his uncle to begin with the story about how he was taken prisoner as a girl. A gourmand does not see the savory dishes awaiting him with more pleasure than did Jacob, preparing himself to listen to his uncle's tale.

"Our prince," began Isak Bamberger, "was, jointly with his neighbor, to furnish a man to the imperial army; but, since he was on bad terms with this neighbor, he wanted for his part to furnish only half a one, and therefore picked my old blind father. Since a young, strong lad is always worth just as much as an old blind man, I got permission to go in his place. I was big and strapping, almost as tall as I am now, but as smooth in the face as a girl.

"While we were stationed on the Belgian border, in the village of Königsdorf, I was carrying on a flirtation with the daughter of a rich miller who lived just outside of town. I had met her in the town, but never dared to visit her, since her father watched her like a hawk on account of the many soldiers. But one evening I got leave and, determined to talk to her, I put on women's clothes to look for work in the mill and in this way at least have an excuse for staying there. I was taken on with open

arms. There was a shortage of hired girls in the mill because two
had recently run off with soldiers. What could be fairer, I said to
myself, than that soldiers in return become hired girls? The
woman found that I was big and strong enough to be a milkmaid,
and only demanded the solemn promise from me that I would not
flirt with the soldiers. And I did make her that promise, with
the intention of sincerely keeping it. When bedtime came and
the hired hands got up, I automatically made a move to go with
them, but the miller's wife grabbed my arm and said, 'Are you
accustomed to that, where you come from? I won't put up with
that here in my house. Please go up and go to bed with my
daughter.' I was already on the way up the stairs when suddenly
there broke out a terrible racket outside the mill and a blinding
glare lit up the rooms. We rushed to the windows—a troop of
Frenchmen was drawn up outside, and Königsdorf was in flames.
'We've got to defend ourselves!' cried the miller, calling for his
hired hands, while the women took shelter in the loft. I stayed
with the men and armed myself with a rifle like the others. The
miller poured out his praise on the plucky woman; after every
shot he fired he looked admiringly at me. Our resistance was
short; the Frenchmen forced their way into the house and a huge
corporal knocked the gun out of my hands and grabbed me,
bursting out, 'That's a woman for me!' 'The Germans are
coming!' cried the Frenchmen now, and just as quickly as they
had come, they rushed off without taking any other booty than
me, whom the corporal held in his enormous arms. I didn't put
up any resistance, just happy at the fact that attention was
distracted from my girl. The corporal took me on his horse, gave
me a big kiss, and off we went through the burning town. After
we had reached the French camp, the whole squadron laid claim
to me, and the dispute was ended only with the corporal's
determined declaration 'I will take her as my wife! I have
abducted her in the knightly fashion, and this is absolutely the
woman for me. Tomorrow the field chaplain will marry us!' They
were all satisfied with this. 'Pierre Lasusse is getting married!'
they shouted. 'Hurrah! The whole squadron is the best man!'
'My friends!' said Pierre Lasusse, 'I will be a happy man. My
wife measures more than five feet, and I myself am six feet; the

children will be at least five feet eight.' 'Ssh, Pierre, your wife will blush at such talk,' said one. 'She's welcome to do that,' shouted Pierre, 'I like red-cheeked women.' 'Jacques,' Pierre went on, motioning to a strapping fellow, 'if I'm ever killed in action, you will step in as my successor—you're the tallest next to me.' 'Won't you also remember me in your will, Pierre?' asked a cheerful little cavalryman. 'You, Arnould?' replied Pierre, measuring him with a glance from head to toe, 'Well, yes, when your turn comes, you can team up with little Jean; together the two of you will have the regulation height.' I was witness to their long-term arrangements concerning me in this way, but decided to wait for an opportune moment to reveal myself. I had *pachat*.[3] The night was spent in the tent in lively conversation. In the morning Pierre took me, accompanied by his comrades, to the field chaplain. In a camp they don't observe many formalities. When the chaplain began the holy ceremony, I interrupted him, trying as well as possible to make myself understood. 'What?' shouted Pierre, thinking it was a straightforward refusal, 'is the lady hesitating to marry me,Pierre Lasusse, corporal in the Anjou Regiment, six feet tall?' I very eagerly began my objections, but nobody understood me. Pierre impatiently shouted, 'What is the meaning of this? What kind of scruples are these? Is the lady perhaps a heretic? Why doesn't the lady want to be my wife?' I screamed as loudly as I could, 'I am not a woman!' and took off my headgear. Pierre stood several moments speechless, then sprang over and pawed me, but immediately let go of me with a painful sigh and covered his face with his hand. The entire squadron burst into roars of laughter, and the chaplain laughed along with them."

Isak Bamberger paused here, and the mother, who was sensitive at this story being told in the presence of the child, took the opportunity of saying, "It seems to me that several years ago you told that same story somewhat differently."

"Well," said Isak, screwing up his eyes roguishly, "several years always cause a change; you also looked different several years ago."

---

[3] Fear.

"But an incident that took place is not a living face; it is in the memory, chiseled in stone," replied Jette, stubbornly pursuing her goal.

"Now really!" cried Isak a little impatiently, "a story is not Toros Mosche[4] either; a tittle more or less in it won't deprive any man of his salvation. Besides, I haven't told the most important thing: how I was arrested as a spy but escaped when the guard saw me in the morning putting on tephilin[5] and realized that I was a Jew just like him. The boy should hear that, so he can know that God does not desert the devout Jew who keeps His commandments and carries his tephilin with him."

But now the Pole authoritatively took the floor:

"Such a tale is nothing for a Friday evening. On Schabbas one should be mehanno[6] with a good meal and memories of God's mercy to those who honor the Schabbas. What I spend to observe my Schabbas God will return to me doubled, as we find in the tale of Joseph Moker Schabbas in the song zemiros. This Joseph was poor, but half of every day's earnings he put back to observe his Schabbas, and on Friday morning when he made his purchases, nothing was too good for the glorification of the Lord's day of rest. Right across from him lived the wealthy Eliezer, who did not care about the Schabbas but on that day, just as well as the other days, worked to increase his treasures. He jeered at his poor neighbor who could never get ahead because on one day he used up the whole week's earnings. One day he met Joseph on the street and jeered at him as usual, adding, 'You ought rather to think about laying something up for your old age and for your daughters' dowries.' 'Don't sin,' answered Joseph Moker Schabbas, 'for everything you own God can give me if it pleases Him.' The wealthy Eliezer became uneasy at these words, and the very thought of the possibility that the Lord could take his wealth from him and give it to his poor neighbor was painful to him. At that time it happened that a great soothsayer came to the place, and Eliezer, who could not overcome his secret dread,

---

[4] The Law of Moses.

[5] See previous note [p. 25].

[6] Regale oneself.

went to him to have his fortune told. 'Don't worry,' said the sage after examining his hand, 'your treasures will not be swallowed up by the ocean, nor will the hand of a thief steal them nor fire consume them. In all your undertakings you will be fortunate; but nevertheless in the end all your riches will only serve to procure Joseph Moker Schabbas a pleasant *Schabbas*.' 'But explain this contradiction to me!' cried Eliezer. 'I have spoken,' said the sage, and was not to be moved to say any more. Eliezer was now seized by fear that the sage's prophecy would come true, and in order to refute it he embarked on the most daring gambles; but they all succeeded. He sent his ships to the furthest seas; but they returned safely. Eliezer's fear grew and grew. Once a conflagration raged in the town, and it drew near his house. He forbade that anything be moved, and when the flames were already licking the gable of the building he joyously lifted his eyes toward heaven. But at that very moment the wind shifted, a violent downpour drenched the town, and the fire was checked. Another time a storm was blowing just as some of Eliezer's ships were expected. A messenger fearfully came up to him with the report that one of the ships was presumed to have gone aground. Eliezer pressed a full purse into the messenger's hand and promised him tenfold if the report was confirmed; but in vain— the storm abated, and the next day his ships sailed into the harbor safe and sound. Eliezer's fear mounted to near-madness. He ordered his storehouses and cellars left open to tempt thieves; the thieves appeared, but the judge, who had expected this, appeared at the same time and thus caught a whole gang. Finally it was heard that Eliezer had suddenly sold all his property and was gone from the town, nobody knew where. In the meantime, Joseph Moker Schabbas continued undisturbed his mode of life, and when on Friday evening he sat at his well-supplied table and recited his *Kiddush*,[7] there was no one in the whole land who was happier than he, and the king himself would not have gotten him to get up and leave his home.

One Friday morning, when he according to his custom came to the market to make his purchases, he saw a large crowd

---

[7] Consecration of bread and wine.

gathered outside a tent. He went nearer and learned that the occasion for the crowd was a fishmonger who was demanding a hundred pieces of gold for a fish. 'A hundred pieces of gold! Has anyone heard the like!' cried the people. 'See if you get it sold, my good man; after it has been lying around for a week, it will undoubtedly get cheaper.' Joseph had to admit that he had never seen finer pike, that he had never had such a delicious dish to glorify his *Schabbas*. 'A hundred pieces of gold,' he thought, 'that is certainly expensive. But our Lord has given me abundant earnings this week—for what else than to observe properly His *Schabbas*?—Get back, people!' he cried, 'the man is right; that is a fish worthy of a king's table; I will buy it in honor of my Lord's *Schabbas*.' He paid the hundred pieces of gold and brought the fish home to his wife. 'It is too big for us alone,' he said, 'I will send word and invite good friends *lekovod Schabbas*.'[8] His wife approved of his idea and proceeded to cut the fish up. How great was her surprise when inside the fish she found a lump, which upon closer inspection proved to be the remains of a glove inside which was a ring. Joseph took the ring and examined it. 'Wife!' he said, 'I have made a good bargain—that ring is worth over a thousand pieces of gold.' He dried it off more carefully. 'Wife!' he cried, 'you could not buy that ring for a hundred thousand pieces of gold!' Finally, when it sparkled for him in all its beauty, he cried, 'Wife! It cannot be bought for a whole kingdom!' The friends arrived, and when Joseph showed them his find, they congratulated him and praised God, who had in this way rewarded his piety. At just that time a kings's son who lived nearby was on the point of getting married, and jewels and precious stones were being sought with great eagerness for his bride. Joseph went to the king's son, who took a liking to the ring and paid him a great sum of money at once and for the balance assigned him an annuity for life. From now on, Joseph could treat himself to *Schabbas* to his heart's content and invite friends and needy people, and then when he was sitting among his guests, he would tell the story of the ring. One evening he had invited, among others, a foreign, wretched-looking man who

---

[8] In honor of the Sabbath.

had only one hand, and he then told once more this story. When he had finished, the poor foreigner broke into tears and cried, 'Great God! So your prophecy came true after all!' Everybody asked about the meaning of these enigmatic words, whereupon the foreigner rose and said, 'Don't you know the wealthy Eliezer any more? Yes, it is I! So far has it come with me, according to God's inscrutable will. See, the prophecy has been fulfilled—all my wealth has only served to procure for Joseph Moker Schabbas a joyous *Schabbas*. You have all heard about this prophecy and how it more and more threatened to come true. Finally I could not stand it any longer. I made the acquaintance of a foreign jeweler who possessed a ring of inestimable value. I offered him my equally inestimable possessions in exchange; he let himself be persuaded, and I went away—far, far away from Joseph Moker Schabbas. I serenely wore the precious gem, for I well knew that it was not threatened by sea nor fire nor thief's hand nor by other such misfortunes that strike people. One day I had gone out to refresh myself in a sea bath, and while I was enjoying swimming, I suddenly noticed that a large fish had greedily approached me. I fearfully stretched out my hand to defend myself; it bit me hard, and half-unconscious I returned to the shore. Imagine my horror and despair when I discovered that my finger was bitten off and precisely that finger on which I was wearing the ring! Poor and helpless, since that time I have wandered about; now I am coming back to die in my birthplace, and now I learn how completely the prophecy has come true.' Everybody burst out in wonder and praise of God's greatness; but Joseph climbed down from the seat of honor, approached the unfortunate Eliezer and entreated, 'Stay with me for the future and share with me; everything is yours, after all!' Eliezer accepted the offer. But in memory of this event we still on Friday evening sing the song *zemiros*. A good Jew ought always to remember what God has done for his entire nation or for the individual members; on *Schabbas* and the high holidays we older people should praise the Lord, on Hanukkah the small children should dance around the lamps and praise Him who freed us from the cruel sovereigns," added the Pole admonishingly.

Jette asked the Pole, "I wonder if that story took place in Canaan [i.e., Slavic Eastern Europe]?"

"That I cannot say for certain," he answered, "but why do you ask about that?"

"Well," Jette went on, "I was just thinking that if a Jew were to go to the marketplace here and buy a fish and say that he was buying it in honor of his Lord's *Schabbas*, we would certainly not hear the last of it!"

"Is there much *risches* here?" asked the Pole, all ears.

"Oh, no, certainly not more than other places," said Philip Bendixen. "We take care of ourselves and mind our own business. If one once in a while hears something, he pretends that he doesn't hear it."

"And if they do yell too loud," added Isak Bamberger, "we are not afraid either of showing that a Jew, too, can fight back."

"*Um Gottes Willen!*" cried the Pole, "*das fehlt noch! der Jed musz mit den Gojim anfangen!*[9] Better be still and suffer a thousand times! Whatever an individual Jew commits against the Christians, even when the latter are to blame, is taken out on all Jews. They saw that in Prague."

"When was that? What happened in Prague?" was asked from all sides.

"It's now over a hundred years ago," said the Pole. "At that time there lived in Prague a Jew by the name of Leiser (Lazarus) Oveiles, with his wife Miryam; they had a 14-year-old son who was named Simon.

"One Friday afternoon an itinerant Pole—like me—came into Lazarus's place and asked him for travel assistance. Lazarus was a pious man and would not permit the Pole to leave his house until he had shared the *Schabbas* meal with him; he showed him to a room, had a bath prepared for him, and then took him to the temple. When they came home, Miryam had lit the *Schabbas* candles and set the table, and, happy and relaxed, they sat down to the savory meal.

"After they had eaten their fill, the conversation turned, among other things, to the persecution which the Jews had to

---

[9] "The Jew should only start something with the Christians!"

endure from the Christians, and the attempts that were being made to lure young people away from the faith of their fathers. At that time the Christians had for some years been at peace with the Turks and with each other, and whenever they are at peace themselves, the Jews are made to suffer.

"Lazarus, who was a strong and robust man, said indignantly, 'Oh, oh! These are hard times! Our own children desert us and in the Christians' temples curse their fathers and forefathers. God be praised that I still have my son and can give him the *Schabbas* blessing!'

"'I hear that in the past week two more Jewish boys have deserted their fathers' faith,' said Leib Löbel, the Pole.

"'Don't talk about it,' cried Lazarus vehemently. 'It only spoils my *Schabbas* joy for me. It is a cursed witchcraft, against which we can do nothing.'

"'Why not talk about it?' asked Leib Löbel. 'That power that seems so dark to you, like witchcraft, I can throw light upon. Yes, it may surprise you when I tell you that during my travel in this country I have been attentively following precisely this matter, and that I have found out the facts of the matter. Be assured—it is the Jesuits. And to reach their goal and entice the Jews' children, they make use of sin, or, to say it right out, of prostitution. They keep evil women who go into the Jews' shops and get the Jewish boys to carry their purchases home to them. When they once have such a poor lad in their meshes, their first job is to persuade him to take off his *arbakanfos*, the sign of purity and the pact with God. When his parents discover that it is gone, in their indignation they seriously punish the child, whereupon he, in fear of new and more severe punishment if worse things should be discovered, generally runs away and takes refuge with the whore, who turns him over to the Jesuits.'

"'If I had such a child, I would beat it to death!' cried Lazarus, shaking with indignation at the very thought.

"'May our Lord deliver you in mercy from such a misfortune!' said Leib Löbel, 'but nonetheless be careful. For the holy fathers, no means is to be despised when it is a question of attaining their goal. Your son is a handsome, red-cheeked lad, and such children are the most exposed to the danger, partly because the evil women themselves by preference select them, partly because the Jesuits use handsome children for their church service.'

"'Merciful God! I cannot bear to think of it!' cried Lazarus, holding his hand before his eyes. 'My son, my dear Simon,' he said, turning to him, 'come and gladden your father's eyes by showing me that I am a fortunate father, that you still wear your *arbakanfos*.'

"Simon, who was sitting opposite him, rose, opened his clothes, and made as if to approach his father; but as he was passing the door he suddenly opened it and scurried out.

"Lazarus remained several moments sitting as if turned to stone; then he leaped up in a frenzy and dashed after his son.

"A breathless tension reigned at the table until, after a quarter of an hour's passage, Lazarus's heavy tread was heard in the corridor. Pale and panting he came in and went over and sat down at his place.

"'Does anyone want more to eat?' he asked.

"No one answered.

"'Then clear the table,' he ordered the servant. 'We would like to *bensch*.'

"'What have you done with your child?' cried Miryam anxiously.

"'My child?' screamed Lazarus, 'I have no child! That bastard who a few moments ago was sitting across from me shall be accursed, his name shall be erased from the earth as it is erased from my heart.'

"'My child,' wailed Miryam, 'you have killed my Simon.'

"'Take courage!' said Lieb Löbel to Miryam. 'Your husband has not found Simon. Do you think that a father could curse his child after he had murdered it?'

"Simon's flight caused a great sensation in the congregation. Until then it had been only poor people's children who had fled; when they had returned and had done penance in the synagogue, the matter was quickly forgotten. But Lazarus was the richest man in the entire Jewish quarter, and everybody talked of the catastrophe that had taken place. It was also known that

Lazarus had promised that he would richly reward the one who brought his son back.

"When some time had passed, there appeared at Lazarus's a young Jew by the name of Manasse, who promised him to procure Simon in return for the promised reward. 'Yes, that is all very well,' said Lazarus, 'but show me some likelihood that this can occur.' 'The matter can well succeed,' answered Manasse, 'although it requires prudence. Your son has been placed in the house of the baptized Jew Franz Kawka, and the servant girl brings him every day to the Jesuits for teaching. But with a baptized Jew everything naturally goes wrong. The servant girl robs him, and she recently sold me two sheets with Franz Kawka's name still on them. I have threatened to denounce her if she does not hand over the boy to me tomorrow at an assigned place.' 'That is another matter!' said Lazarus, happy to hear that Simon was still taking instruction and therefore was not baptized; he gave Manasse ten pieces of gold immediately and waited impatiently for the next day, which was to bring his son back to the the house of his fathers and the faith of his fathers.

"The next day Manasse appeared precisely at the assigned time and place. When Simon saw him coming, he cried to the girl, 'That man knows me and may want to hurt me.' But the girl held onto the boy, Manasse dashed up, threw the sheets to her, seized Simon, whose scream he smothered by holding his hand over his mouth, and carried him quickly into the Jewish quarter.

"Here a large crowd quickly gathered, which with shouts and imprecations accompanied Simon and his abductor to Lazarus's house.

"Meanwhile, Lazarus was pacing agitatedly back and forth in his room; Miryam and Löbel were sitting silently in anxious expectation. Lazarus had expressed the decision to send his son to his father-in-law, Rabbi Feibel, in Fürth in order to avoid the shame of the boy's doing penance in the Prague synagogue. Now he was awaiting with dread and suspense the favorable outcome of Manasse's undertaking, and yet he shuddered at seeing his renegade son again.

"'Yes, that's the way it will be,' he said, 'he must go to Fürth; Rabbi Feibel will keep a tight rein on him, and I never want to see him again. But first I will give him a serious punishment to remember.'

"'Are you going to beat your son in your temper?' asked Miryam.

"'Haven't I given Manasse ten pieces of gold? Hasn't he caused me enough sorrow and anxiety and expense in the bargain?'

"But the combined entreaties of Miryam and Löbel succeeded in persuading him to promise that he would not see his son at all, and that Löbel alone would receive him and take him to a side room.

"When Simon had been brought into the house and Lazarus heard the loud clamor of the Jewish throng outside, he thought that it was in congratulation to him on his son's return. But when the uproar continued, he stepped out of his door and asked the crowd, 'What do you want, my friends?'

"'Punishment!' cried the mob, 'you must punish your son!'

"The rich man's pride was aroused, and he said, 'Whether I punish my son or not does not concern you.'

"But the din only increased at this, and someone shouted, 'You have pampered your son; it is your own fault that he has fallen away and gone over to the Christians! Now you won't even punish him! Poor people's children have had to do penance in the synagogue, so that everybody came up and beat them, and they had to give thanks for the kindness, but you are sending your son to Fürth! Is he to do penance there? But it is here that he has insulted our holy religion; it is here that he must atone!'

"The mob expressed its approval by loud shouts, and some screamed, 'If you won't punish your son, then we will!'

"One can imagine what the proud man suffered at these words, precisely because he felt that he was rightfully humiliated in this way.

"His entire wrath turned against the one who had given rise to this dishonor; the thought of Simon's apostasy aroused anew his frantic rage.

"'Wait!' he cried to the mob, which was making a move to force its way into the house; 'I will show you that I am just as good a Jew as anybody.'

"With these words he seized a stick and raced up the stairs to Simon's room. Löbel heard him coming and locked the door, but Lazarus broke it down with his foot and threw himself on Simon; in vain Löbel leaped in between to hold him back. The raging man hurled him against the wall, so that he fell dazed.

"'Bastard!' shrieked Lazarus, gnashing his teeth, 'why did you want to be Christian?'

"'Dear father,' wailed the boy, almost swooning with fear, 'I will confess everything, only don't beat me.'

"'Bastard! damned, accursed bastard! Confess, why did you want to be Christian?'

"'Because Doktor Münzer, the rector of the college, said that Jesus Christ the crucified is the son of God and our Messiah.'

"These words, spoken in mortal fear, drove Lazarus completely wild. He flailed at his son with the heavy stick, screaming, 'There! That's for Jesus!'

"His son shrieked, 'I am and will remain a Jew! *Shema Yisroel, Adonoi Elohenu, Adonoi ehod!* Hear, O Israel, the Lord your God is the one eternal Being!'

"But Lazarus heard no more. 'That is for Christ! That is for the Crucified! And that is for God's Son! That is for the Messiah!'

"Here he stopped, for Simon was no longer screaming and was bleeding heavily. He wrenched him up and laid his hand on his chest; he was not breathing.

"At that moment the room filled with a clamoring, alien mob. It was Christians who had noticed the abduction and the din in the Jewish quarter, and who in ever growing numbers had invaded it. When they saw Simon lying dead, they cried, 'That was a Christian child! The Jews have killed it!'

"Raging, they fell on Lazarus and beat him almost to death, as they did Löbel and poor Miryam. Then they spread out in the house, looted it, and finally set it on fire. Then they fell on the other Jews, ravaging and looting and burning until soldiers arrived and chased them off.

"A month later Lazarus, Löbel, and Manasse were executed under fearful tortures. Miryam had already died. Simon was of course also dead. Thus was Lazarus's curse fulfilled—that his line should be eradicated from the earth."

The Pole was silent. A profound emotion was stamped on all faces.

"It is late," said Philip Bendixen after a pause, "let us *bensch*."

He ceded to the guest the rightful honor of leading the singing of the prayer, and when it was ended, they went to bed.

Chapter 7

OTHERWISE STRANGERS WERE very seldom seen in the house. With the exception of the municipal bailiff and the customs inspector who, when they appeared in the shop, were invited inside, visitors were received only on the Jewish high holidays, in the persons of the few Jewish families who, besides Philip Bendixen and his brother-in-law, lived in the town. The perpetual petty enmities inhibited a frequent social gathering, and whenever they did get together in friendship, the assemblage's elements did not have sufficient intellectual and social refinement to control their irritability and passion. A bit more business at a neighbor's than at one's own place, a little increase in splendor whereby the neighbor's wife eclipsed one's own wife, and the like gave rise to a secret resentment which on occasion burst forth. Thus for the greater part of the year they looked askance at each other and spat before each other on the street, reduced the price on their wares to hurt the competition, and caused as much injury to each other as possible.

In all justice, it must not be denied that there was etiquette and ceremonial enough whenever they came together—perhaps etiquette and enmity were closely related. No one gave away anything of his dignity by visiting another more often than he received visits from him; attention was paid to the most insignificant words and looks of the host and hostess; if another received a more friendly smile or more questions concerning the state of his health, one suddenly became as silent as death, got up shortly after, and left with the firm resolve never again to darken this threshold with one's shadow. But all perils and difficulties were herewith not yet overcome, for the matron whose husband was rich expected to be received with greater marks of respect than the one whose husband was less rich, and the latter in turn watched with jealous meticulousness to make sure that the other was not given preference over her because she was richer—so that it seemed almost impossible that a gathering could end without enmity.

History reports that, while the Romans besieged Jerusalem, the various parties among the Jews raged just as violently against each other as against the enemy standing outside. A strange people, who in your exile display the same image! Was Jerusalem your mother, and have you imbibed discord along with your mother's milk? You live scattered among a foreign people, and while you feel yourselves hated and despised, you so often reciprocally hate, envy, and despise each other—a sign, as it were, of the final dissolution to come. And what is the yardstick for your reciprocal admiration? Money! The rich man is your nobleman, and you bow just as low to him as *kemech* bows to the star and the ribbon of nobility—well, the star and the ribbon anybody can turn out, but gold . . . You are right! Of the two of you, it is you who are right. And hasn't gold been your sword and your shield, haven't you bought with it the air you breathe, your children's life, and the peace of your burial place? Haven't you from time immemorial been commissioned, "Bring gold!" and can one then be offended that you have sought it?

And doesn't the Christian love gold, does he contemptuously throw it to you, that you can gather it up and rejoice in it? Are you alone infected with this illness, or does the worm sit and gnaw all mankind? . . . The misfortune is only that some of you have the bad habit that your eyes glitter and your fingers contract convulsively when gold gleams. Get rid of this ugly habit and learn some pretty phrases about virtue and human worth and money's filth—but pronounce these phrases without an accent.

There was finally a fairly general peace in the town on *Rosh hashana*,[1] so that Philip Bendixen's house could be honored by the visits of the other Jews. The men had only gone home from

---

[1] The year's head, New Year's.

the temple to get their wives[2] and now arrived one after the other in the entrance hall, where Jette and her husband received them with the most zealous attention. After many compliments the company was settled in the sitting room under the cheerful influence of the holiday's holiness and peace. Leib Essen, the last arrival, rubbed his hands together and said, "Today we had a proper *Schul!* It went off so *mejuschuf,*[3] that I really enjoyed it."

"So did I," said Philip Bendixen, "not since I was in Copenhagen have I heard anyone blow the *shofar*[4] as well as Rabbi Jokuf. He is a great *bal tekeio.*"[5]

"Just think," said Mosche Nyborg to his wife, "Leib Essen was *mechabot* to me today with a *mitzvo;* I had *gelilo.*"[6]

---

[2] In the temple the men and women sat apart from each other. Wherever the temple has not been arranged accordingly, the women could not come to the common religious service.

[3] Nicely and respectably.

[4] On the High Holidays Satan appears before the Lord's throne as accuser; on this account the *shofar* (a horn) is blown, and every note proceeding from it becomes an angel who defends the congregation against Satan's accusation.

[5] Master of horn blowing.

[6] The Jews' religious service is based on the principle that the people themselves are to perform it, and knowledge of the Law and the ceremonies is thus not to be the monopolized property of one single class. Since the sacrifices ceased after the fall of Jerusalem, the priest has nothing at all to do with the religious service, and can be altogether dispensed with; a member of the congregation leads the reading of the prayers, when there is no paid cantor (*hazan*). On Mondays and Thursdays three, on Saturdays eight, sections of the Torah are read aloud by the congregation itself, so that each section is read out by another member. Great care is taken that, for example, anyone with a defect or a domestic misfortune or who has committed a sin does not by accident read out a section that might remind him of the misfortune or contain a reproach for him. The Torah stands in the Holy Ark; God's spirit is thought to be enthroned with it. The ceremonies connected with taking out the Torah, when it is to be read aloud, resemble in pomp and protocol those used in a Christian church. One member, reverently bowing, draws the curtain, opens the Ark, and takes out the Torah to hand it over to the cantor; his task is called *Hautzoa vehachnoso;* when the Torah is laid on the lectern by the cantor and has been read, another has the task (*Hagbo*) of lifting it and holding it out toward the congregation, calling out, "*Thoros Mosche emmes*" ("The Law of Moses is truth!"), which is repeated aloud by the congregation. Now a third member steps up to roll the Torah scroll (*Gelilo*) and wrap it in the *Mappo,* a piece of cloth resembling a child's blanket, and then put on the cover of velvet or silk with the appurtenant silver ornaments (which are donated to the temple by devout people, like alter cloths or the like among the Christians). The *Maftir,* the one who last reads from the Torah, brings it back to the shrine; the one who took it out then takes it from his hands, places it in, and shuts the Ark, bowing. Anyone who touches the Torah kisses it before he passes it on, likewise the spot on his finger which has been sanctified by

"No! Just think of that!" cried his wife, looking at Leib Essen in a friendly way.

"That was to strengthen our reconciliation," said the latter good-naturedly, extending his hand to Mosche Nyborg.

"I'll certainly remember to pray for you on *Yom Kippur*," said Mosche Nyborg's wife, "blessed *Yom Kippur*! in nine weeks we'll have it. Do you fast on *Yom Kippur*?" she asked Jacob, discovering him beside her.

"Yes!" cried Jacob proudly, "I already fast half a day, and I fast a half a day on *Tishebeaf*."[7]

"You are a good boy!" said Madam Nyborg, handing Jacob an orange slice.

Between his father and one of those present there now ensued a subdued conversation about the son's good qualities, and a lull settled over the gathering.

"To be sure, it went off very *bekovod*[8] today," Schol Bernburg said finally, "but it really is nothing compared to Copenhagen! What I wouldn't give to hear a proper *duchno*[9] again! *Das Lef thut Anem weih*."[10]

---

touching it. All these various tasks are deeds pleasing to God (*Mitzvos*) and are bought at auctions held on the spot, but one can present to another the *Mitzvo* which one has bought for oneself, and this is done when the other person is having a domestic celebration or when one wants to demonstrate his friendship. The money collected at the auction goes to the synagogue. In Copenhagen, where everything generally is arranged with great orderliness since the new synagogue was built—perhaps even a little aristocratically—this democratic arrangement with auctions is no longer found; *Mitzvos* are bought privately from the cantor a day in advance. The religiously displeased find it easy to console themselves, since a gathering of ten Jews forms a congregation and temple in an attic, under the open sky, on sea or on land, anywhere.

[7] The tenth day of the month of *Av*, the anniversary of Jerusalem's destruction. This day is a fast day, and on the nine preceding days no meat is eaten, in memory of Jerusalem's tribulations.

[8] With honor, properly.

[9] On the High Holidays all the *Konim* (descendants of the high priest's caste) stand forth on the raised platform in front of the tabernacle and, shrouded from head to foot in white *Talesim*, they recite in a distinctive tone and with mysterious monotonous gestures the blessing over the congregation. They must not be looked at while they thus are representing the divinity. This ceremony is called "to *duchne*."

[10] "One's heart aches from longing."

"Why didn't you stay in Copenhagen?" cried the fat Wulf Mendel. "You are always talking about it; in your place I would have stayed there!"

Schol Bernburg had had to leave Copenhagen on account of an awkward bankruptcy; he bit his lip but kept silent so no one would notice that he had understood the allusion. But the others understood it, and the conversation ground to a halt again.

In order to say something, Philip Bendixen went to the window, looked out as if he were looking for someone, and said, "God knows why we don't have the honor of Simon Nasche's visit today?"

"He probably knew that he would meet me here," remarked Wulf Mendel with a malicious smile.

"Are you on bad terms?" asked Philip.

"Bad terms? That fellow stinks of *gavo*[11] so that you can't come near him. Now listen to this. The other day he comes to me in my shop, and since there was nothing to do, I chat a little with him. He talks about the hard times, about the bad luck—*bei ihm bleib' es!* [may he be stuck with it!]—he had a while ago, when the customs inspector took some goods away from him, and complains about the fact that he doesn't know how he is going to pay the note he took out on the goods. Well, I say, don't let your wife run around with as expensive silk material in her dress as my wife! Am I not right? Such a good-for-nothing comes and complains that he hardly has bread in the house, and when you see his wife, you'd think she was married to the richest man in town. What do you think he answered me? He spat in my face and yelled, 'May things not go well for you right up to the end! Be careful, or God will punish your innocent children for your pride! For the Lord, the God of Israel, is a just God who punishes the sins of the fathers. . . . ' I didn't hear any more; I ran inside to escape his evil words, and he ran off. May his own curse strike him!"

"But you, too, were too hard on him, Wulf Mendel," said Philip Bendixen reproachfully. "Everybody does like to see his wife dressed up. Doesn't Abba Hilkia say, 'The man shall give

---

[11] Pride.

his wife finery so that she can strive to please him, and so that he shall not find pleasure in other women'."

"Listen, Philip Bendixen," cried Wulf Mendel, flushing blood-red, "I won't put up with any reprimands from you! You are not yet a *rof*.[12] Maybe you think, because you have a couple of pennies more than I, that you can lord it over me? The Lord stands against the haughty. . . ."

His wife covered his mouth so that he would not pronounce a fatal word, but the furious Wulf Mendel got up to leave.

"Don't let the blessed *Yom tov* be disturbed by discord!" implored Philip Bendixen, taking his hand, "I didn't say that to offend you."

Wulf Mendel allowed himself to be pacified and resumed his seat.

"There goes old Marthe," said Isak Bamberger, pointing out the window in order to distract everybody's thoughts from the painful scene just past.

Hardly had he made this movement when a shrill voice resounded from the street: "*Ausgerottet soll't Ihr werden!* [You should be exterminated!] There you sit and gorge yourselves while a poor old woman like me doesn't even have the means to put a *kuggel* in her *scholunt* for *Schabbas*.[13] But the Lord will not forget that!"

Isak Bamberger goodnaturedly replied, opening the window, "Well, then, come on in and refresh yourself with us. Come and eat a piece of *Butterkuchen*, saved for you from last night."

"*Butterkuchen* you have on Friday evening, while another child of Israel roasts a piece of *bersches* [Sabbath bread] and lean meat!" cried the old woman, slapping her hands together. "But I won't enter your house. I would come only as a beggar to the rich man, and you are no Boas. *Jemar Schemecho!*"[14]

---

[12] Rabbi.

[13] Since Jews may not cook on the Sabbath, a soup is cooked on Friday, which is kept on glowing coals until Saturday. It is called *scholunt* (literally translated: something that has stood over night). A dumpling that goes into the soup, made of flour, sugar, and fat, is called *kuggel*.

[14] "Your name shall be eradicated."

Disappointed over the unsuccessful outcome of his efforts to bring about a livlier mood, Isak shut the window; but to make one more effort, he forced himself to smile and said to the assemblage, "I am no Boas, she says; she is certainly no Naomi (i.e., charmer), either."

They laughed, and one of the women present began, "Who cares what old Marthe says! If you gave her all your clothes down to the skin, she would curse you because you didn't give her the skin, too. Yesterday she came to me to get her usual *Rosch-ha-Hodisch-Schank*.[15] I usually give her six coins, but I had only exactly four in small change, and I gave them to her. What did she do? She threw them on the floor and said, 'If you cannot afford to give me six, then I can afford to give you six.' With that, she laid six coins on the table and left with a curse. Yes, what one puts up with, with such a needy Jew as that!" She went on, "If you give a *goy* one coin, he doesn't know enough blessings to bestow on you, but for the Jew, alms are a *Musz* [a must, an obligation], and he himself decides what you are to give him."

"In your place, Memmele, I would have done with Marthe what I once did with Black Ephraim from Assens," said Isak Bamberger. "You remember that he went around here and took up a collection when he had had a fire? He came to me, too, and I started to give him a two-rix-dollar bill. 'Excuse me, Mr. Bamberger,' he said, 'your brother-in-law gave me two of these bills.' I stuck the bill in my pocket and answered, 'Excuse me, Mr. Ephraim, then my brother-in-law gave for me, too'."

"God protect me from daring such a thing with Marthe!" cried Memmele, laughing. "But you surely know, Jette Bendixen, that you can consider yourself lucky that Marthe didn't see the nice new dress you have on today; she would have cursed you the whole night," she added with a sidelong glance at Jette's dress.

"This dress is not new; it's an old one that I made over and dressed up. One gets by the best one can."

"That's a different matter," said Memmele mollified.

---

[15] *Rosh-ha-Hodesh*, the head, or beginning, of the month. Alms are given preferably on Friday.

"Since we're talking about Marthe," began another woman, "have you heard how she behaved the other day at Schol Esser's? It was on Friday, the day after he had gone bankrupt, and she turned up to receive her *Schabbasschank*. When she started to knock on his door, her daughter, who was along with her, said, 'Mother, isn't it better now to give him his gift; he has after all gone bankrupt.' 'Well, so what?' answered Marthe crossly, '*wer schenkt mir was* [who gives me anything]?'"

"That's just like her!" cried Memmele.

"I don't know what more the poor in a *kille*[16] could ask for, than they get," remarked Gidel, a plump little matron. "Aren't bread and meat distributed to them every Friday, and don't they receive money in the bargain? Don't they receive their *matzos*[17] on *Pesach*, and aren't they remembered on *Purim* with *schlachmonos*?[18] Does ever a *Yom tov*[19] go by without their receiving their share of the gladness? Do you think the Christians do that much for their poor?"

Now old Rabbi Jocub (i.e., Jacob) got up. This was a little gray-haired man, quiet and inoffensive by nature. He lived on a small pension and stood in high repute for his learnedness in the Scriptures, for which he was usually given the title of rabbi. He said, "The merciful God looks at the attitude, not at the gift. When your brother asks for bread, you shall not give him a stone; but an unkind attitude turns the bread into stone. You give old Marthe alms and want her to thank you. Do you remember the time when she was rich? Then she was met by a fond '*Boruch habo*,'[20] when she opened the door, and she sat in the place of honor. *She* remembers that time when she accepts alms at that same door. She does not look at the gift, but her ear and her heart are torn apart by that '*Boruch habo*' that she no longer hears. Let us praise the almighty God, who deals out afflictions."

---

[16] Congregation.

[17] Easter biscuits.

[18] Presents.

[19] Holiday.

[20] "Blessed be your arrival."

"Tell me, Wulf Mendel," the indefatigable Isak Bamberger began again, "how is your lawsuit going? Is he still making it hard for you to get your money, this merchant Jensen?"

"All my afflictions on his head!" cried Wulf Mendel. "If a Jew treated a goy like that, we'd hear about it! It's now already a year and a half since I ought to have had my money, according to his legal note, and he has dragged it out all this time under the pretext that the goods were not worth so much. Did I force him to buy my goods? And in every plea in the court he calls me the Jew Mendel. But just wait! The judgment will be handed down soon, and if I then have to sell his last comforter, I am going to get my money. Every time he sees me, the adsus ponim[21] laughs right in my face. But just wait!"

"There is no doubt that you are right, Wulf Mendel," said Isak, "but this Jensen is making a frightful risches in town. He hangs around the whole day at the tavern and tells everybody how the Jew Mendel wants to put him and his children in their grave."

"Um Gottes Willen [for God's sake]!" several cried out fearfully. "Do be careful that there won't be risches, do you hear, Wulf Mendel!"

"Am I supposed to make him a gift of my money into the bargain?" cried Wulf Mendel furiously. "Do I find my bayis horo[22] on the street? In order to reach a settlement, didn't I myself offer to be satisfied with whatever value three Christian merchants would place on the goods? Didn't the scoundrel refuse that? Even if it costs me my life, he is now going to pay me every last thing he owes me. Yes, the Jew Mendel will put him and his children in their grave!" added Wulf Mendel, grinding his teeth.

---

[21] Obstinate and mocking face.

[22] Goods.

The mood was now no longer to be restored. Most had turned their thoughts anxiously to the consequences this lawsuit could have for all the Jews in the town; Wulf Mendel was mulling over his indignation. "*Ausgerottet soll't Ihr werden!*" It was again the shrill voice of Marthe, now on her way back, resounding outside the window, and with ominous feelings the company broke up after forced compliments and protestations of friendship.

Chapter 8

Pogrom

Among the letters which Philip Bendixen received in the mail one morning was one that made him throw up his hands in fear and desperation. It was from his brother in Copenhagen and read thus:

Dear Brother!

When you receive this letter, the rumor of the dreadful days here will already have reached you, and I am writing you so that you can see that our lives are safe, the Lord be praised! But how will it go later on?—that is what we are anxiously asking each other, and nobody knows a reassuring answer; but every day we face the evening in mortal fear. *Kemech* are like absolute lunatics; they are smashing in the windows of all the Jews, and woe betide the Jew who dares to go out among them! Rabbi Jehudo, who was beaten and kicked by them as he walked home, has died, and several other devout Jews have been badly beaten up. My father-in-law fell into the hands of two sailors who threatened to kill him if he wouldn't dance for them. What was the old man to do? He had to dance, after which they spat in his face and said, "That's what you get, kike, because you dance so badly." But they did take him home unharmed. Now he is in bed mortally ill from fright. It has come here from Hamburg like a plague that spreads from one country into another. If it only were a plague they had caught! During the daytime they are calm and watch the windows being put in. It is for their amusement in the evening. We have considered fleeing from this Gomorrho and take refuge with you, but the chief of police, old Haagen, has persuaded us to wait a few days more. When I went to him to ask for a passport, he talked to me in his peculiar way; you probably remember it from the old days when he visited our mother's house: "Are you afraid, Marcus? Don't you think we can protect you? Just wait a couple of days, until the king confines the soldiers to their barracks and leaves everything to me and my good police clubs! I know my Danes better." May the Lord put His power in the police clubs! But if that doesn't happen soon, then I'll leave with my wife and children and hope that you will give us shelter until everything is back to normal. Greet your good wife and your little son, just as you yourself are greeted affectionately from all of us.

Your faithful brother
Marcus

In unutterable anguish Philip Bendixen hurried over to his brother-in-law to inform him of the terrible news. There he met more Jews who had already received similar letters in which the calamity in part was described even more strongly. The military refused to serve, it was said; the civil guard would join with the rioters; the king was on the point of sacrificing the Jews to save his crown; all Jews were to be slaughtered on the same day throughout the whole kingdom, etc.

A terrible fear of the threatening calamity and a fervent compasssion for their fellow Jews who were already engulfed in it seized those present. The men wept like children and beat their breasts in this misery, for which they knew no remedy. "Fortunate are those who are resting in their graves!" they cried, "their eyes have closed in peace. It is as if we were in the Flood; the catastrophe is advancing, and nowhere is there a hiding-place. Woe, woe, woe betide us! The Lord has turned his countenance from His people, and it is coming to pass, as it is written: your festival shall be transformed into sorrow, your joy into lamentation!"

"What good is there in whining?" Isak Bamberger broke in. "Our brothers are in God's hand, and we cannot help them. But we can help ourselves, if we stick faithfully together and don't lose courage."

"What do you mean?" they all asked anxiously.

"We are only a few," said Isak Bamberger, stepping in the middle of the assemblage, "but we are enough to defend a firm, solidly built place. I once saw a handful of Frenchmen defend themselves in a cemetery against an entire regiment, and they didn't surrender until cannons were used against them. *Kemech* here don't have any cannons. Let's assemble with our families and defend ourselves to the last drop of blood. I offer my house for this."

"You speak well enough, Isak Bamberger," cried Wulf Mendel, "are we others all supposed to leave house and property to help defend yours? And who says that we all will be attacked? Maybe they will be satisfied with individuals and spare the rest, the most peaceable. But if we are assembled and are attacked, then we will all fall."

"And how are we to defend ourselves?" said another; "we are no soldiers, no Frenchmen. That's good for people who have learned nothing else. If I were to to stand and defend a house, and they came marching up in howling mobs, from fear I would fall out the window into their midst. I won't make myself out to be a greater hero than I am. Caleb was a warrior, but Aron was a man of peace."

"From the time that Jerusalem fell," said a third, "it has been Israel's fate to suffer defenseless. I am going home to await whatever the dear God will ordain for me."

The rest were of the same opinion, and resignedly each slunk home.

Isak Bamberger went over with Philip to reassure and comfort the latter's wife.

In the meantime the news had also reached other residents of the town, and at various spots they had gathered to discuss it.

The local administrator and the customs inspector were at the municipal police chief's.

"I have received orders to nip any possible attempt here in the bud," said the police chief. "They are relying on my discretion. God knows what I am to do if it really breaks out! I have two police officers, of whom one retired from the customs on account of age and infirmity, and the other was appointed a police officer because in 1807 he was relieved of his job because he lost a leg. That is my entire force, but I still think that it will probably be fairly calm here. I am on good terms with the townspeople, and a couple of reasonable words used at the right time can accomplish a great deal."

"If the Jews could get a little scare so that we in the future are free of them, I wouldn't have anything against it," said the administrator. "I am not intolerant, but I admit frankly that I do not like Moses' people. This loathing for the Jews must also have deeper grounds; it is in all our blood."

"It's more likely in upbringing," remarked the customs inspector, a friendly grey-haired man nearing old age. "They are brought up separately, as are we, and we absorb prejudice against each other from childhood on."

"But it is such an avaricious, dirty race," resumed the administrator, "and even the better among them, such as Isak Bamberger and his brother-in-law Philip Bendixen here in town now, still have something unpleasant, a certain—I don't know what—about them. With them, one feels as if one were in another atmosphere . . . maybe it's the garlic atmosphere," he added with a chuckle.

"Bamberger and Bendixen are two good and decent men," said the customs inspector, "and I would be sincerely sorry if the slightest harm came to them. And have you seen the delightful, bright boy Bendixen has? Whenever I see the boy, I am really sorry that he is a Jew."

"You see!" cried the administrator, "you have the very same feeling I do. When you find something good with the Jews, you think that it doesn't belong among them."

"You misunderstand me, and I perhaps didn't express myself clearly enough, either," said the customs inspector, smiling and shaking his head.

"I'm going out; I'll go around to the Jews and cheer them up," cried the police chief, "it will also make a good impression on the townspeople when they see me going to the Jews."

The police chief took his uniform cap and his little cane, and the three officials strolled down the street.

At the tavern another gathering was occupied with the same subject. The main room was almost full, and the noise of the billiard balls and clinking schnapps glasses was pierced by excited voices. Larsen, the fat distiller, was sitting with his back to the open window and holding forth. "Yes," he shouted, raising his right hand with his large meerschaum pipe, "the Copenhageners are plucky people. They don't talk, but strike."

"The king is supposed to be in a bad pinch," remarked the barber with an important and mysterious look, "they have sent him word that if he will let them treat the Jews as they want, he can sit absolutely without being disturbed. If not . . ."

"He'll have to take the trouble to have them thrashed to scatter them," the young Dr. Flor interrupted the speaker.

"You are always so humorous, Doctor," said the barber with suppressed annoyance; "the Copenhageners are damned well not to be trifled with."

"No, the Copenhageners are plucky people!" cried the distiller, "hurrah for the Copenhageners!"

"Hurrah for the Copenhageners!" resounded in chorus.

"I'd like to see the faces the Jews make when they are on their knees being beaten and praying, 'Abraham, Isaac, and Jacob, help us!' and Abraham, Isaac, and Jacob ignore them," shouted the young shopkeeper Petersen laughing.

"That sight wouldn't be so difficult to get to see," said the butcher Carstens with a meaningful look.

"What sin would there be in killing a Jew!" cried the misshapen sexton Green; "it was the Jews, wasn't it, who slew Christ."

"And now they are sucking us Christians dry!" bawled another.

"And such scum as that think they're too good to eat with us Christians," said the butcher. "I can butcher to satisfy everybody except the Jews. There is a reciting and a washing whenever an ox is to have the honor of being eaten by them. Who do those scum think they are?"

The proprietor bawled, "There they are, sitting on their money, which they cheat us Christians out of. I serve the foremost men in town, but never has a Jew granted me so much business as a schnapps. To hell with that trash; what are they good for?"

"It's no more than a week ago that that fat Wulf Mendel cut off two more rix-dollars for the work I did at his place," related the carpenter Hansen; "you can't earn anything from that kind of people."

"Wulf Mendel—he was also the one who put Jensen in the poorhouse," someone said.

"Yes, he is a real scoundrel!" cried another.

"They are all the same!" bawled a third.

"They ought to be taken out to the border and given a kick!"

"They ought to be killed like mad dogs!"

But the crowd got no further than what "ought" to be done to them, and since noon was approaching, they one after another went home.

But up at the poorhouse, the former shopkeeper Jensen was running about. He had been there now for two years, since the unfortunate outcome of the lawsuit with Wulf Mendel. He had become terribly thin, and it was apparent that a devastating consumption was draining his vital forces. But his otherwise dull blue eyes blazed with a sinister fire, and on the pale, sunken cheeks small red spots came and went.

It was as if a subdued insanity had taken possession of him at the prospect of the hitherto unattainable vengeance being so close. He ran around with strange gestures like those men sometimes seen in dreams who seem to the dreamer to be imparting their words by touch more than by speech. From his workbench he darted now to one, now to another, elbowed him and whispered, "The king has commanded that all Jews be killed tomorrow.—Hey, you! Tomorrow we'll rob the rich Jews and kill them.—Have you seen the king's command? Tomorrow I'll pay back Wulf Mendel.—We'll call in the farmers; they're supposed to help us to rob and kill them."

His mood seemed as if magnetically to communicate itself to the others and increase in energy under the guardedness imposed on them by the presence of the superintendent. When working hours were over, they went with him down the street to the market where the farmers gathered. There he again ran from one to the other: "Have you heard the king's command that all Jews are to be killed? Come tomorrow with your flail and pitchfork, and we'll kill the Jews and take their money." "No, is it really so?" said the farmers, "yes, we have heard whispers about it all day. Yes, if the king commands it, then we'll obey." "Yes, come tomorrow and make your purchases as usual; tomorrow evening, when it gets dark, we'll kill the Jews."

"Who is that fellow?" asked some of the farmers. "It's him, Jensen, who was formerly a shopkeeper," replied others; "he's a smart fellow; he must know it." "In Copenhagen they have been killed; tomorrow we're supposed to do the same, and we'll take their money!" In this way he continued his goading until the farmers had gone.

From the market he hurried homeward, and wherever a Jew lived he stopped and shouted, "Just wait till tomorrow!" and the whole mob joined in the hoarse cry, "Just wait till tomorrow!"

In the evening he was sitting alone with his wife in their wretched little room. "Tomorrow," he said, "I'll get Wulf Mendel paid back. I just knew that God could not let me die before that, even if He had to perform a miracle."

"In the name of Jesus!" said his wife, "he did put our two little ones in the grave. The poor things died of poverty and misery," she added weeping.

"Tomorrow!" he went on, "and then I will gladly die. I know that you will follow me soon, won't you, Ma?"

His wife wept silently.

He continued, "It was three years after we got married. Then I took you to the poorhouse."

His wife sobbed.

"And now for two years, day in and day out, I have seen you wearing this coarse dress while his wife has been dressed in velvet and silk. But tomorrow we'll settle accounts, Wulf Mendel!"

"But he did offer a settlement," said his wife, impelled by that sense of justice which women so often possess to a higher degree than men.

"Didn't he know very well that I could not pay? Could I help all the bad luck that struck me? And what were the couple of hundred rix-dollars for the rich man? For me they were everything! They have cost me health and happiness and my two children! That was a high price, Wulf Mendel! But tomorrow we'll settle accounts."

"Let's sing a psalm, Ma!" he said after a pause, "it's a long time since we sang together."

He took the psalm book, opened it, and struck up the first psalm that caught his eye, and now the couple's singing was heard outside:

"I know that the grave is my lot,
And I must depart from here;
But when? Oh God, this Thou hast not
Wanted to me to make clear.
That is known only unto Thee.
Thou in Thy world here did place me,
And Thou numbered all my days."

The notes died away, and stillness descended on the large, cheerless building.

Early the next morning Isak Bamberger came over to Philip Bendixen's.

"Philip Bendixen!" he said gravely, "we have now for many years stuck together like brothers. If you feel as I do, we'll stick together to the last."

Philip silently clasped his hand.

Isak went on, "The police chief has directed us to keep our shops open the whole day and act as though nothing were wrong. I'll do that. But as soon as it begins to get dark I'll close shop and come over with my wife and my best things to you. You have more to protect than I, Brother! You have a son."

"My son! My poor child!" said Philip, tears coming to his eyes.

"We will protect him!" cried Isak in a firm voice; "as long as I can swing an ax, nobody is going to get near him."

"My poor child!" wailed Philip.

"Be a man, Philip!" cried Isak, clutching Philip's arm; "it doesn't help to whine. Protect your son, don't weep for him."

"Oh, Isak!" moaned Philip, "you don't know what it is to protect a child. Won't any blow struck at attackers fall doubled on the child's head?"

Isak brushed his eyes with the back of his hand and went home.

Never have sellers been more reluctant to sell and buyers more eager to buy than that day. The Jews thought they could drive away the farmers out of their shops by jacking up prices to the astronomical, but the farmers paid whatever they demanded, and saw the money glide into the till with an expression that seemed to say, "We'll certainly find you again this evening."

All over town the farmers were carousing and were exceedingly merry, but nothing suggested the catastrophe that was prepared for the evening—a peculiarity that scarcely has its match in any other race than the deliberate Danish farmer. The farmers thought they had the Jews absolutely in their power and now were playing with them as a cat plays with a mouse. The Jews would gladly have been the mouse—just to be able to creep into a mousehole.

When it began to grow dark, all the Jews shut their shops, and the farmers gathered on the marketplace. The inmates of the poorhouse, journeymen and apprentices, and a few townspeople joined them, and now, without noise, in an orderly procession they proceeded toward Wulf Mendel's house.

At first the mob was intimidated by the profound stillness that reigned, but when no signs of resistance were to be seen anywhere, the doors were soon kicked in and they broke into the shop. In an instant the shelves and drawers were emptied into the sacks that had been brought along, and the indefatigable Jensen led the attackers into the private rooms. When the door to the innermost room had been broken down, they saw Wulf Mendel standing before his wife and grown daughter and money chest. The women were deathly pale and could scarcely hold themselves upright. Wulf Mendel was trembling, but his fear was mixed with a convulsive fury at seeing the danger threatening his money chest. But hardly had so much time passed as is here used to describe his condition: the two enemies stood face to face.

Without uttering a sound they threw themselves at each other. Wulf Mendel's powerful hand struck his enemy's diseased chest, and a tremendous blow from the latter's cudgel fell on Wulf Mendel's head. The two enemies fell fraternally side by side.

This scene gripped the farmers spontaneously, just as any intense outbreak of human passion grips the sensibilities; one sees a volcano opening, the possibility of which everyone bears in himself. Some looked to Jensen, while others carried Wulf Mendel along with the two unconscious women out of the house and turned them over to the next-door neighbor, Simon Nasche, whose door they broke down. As if his house had been consecrated by their victims' presence, they moved on without inflicting any damage to it.

The Jew living closest was Philip Bendixen, and the procession now moved toward his house. The doors were broken down, and the family retreated slowly from room to room, finally to seek refuge in the cellar, where their best wares had earlier been brought. The attackers could hear the cellar door being hastily slammed shut, but hesitated a little in pursuing through the winding subterranean passageway.

"I know the way!" cried a farm hand, placing himself at their head, "I have worked here in the house."

They advanced, but again stopped at a turning.

"Just follow me!" shouted the farm hand, dashing ahead of the others.

A dim flash was seen, a short, muffled yelp was heard, and the farm hand dashed back with a loud scream.

"What is it?" several cried.

"It's the Jews' god sitting there!" cried the farm hand, almost beside himself with terror and pain, "didn't you see the little black thing? There he is again!"

Seized by panic, he plunged back, taking the rest with him out of the passageway.

Up in the living quarters they ran into the police chief. He was dressed in his red uniform coat, armed with a stick and badge and accompanied by his two officers, who at least could function as supernumeraries. "What are you doing here?" he barked harshly at the intruders.

Nobody answered.

"And what's wrong with you?" he asked, catching sight of the bleeding farm hand staggering out. "It serves you right. In the king's name I arrest you!"

He laid hands on the farm hand, who collapsed from loss of blood and terror.

The words "in the king's name!" affected the farmers like a thunderbolt.

"In the king's name!" repeated the police chief harshly. "I command each of you to go to his home; whoever I meet again will be punished as an insurgent guilty of high treason. Do you understand me?"

The farmers slunk silently away, leaving the filled sacks.

Meanwhile, the family had listened in breathless terror to the rumbling procession and with a silent prayer thanked God when it unexpectedly departed.

"Jacob! where are you?" his anxious mother said at last, groping for him.

"Where are you, Jacob?" she called more loudly when she did not find him. "Where is my boy? Didn't I have him go ahead of me into the cellar? Where is he? Where are you, my son, my Jacob!" she cried in maternal fear.

"He has probably crawled into a corner," said his uncle, "maybe he has fainted from fear. I do remember that he was born in fear of war and unrest."

They searched in all corners, but he was not there.

"*Schema Jisroel!* They have found him and taken him along!" cried his mother in utter desperation. "They are killing my child! That's the reason they are so quiet."

"Then come on, Isak, and keep your promise!" screamed Philip Bendixen, tearing open the cellar door and leaping out with an ax in his hands.

"Father!" said a soft voice when he had gone a few steps.

"Jacob! God in heaven! Is it you?" called his father, letting the ax fall.

There sat the boy on a stone, and in his hand he was holding his dagger. It was bloody up to the hilt. The weak lighting falling in the passageway revealed to the father and the uncle the boy's pale face and the bloody weapon. With one glance they guessed what had happened.

With a strange feeling of fear and admiration the father bent over his child, who fell unconscious into his arms.

The uncle said, "Now there is blood between him and the Christians."

The police chief came to find the family and led it back in triumph to the living quarters. He took the unconscious child from the father and carefully put him to bed, while he scolded the maidservants because they didn't spread the covers quickly enough on the sofa. Then he took Isak Bamberger aside and whispered to him with a meaningful look, "A farm hand was stabbed with a knife down there. I don't care who did it; he got his just deserts. It's not you, of course, Mr. Bamberger."

Isak found it better by his silence to confirm the police chief in his conviction than by a denial possibly provoking an investigation.

The police chief now turned to the others. "And now tomorrow open your shops as usual. I will guarantee you that no one will raise a murmur to you. Don't be frightened any more now, Madame Bamberger, and you either, little Madame Bendixen. I hope the little one is better soon. Good night!" He shook hands with the men and left.

But the thoughts of the others were completely elsewhere than where the police chief believed. They were silent, but all felt that they could not separate yet. There was something among them that they avoided discussing, but each one knew that the other's thoughts were occupied with it. There was a secret, not from the world, but from each other; they were afraid of lifting the veil, so to speak, in order not to get to see more. To them it seemed that what was concealed would show itself if it were discussed, but through silence would remain in the depths.

When the child opened his eyes, his mother asked if he didn't want to eat. The boy said he did and greedily fell upon the food that was brought in, and seemed to eat eagerly. The others looked at each other with lightened hearts, and a little afterward they went to bed.

Chapter 9

AFTER A STORM AT SEA the waves do not subside immediately. A long time passed before spirits returned to their accustomed stillness and calm; at least among the Jews the sight of any Christian face aroused memories of the hatred directed at them and of the terror it had recently caused them. The more cultivated Christians who with word or deed had taken part in the Jewish persecution were secretly ashamed when they saw a Jew, and were afterward annoyed that they had to be ashamed because of a Jew. The simpler townspeople, on the other hand, and in general those who owed the Jews money, came to them immediately after the pogrom with friendly faces, and each assured them with the most ingenuous expression that he had had no part in the persecution.

There is in the world far less dissimulation than one reads in novels, but far more than one believes in daily life. Those faces on which simplicity or stupidity seems to have set its stamp can conceal exceedingly well one or another cunning thought that has sneaked in—how indifferent can it not look, when it is most clever not to show sympathy, how amiably can it not smile at an enemy who is too strong or who is needed! And in general how much comedy we all act with each other, almost without noticing it, without feeling any effort? When are two people completely candid, even when they sit down to talk quite sincerely with each other? How many families must there be in which there is not hidden one or another small secret, at times even a large one? When you are sitting gathered around the table, apparently occupied only with each other, with the little world within your four walls, and each one suddenly should have to tell what his or her thoughts were, or where they earlier had been—if the wife should talk to her husband, the husband to his wife, the daughter to her mother, the bridegroom to his betrothed, and circumspection did not stand guard on the floodgates of the heart—oh, that would be asking for too much, that would be seeing the white skin drawn back from muscles and sinews, that would be seeing the heart beating in the breast—let it remain closed!

Another year now passes in the accustomed stillness, and our attention is directed at Jacob only when, one Saturday morning in the summer of 182-, he is led by his father down the street to the building where the synagogue was located. Both were festively dressed, Jacob for the first time in his life in a dress coat, hat, and frilled shirt front. Today it was Jacob's *barmitzvah*, the first Sabbath after his thirteenth birthday and when he was to be admitted into the adults' community by blessing the Torah.

In the synagogue the *Aron hakodesh* (the shrine in which the Torah is kept) was ornamented with a new silk curtain which Philip had donated; two large yellow wax candles burned on the *shulhan* (the lectern where the Torah is read aloud), the chandeliers were lit, and the entire little congregation, festively dressed, was gathered.

When they had entered and had bowed reverently before the *Aron hakodesh*, the father took out a brand new *tallis* woven of the finest wool and edged with a purple border and a wide fringe of gold, and placed it around his son's shoulders. Then they both silently took their places and softly recited the prescribed prayers which the cantor read out aloud.

Now came the time when the Torah was to be read aloud. Singing loudly, the member of the congregation who had bought this service approached the *Aron hakodesh*, pulled the curtain aside, and took out the Torah, accompanied by the audible prayers of the congregation. Anyone who might have heard the loud shout of the assemblage at this moment and who did not understand the ceremony would have thought that the cantor was committing burglary, and that the rest with their warning shouts were trying to prevent him from doing this.

The cantor received the Torah and, amid the general silence, spread it out on the *shulhan*; he sought out the place where that

day's reading was to begin, called up, one after the other, seven of
the congregation to read aloud, and finally extended the silver
pointer and called out, "*Yaamod Rabbi Jainkes, Ben Rabbi
Pfeivos!*" ("Step forward, Mr. Jacob, son of Mr. Philip!"). The
father whispered a blessing, but did not move to accompany him,
for alone and unassisted the youth must go to the consecration.
More anxious than he ever was later at his university
examinations, pale and with trembling knees, he went through
the close-packed row of Jews and climbed the stairs. As he had
been painstakingly taught, he touched the Torah with the *tsitsis*
of his *tallis*, kissed them, and then recited, in the distinctive
traditional sing-song tone, the formulaic blessing: "Blessed art
Thou, God, Lord of the earth, Who hast made us blessed over
other nations and hast given us the Law." And now he proceeded
to the studied, rhythmic reading of the verse in the Torah which
chance had chosen for him, while his stern, pitiless judges stood
and listened for the smallest mistake he might possibly commit.

Many Jews believe that, when something good is contained in
the verse which they read on this day, it is a prophecy for their
entire life. If there is something bad, they consider it pure
chance. Jacob read:

"The Lord God said to the serpent, 'Cursed are you above all
cattle, and above all wild animals; upon your belly you shall go,
and dust you shall eat all the days of your life.

"I will put enmity between you and the woman, and between
your seed and her seed; he shall bruise your head, and you shall
bruise his heel.'"

After again touching the Torah with his *tsitsis*, kissing
them, and pronouncing the blessing, he turned to climb down; in
his confusion he mistakenly started to go down the same side he
had come (which one dare not do), and the cantor had to take
him by the arm and lead him the right way. Everyone looked
down in order not to notice this unusual occurrence, and when
Jacob climbed down from the last step, he was met by his father's
and the congregation's loud congratulations. The old Rabbi Jocub
pinched his cheek and said, "*Ä koscher Jüngelche*" ("A pure, good
youth"); but he added softly, directing a prayerful glance toward
heaven, "*Für die guten Kinder Jisroel soll Gott schomar und*

masol sein" ("May God preserve Israel's good children for the nation!").

When the rest of the religious service was over, the well-wishers were invited home for a celebratory meal.

Jacob was dazed and hardly knew how he got home. But later in life he was able to recall with such strange clarity every single face that had looked out the windows at the homeward bound crowd; he remembered quite distinctly how each person had been dressed in the synagogue; yes, he thought he could give precisely the length of the wicks on the tall, drowsy wax candles which he really had not noticed at all in the synagogue. And although in later years his heart often throbbed with pride, although hours came when intense, passionate, happy feelings caused the blood to storm through his veins, there still was no day and no hour that was fixed in his memory in such a dawning, magic radiance as this one.

In the afternoon after the guests had departed, his father and his uncle were sitting on the sofa; Jacob was standing with his mother by the window, looking silently out at the street. His father seemed only with difficulty to tear himself from his thoughts; in an unusually soft voice he called to Jacob, "Come over here, my dear son, so that I can talk to you."

Jacob went up to him; his father placed his hands on his head and said, "Now, my son, you are a man, a Jew. You are no longer a branch on my trunk, but are yourself a tree."

"A nice, tall tree!" his uncle interjected, holding the palm of his hand a couple of feet from the floor.

His father continued, "Up to now I have answered to God for you; for the future you yourself are responsible before God for your sins. You are a grown man."

"And can get married, if you want to," his uncle broke in again, taking him from his father and setting him on his own lap.

His father went on, "When I was *barmitzvo* my mother said to me, 'Go, support yourself.' But I will share with you, Jacob, as long as I myself possess anything."

"*Chri bekan berero!*"[1] cried his uncle, "just let your father try to say, 'Go, support yourself'! We'll stay anyway."

Jacob's eyes wandered to and fro between his uncle's cheery face and his father's friendly but serious face. Inwardly he vacillated betweeen smiling and weeping; the more his uncle joked, the more melancholy seemed his father's gentle, affectionate seriousness. His throat seemed constricted; he felt so infinitely at peace, but at the same time so infinitely sad. Then his mother came over and took him in her arms and kissed him. And this silent assurance that she, too, would stand by him resolved the spasmodic struggle, and he burst into tears.

His uncle looked at him wide-eyed. "What the hell has come over the boy? Is he sick? Who hurt him? Did I hurt you, Jacob?" he cried, clutching his arm.

"No, uncle," he replied, trying to stop his tears, "but you were joking so oddly."

"Well, there you are!" said Isak crossly, "I didn't want to have anybody speak solemnly or gloomily to the boy today, and so I was speaking cheerfully, and then he weeps at my cheerfulness. It's a good thing that we'll soon be rid of him!"

At these words Jacob wept still more violently.

His father, touched, was silent for several moments and then said, "Now don't cry, Jacob. Don't be childish; today you became a man, and it is my duty to speak seriously to you. In a few days you are leaving my house, where I have cared for you and brought you up, as is fitting and proper for a devout Jew. When the accusing angel stands before God's throne and I humbly await judgment, you will be able to step forward and give me this testimony, won't you, Jacob?"

"Yes," he sobbed.

His father resumed, "Before you leave me, I will also give you the best piece of advice that I know; let your ears be open to my fatherly words."

Jacob dried his eyes and looked attentively at his father. His father drew him closer and went on.

---

[1] Rending one's clothes without bereavement, i.e., virtue out of necessity.

"My soul is anxious on your account. If only you never take the wrong way, when you go from my side!

Preserve the good teachings you have received from your father, your mother, and your uncle; they have been given with the best will and have your welfare at heart.

The Christians will teach you much that is new and good, but you must not therefore forget what is old. Say your Jewish prayer every morning and put on your *tephilin*; the day is well begun when it begins with God.

Take care that your *tsitsis* do not become *posul*; God's eye rests on purity's pact.

Say your *krischmo* [i.e., *k'rias Schema*, Deuteronomy 6:4–9] in the evening; then God's spirit will watch over you during the night when your father is far away.

Go to the synagogue on holy days. What you miss in school you will easily make up, for God strengthens the mind on days of rest.

Be gentle toward your comrades and social friends; it is better to suffer than to commit injustice.

Show respect to older Jews; it secures a good name, and a good name is the best inheritance.

For the rest, may the almighty God bless you!"

And with these words he clasped his son to his breast and kissed him and mixed his own tears with those of his son.

Late in the evening Philip Bendixen was standing alone in his office putting papers together. "Once I have said 'A' I must also say 'B'," he said, "if he is going to be a university student, he is not going to be a shopkeeper. Ha! in one respect my son won't need to be a Jew after all." He sealed the bonds and wrote on the outside "My son's property."

There was a knock on the shutters, and Philip Bendixen cautiously went to the window. When he opened the shutter, he saw his brother-in-law. "Open the window!" said the latter. When this was done, a bag appeared at the edge of the window, and it gave a hard clink when Isak set it on the sill.

"When I was sitting over there," said Isak, "I regretted that I had caused the boy to cry today, and then it occurred to me that I also had not given him a present for his *barmitzvo*. Now you take this money and put it away for him . . . before I count it over again."

"Isak!" said Philip, touched.

"Put the money away!" cried Isak almost fiercely. He added as a kind of joke, "If it remains at the window tonight, I cannot be responsible for it."

When Jacob, several days later, stood with his father on the ship carrying them to Sealand, and dazed with the pain of leave-taking stared out at the disappearing shore, at the spot where he had fought his first battle, a long-forgotten picture flashed unbidden before his fantasy. It was the face of the boy with whom he at that time had fought so furiously. Instinctively he fixed his thoughts on that scene in order to distract his yearning and thoughts from home, and the picture of his first enemy followed him until pain and fatigue forced him to go to rest.

Chapter 10

WHEN THEY WENT OUT TO LOOK for a school near where Uncle Marcus lived, in which Latin was taught, they were lucky enough to stumble upon one of the best humanistic schools in Copenhagen.

The director of this school combined energy and strictness with a warm interest in his calling. In contrast to most of the school directors of that time, whose conscience was content with inculcating in the pupils that quantity of knowledge established by the university administration and seeing to good discipline and order within the confines of the school, he sought to affect not only his pupils' intellect but also their soul; he wanted not merely to stand over them as a disciplinarian and hired teacher, but also to descend to them as a guide and mentor—although these efforts under the then (and still) prevailing separation between upbringing and education had perforce to manifest themselves weakly and as rare exceptions.

The devoted educator for the most part had to be satisfied with exchanging observations with the other teachers, since a really lively interplay between him and the pupils was not possible. Jacob, who was so far from home and who was specifically commended to his care by his father, was nonetheless entrusted to the school only during lessons since he was living with his uncle, and therefore even regarding him the director had to limit himself more to attentiveness and observation than to an immediate contact.

"When I," he said one day to some of the teachers a short time after Jacob's admission into the school, "when I see this boy with the oriental face sitting in the lowest class among the blockheads of the class, there are moments when my school seems to me a collection of domestic animals among whom a tame panther cub has appeared. If only the other whelps will treat the panther cub well so that its nature is not aroused." These words were as much in jest as in earnest, but to his astonishment the director was soon to see that they were absolutely correct.

At first, Jacob swam in ecstasy. Since he, with his intellect developed by Talmudic acuteness and with his memory filled by fragments from so many sides of human knowledge, came to the school without knowing a schoolbook, he was like a person who can play an instrument but cannot read music. He was examined like any of the other boys, and he could not answer a word. But when he began to take part in the instruction and the interspaces, so to speak, between the fragments thus began to fill up and he himself came to an awareness of his own knowledge, he made dizzyingly rapid progress in the judgment of his teachers.

And what a delight for him to sit there on the bench among other boys! To be thought just as good as they, sometimes even to be preferred over them, not to feel any other difference than that erected by industry and ability! How diligent he was, how he every evening longed for the next day, which would renew the glorious contest!

What delight to sit there on the bench among other boys—but this was also only during the lessons, when the boys were bound like soldiers under discipline. Hardly would the lesson be ended, before Jacob would hear that he was a Jew. Nothing more was necessary to distance him immediately from his schoolmates and leave him standing just as alone as if the board fence had separated him from them.

As long as school life was still new to him and the competition with his schoolmates had all the allurements of novelty, he did not especially feel this new persecution; his whole soul hung on the lessons and the subjects which were taken up in them. But gradually as his youthful enthusiasm waned, he became more sensitive to the teasing of the other boys. When the whole class swarmed around him and laughingly shouted "Jew!" or "*Ach wai mir!*" or "*Hep, hep!*" he put up with it with a certain lethargy; it was as if he were hearing the whole world shouting at him and he had to bow before its voice. But when one individual ventured too close and with the cry "Get out of the way, Jew!" or the like, and shoved him, then it seemed immediately like more of a personal insult, and like a wounded tiger he flexed his firm, lithe limbs for a spring at his tormentor. It then always ended with several coming to this one's aid and with Jacob getting a beating.

One evening the janitor found a boy lying unconscious on the floor, bearing clear marks of violent treatment. From a wound on his head blood trickled along the floor. The boy was carried home unconscious.

The next morning when the pupils arrived they all were commanded to go up to the large hall, where the teachers were already gathered. The rector ascended the speaker's platform and related the incident of the previous evening, adding, "There is, of course, only slight hope that the guilty one will come forward, and the injured boy, when he has recovered his health, will perhaps conceal his name, out of comradely loyalty. But whoever the guilty one may be, may he bear the awareness that his teachers and every honorable schoolmate regard his conduct with the deepest indignation. And I expect of each one among you who takes the honor of the school to heart, that he will not conceal what he knows, out of misunderstood comradely loyalty, but will do his part in discovering the perpetrator, so that suspicion will not rest on an innocent person."

The rector looked sharply around the circle, but everyone was silent. Then Jacob Bendixen rose and said, "I am the one who did it."

"What?" cried the director and stepped a pace forward in astonishment. "You, Bendixen, the most modest and quietest of all the school's pupils? I cannot believe that about you."

"I am the one, as I say," Jacob persisted firmly.

"But by what accident did you come to do it? For it is surely impossible that you did it deliberately?"

"Yes, I did it deliberately," Jacob insisted in the same tone of voice. "He is always the worst in calling me kike, but always hides behind the others. Yesterday evening I stayed behind alone with him, and when I started to leave, he ran up behind me and shouted, 'Out of the way, Jew!' and shoved me into the door, so that I hurt my knee. So I hit him until I thought he was dead. I know very well," he added, advancing a few steps, "that you side with him and also call me kike, but don't do it when we are alone!"

Jacob's lips trembled, and his cheeks were chalky white. A deathly stillness reigned in the hall; the rector stared fixedly at him. The other teachers went up to the speaker's platform, and after several moments of soft whispering they went out with the rector. When they had shut the doors behind themselves, a few boys, with subdued voices and threatening gestures, shouted at Jacob, "Now, Jew, now you'll get it!" But most of them were silent, and several minutes passed in an expectant pause. Jacob remained standing motionless, without hearing anything. Finally the teachers entered, and in a profound stillness the rector again stepped to the speaker's platform.

"Jacob Bendixen!" he said, "the insult of which you have been the object is so base and despicable, and I feel so distinctly the impression which it, continuously repeated, must have made on your spirit, that I do not consider myself justified in punishing you." The rector paused and looked at Jacob, who on being addressed in this unexpected manner stood as if thunderstruck. Then he turned to the other pupils and said in a stern voice, "He, whom Bendixen has punished, has only gotten what he deserved. And you others! Pay attention to what I am now going to say to you! If the cultured and humane feelings which the school seeks to inculcate in you are not strong enough to elevate you above the rabble, then expect the most serious chastisement every time such an outburst of brutality comes to my attention. And now I hope, Bendixen," he went on, turning back to Jacob, "that you have so much confidence in me that in the future you will not take the law into your own hands, but, no matter how harshly you are insulted, will remember what you owe the school, and turn to me for help against those who insult you. Now go, all of you, quietly down to the playground and wait till the next lesson begins. I hope that this lesson period, even though it has not been used according to schedule, will not have been wasted."

When all the pupils, including Jacob, had gone down and the teachers were left alone, one of these said to the rector,

"Wouldn't it have been more correct to keep Bendixen up here than to let him be alone among them now?"

"On the contrary!" cried the rector. "Should we, at the same moment we are trying to bring them together with him, separate him from them? If he were separated from them at this moment, then no reconciliation would be easy in the future. A wound must be closed while it is fresh, if it is ever to be healed. And if this is perhaps painful for him at the moment, he also has to suffer something; his temperament must also be bent."

"I would not have expected such energy in a child of that nation," remarked one of the teachers. "In other schools where I teach there are also Jewish boys; they put up with blows and abuse as if it were in the order of things. I have often been genuinely annoyed at seeing their submissiveness—here I must not be annoyed at precisely the opposite."

"I cannot forget that scene," said the rector. "I frankly admit that I was downright impressed when Bendixen said, 'And then I hit him until I thought he was dead.' Only at that moment I felt that I could not punish the boy. Only then was it clear to me that this was not some schoolboy fight; it was rather a battle of nations. I pretended not to hear those words, for what is one to use against such a spirit other than gentleness."

"And what a challenge he hurled at them!" said another teacher. "I assure you, I was almost frightened when he stepped forward. He hits hard, the little devil; that we have seen."

"Yes, what despair there must have been in the boy's soul!" the rector resumed, staring into space. "He thought he was alone among nothing but enemies and now would really be overwhelmed. This boy must be treated gently."

"You were a sort of prophet when you compared him with a panther cub a couple of months ago, do you remember that?"

"Yes, a better prophet, unfortunately, than I myself believed."

The instruction was continued as if nothing had happened. In the evening, when the school day was over, the rector called Jacob into his office.

After sitting down and having Jacob take a seat, he said, to begin at the beginning, "Tell me, what do you do on an evening like this, when you come home from school?"

Jacob, who had expected that his punishment was just to begin now, answered with relief, "I study my lessons."

"And when you have learned them, what do you do then?"

"Then I read other things to pass the time."

"Do you never go out for a walk with any of your schoolmates?"

"No," replied Jacob, casting his eyes down.

The teacher felt that he was almost touching a sore spot and went on, "But your uncle has children—don't you play or take walks with them?"

"He has two sons, one of whom is the same age as I, the other a little older. But one is apprenticed to a haberdasher, and the other to a greengrocer, and they rarely come home except on Friday evening."

"Doesn't he have any daughters?"

"Yes, three, but one is quite small, and I sometimes give her reading lessons, and the two older ones make fun of me because I want to study at the university. They say that I ought rather to study to be an officer, for officers are much more dashing than university students. But I want to be a university student."

The rector smiled imperceptibly at casting this brief glance into two Jewish girlish hearts.

"But when you have studied and read, what do you do then?"

Jacob hesitated in replying.

The rector became curious at this hesitation and inquired, "Is there nothing at all that you do for fun?"

"Yes," he answered, looking at the floor.

"Well, what is it, then? Oh, go ahead and tell me, don't be so timid."

"When I am tired of reading," he said at last, hesitatingly and shyly, "then I imagine that a bird comes and takes me home to my parents and my uncle, and then I am at home the entire rest of the evening."

"Is that all your amusement?" asked the rector, touched.

"Then I am so happy," said Jacob, a faint blush coloring his cheeks. "I can smell the flowers in the garden and the seaweed from the beach, and I can hear my mother singing very softly, and I can see my father and my uncle, but they cannot see me. Finally I start crying, and then I go to bed."

The rector looked at him silently a long time. He got up and took out a volume of Oehlenschläger's poems, which at that time had just come out, and handed it to Jacob. "Read these," he said, "then there will also come a bird and take you, though not exactly to your parents, but it is good for one to look around a little in the world. And since you have so much time to spare, what do you think of visiting me from time to time and reading a little more than is read in school? You will be the better university student!"

Jacob dutifully thanked him, and the rector let him go home.

Chapter 11

SCHOOL LIFE CONTINUED, but it is difficult to say whether Jacob had grounds to be more satisfied with his position among his schoolmates now than before. He was spared the loud shouts and abusive words, the violent persecutions, but the profound silence and coldness that had taken their place were almost more painful to him, since he well knew what it meant. It spoke loudly in all its silence, but it was soundless words that he could not seize and punish. Those glances and gestures—he well understood how to interpret them, although he did not dare to interpret them for fear of making himself ridiculous. He often felt the same as when one in the night is afraid of something and wishes that the unknown would appear so that one can put an end to the uncertain dread.

With that almost legalistic cunning peculiar to schoolboys, his schoolmates often understood how to say to him what they wanted to say without his being able to do anything to them in return. One would begin to tell longwindedly about something at home so that the whole thing would become a tangle of words ending in *-ew* and *-ike*. Right in the middle, another would interrupt gravely, "Now, you be careful! You are talking about a kike, and Bendixen is listening." "I was not talking about a kike!" the storyteller would reply, equally seriously. "Yes, you were, and you even said 'Jew.' I'll go and tell the rector." "Oh, what a lie! Was I talking about a Jew, you others?" "Yes, you were! You called Bendixen a kike, we heard that. Bendixen, go up to the rector."

As young as Jacob was, necessity had already taught him so much self-control that he was able to sit still and pretend that he did not hear such things. He would have liked to throw himself at one of them, but who was the guilty one?

After a couple of months passed, the injured boy came back to school and took his place as if nothing had happened. There was no trace of vindictiveness against Jacob; it was as if he and Jacob had never known each other. It is a peculiar trait of the Danes that a certain good-naturedness often robs them of intellectual energy, but also frees them of the energy to hate, to hate for a long time. Among the common people one can even see a man cured of his enmity by receiving a proper slap from his enemy's hand; he good-naturedly and impartially acknowledges a superiority. Among a more fiery people a conflict such as that between Jacob and his schoolmate would have bred an enmity that from school would have spread out over their entire lives, but the Christian boy seemed on the contrary even to have overcome part of his former animosity toward Jacob. The latter, who made his inferences on the basis of his own nature, was struck by the unexpected stillness and gentleness with which the boy now behaved, and he began to feel regret over what he had done. One day the boy was standing in front of him at the desk and was looking in a book. Jacob looked at his pale, sickly features, and sincerely moved, he seized his hand and looked at him with tears in his eyes. But the boy withdrew his hand and cried, "Oh, are you going to beat me again, Jew?" Jacob's swelling heart shrank convulsively and he thought, "Now we are even!"

In this way time passed; weeks followed weeks, months followed months. Jacob went to school and frequently visited his rector at the latter's invitation, learned from him, and was without himself knowing it the object of his attention and care. On the isolated holidays it sometimes happened that Jacob was with him from morning till evening, and once it even happened that he took Jacob along to visit a family. To be sure, it seemed to Jacob that he could tell by the friendliness they showed him that the rector had spoken about him beforehand, and he thought he could detect the pains with which they, in his opinion, sought to restrain any allusion to Jew and Judaism; but all the more interesting he found the family and social life which he saw here for the first time. The lively and joking conversations between young ladies and gentlemen, over which the erotic element rested with an unmistakable fragrance, the delights of the table, and even the table setting and the courses with the many dishes forbidden to Jacob—which precisely for that reason seemed to him to be all the more savory—and finally after the meal, song and music and a little improvised dance, all this Jacob saw with a strange mixture of ecstasy and heartache. It was the realization of the fantasies he had dreamed in his early childhood, but he seemed to stand even further removed from them than at that time, because he did not at all understand how to take part in them. These people seemed to him to belong to a favored caste, to have learned a secret art with the aid of which they could create for themselves such delights out of nothing. He was seized by a painful longing; he wished he had been born in this caste.

One holiday he came, as appointed, early in the morning to the rector. The latter was in the act of getting dressed, and Jacob waited for him in his study. The rector entered in his shirtsleeves, put on a light morning coat, went to the open window, and cast a joyous glance toward heaven, taking a deep breath of the fresh spring air; then he sat down with a happy face at the coffee table. For Jacob, each of his movements was the object of attention. This manner of holding morning prayer—greeting his God with a joyous glance—was so easy and uninhibited in comparison to his own morning prayer: putting on *tephilin* and half-thoughtlessly reciting long, partially incomprehensible Hebrew prayers; and the rector's contented countenance demonstrated quite clearly that this could take place with a good conscience. When the rector this morning recited the chapter of Herodotus in which is told of the Spartans at Thermopylae who anointed and crowned themselves with laurel wreaths before they went into battle, Jacob noticed in this story for the first time that his heroic, almost worshipped Spartans had not put on *tephilin*.

The next morning he omitted for the first time in his life putting on *tephilin* and sneaked like a criminal past the silk pouch in which they were hanging, out of the house. But when the whole day, and even the evening to boot, passed without heaven crashing in or some other terrible event taking place, he regained his calm, and he decided to test it again and pray like

the rector. He tried it again and again; he became accustomed to
it.

Faith, whether it is composed of ceremonies and superstition
or is purely spiritual, is not to be compared with a building from
which one can take out a single stone and set another one in its
place. As soon as doubt sets in with it, the entire building
totters; it collapses, and the materials cannot even be used to
erect a new one. Doubt is not deposited on faith like a rust spot
that slowly corrodes; it is like that poison that needs only to
touch the tongue to spread instantly throughout the entire
system.

Jacob had immersed himself in Oehlenschläger and had
submerged himself in the nordic heroic age and pagan times. The
only thing in which he had not been able to participate along
with the warriors was the mealtimes in Valhalla, where they ate
so much pork. But now he acquired courage enough to ask himself
what offense the deity could possibly take if the flesh of this
animal or that animal touched his lips. Is it thinkable that the
various means of nourishment that enter my stomach can offend
the divine moral law? he asked. Is God supposed to sit up there in
heaven and make sure whether I let precisely one hour pass after
having eaten butter, before I eat meat? He ventured to eat
buttered bread with meat at the rector's, and experienced no
great inconvenience from it.

He had read about the Turks who came to Skanderbeg's grave
and draped themselves with his bones as amulets that could
protect them from perils, and he had smiled at the Turks'
superstition. These were after all only bones of a dead man—
what power could they possibly have? Now he suddenly realized
that he himself wore an amulet, his *arbakanfos*. It was after all
only a piece of woolen cloth—what power could it have? And he
took off his *arbakanfos*, which he had worn since his sixth year,
the sign of the pact with the God of the Jews.

With such struggles and investigations, which remained
hidden from the entire world, Jacob now spent a long time. At
isolated moments there certainly appeared before his soul a dark,
frightening thought: that the rector, who had given the first
impetus to these new ideas, could be one of those dangerous

seducers who had gotten little Simon in their snares; but he soon felt fervently that it was a higher spirit he had himself discovered, which was at work in him. Nevertheless for a long time he would dream every night that he was sitting at the *Schabbas* table, and that his father would say to him, just as Lazarus said to little Simon, "Let me see your *arbakanfos*, my son!" and that he shamefully and fearfully would sneak out the door, away from his father.

But it was in the dark of night that the old, mystic memories menacingly appeared before him, just as the legends of the elf maidens and nymphs awaken in the wanderer in the dark woods. When the bright day shone, the pictures disappeared, and he lived in the free and clear light of the intellect.

It was the Jews' Pentecost. Jacob had to stay home from school for several days to celebrate the festival, and one morning he accompanied his uncle to the synagogue. With strange feelings he found himself after a long time in this place. For a moment he became horribly empty inside. He had divested his God of all his attributes, and what was left over of this God's being was next to nothing. But over this divinity there seemed to him to soar a higher esthetic being, just as the concept of the Father of the Universe in the mind of the pagans soared over even Odin, and with the most passionate fervor he addressed that higher being in prayer: "You dear, great God! You are the one who led the Jews out of their enemies' land! I want to belong to you, I want to believe in you; but forgive me that I cannot believe all that which I no longer believe." And he joined in the congregation's loud cry, which now resounded: "*Schema Jisroel! Adonoi Elohenu Adonoi echod,*"—"Hear, o Israel, the Lord your God is the only eternal Being!" Strengthened by his simple prayer, he refrained from reciting the remaining Hebrew prayers, and saw with a mixture of pride and sorrow the rest of the congregation praying in simplicity and fervor. But when the moment came when the Torah was to be brought out of the *Aron hakodesh*, and the congregation pushed forward to kiss the parchment scroll or just to touch it with a finger and kiss the finger, he said to himself, "See, these people kiss the dead parchment and the dead letters and believe that this is the living spirit."

When the other members of the family came from the synagogue at noon to enjoy the festival meal in peace and joy, there was in Jacob a certain bashfulness; he felt that he did not deserve to take part in this joyous tranquillity since he had not taken part in the prayers. He well remembered the time when he had entered the pleasant room with equally religious feelings, and with just as great satisfaction had sat down to the decorated festival table, and although his intellect told him that he was on the right path, still there was in his heart a secret remorse and lamentation.

But without knowing it, they came to his aid in this silent battle.

During the meal, the aunt was carving a delectable chicken. In anticipation, Marcus picked up a small piece for a taste. "Believe me," said his wife, "I got a real scare when I cut up the chicken and found a pin in the crop."

Her husband grew deathly pale and hastily took the meat out of his mouth. "And you tell me that only now?" he cried horrified. "Are you crazy, woman? Do you want to make the whole house *terefo?*"[1]

"Oh, don't get excited," answered his wife, continuing to carve, "I sent to the *rof* [rabbi] and let him see the crop with the pin in it, and he answered that it was quite all right for us to eat the chicken, but we had to bury the crop first. And I did that."

With a sigh of relief her husband turned back to the chicken.

"It's odd," said Jacob, "that the chicken could become *koscher*[2] because the crop was buried. One would believe that the crop had already made the chicken *terefo*, and that it could not help to bury the crop afterwards. It is the same as wanting to put an antidote in the poison bottle after a person had drunk from it."

"Don't sin, Jacob," said Marcus Bendixen, "the *rof* must know that better. There are many mysterious things that one

---

[1] Unclean.
[2] Clean.

must believe without being able to explain them. What is *die Tekufo*, for example?"

"Yes, what is *die Tekufo?*" asked Jacob.

"Four times a year *die Tekufo* falls from heaven," replied Marcus. "It is a drop of blood; where it comes from I cannot tell you—one does not speak of that to children, but it falls into butter or meat or the like, and the person who eats any of whatever the *Tekufo* has fallen into, must die. For that reason on those days every devout housewife places a nail beside the articles of food she has in the house, for then the *Tekufo* does not fall into her house."

"A nail!" said Jacob. "Would a dead object really have the power to withstand God's will?"

"Doesn't a lightning rod deflect lightning?" answered his uncle.

"Yes, it does, but lightning is also a force of nature that is deflected from its path by another force of nature; God has not placed His will in either of them. And would God need a nail as a sign in order to distinguish among the devout? Doesn't he know the heart itself?"

"The Lord demands a sign from people in order to see that they are receptive to Him and remember Him. Didn't God command that the Jews brush their doors with blood of the paschal lamb so that His angel could distinguish their houses from those of the Egyptians?"

"God is omnipotent," began the eldest of the cousins with rabbinical unctuousness, "but He sometimes does not use all His omnipotence. He could have created man out of nothingness, but he formed him out of earth. Why did Adam not get to be a thousand years old? It was determined that Adam would be a thousand years old and that David would be stillborn. But for the benefit of the Jews the Lord took seventy years from Adam's age and gave them to David. Couldn't the Lord well have created seventy years alone for David?"

"But such things belong under mythology," cried Jacob, "and don't need to be believed, no more than the legend about Saturn, who ate his children."

The uncle said sternly, "Nothing of what is written for the Jews belongs to . . . what was that you said, Jacob? What kind of a word was that, the *goyim* have taught you? . . . Nothing of what is written there does not need to be believed. If we listen more closely, then maybe one does not need to believe in *Yom Kippur*, one does not need to fast and pray and confess his sins, eh?"

"Yes, one does," cried Jacob, abandoning himself with his whole soul up to the images which this festival's name evoked, "yes, *Yom Kippur* is a beautiful and poetic festival! For its sake alone it would be worth being a Jew! When the entire congregation stands in the white shrouds; when the *hazan* and the two elders climb up before the Torah and apologize for the gathering 'before the court of the higher regions and the lower regions, on behalf of God and on behalf of the congregation' in case it is praying with unrepentant sinners in its midst, when the *tallis* are consecrated and the congregation covers itself; when the *hazan* recites the affirmation, and at the word *kor'im*[3] everybody kneels; when the white figure invokes the names of the dead and wishes them a blessed rest; when the Levites bring water for washing to the Kohanim and the latter, after having washed themselves, come forward and pronounce the holy blessings; when the horn sounds and enemies shake hands with each other—then I believe and pray as well as anyone, then I am proud of being a Jew!"

"*Jeschar-koach*! Thanks! What Jew is not proud of *Yom Kippur*?" said his uncle. "It was on a *Yom Kippur*," he went on, "that the great Roman commander Pompeius stormed Jerusalem. When the first warriors broke into the Temple over the broken-down walls and overcame the Jewish heroes and the frightful blood bath began, inside the Temple they were at *Maskir neschommos* [the requiem]. A priest went to the high priest and told him that the enemy was coming and now all Jews would be killed. But the high priest continued undisturbed to call out the names of the dead, and when Pompeius burst in and saw the shrouded silent rows and heard the high priest's calm voice, while everything outside was blood, burning, and death

---

[3] "They knelt."

cries, Pompeius drew back; he did not touch the Temple's vessels or treasures and remained a friend of the Jews until his dying day in Mizraim (Egypt). So! You are proud of *Yom Kippur? Jeschar-koach!* Many thanks! What Jew is not proud of it and of his entire religion?"

"Yes, certainly!" Jacob continued, "there is much that is beautiful in it. But," he added a little more softly, "there is, however, also much ridiculous superstition mixed in."

"Jacob!" cried his uncle, "you dare to say that in my house! Name me the slightest thing that is ridiculous! Let's hear it! Speak!"

"Well," said Jacob with a slight smile, "that is not difficult; there is, for example, the care with which you on Friday afternoons clip your nails, gather up the clippings, cut a little splinter out of the table or window sill and burn it along with the nail clippings."

"*Am ho-oretz!*"[4] cried his uncle, "don't I do that so that on Judgment Day, when the Lord calls, I won't have to go around and gather up the nail clippings? Aren't the splinters my *eidim*, witnesses, that I have burned the nails? Next time don't mock at things you don't understand! Beware that on Judgment Day you don't have to remain on earth to take care of the things you have neglected!"

With these words he turned angrily away and said to the others, "*Rebbosai! Wir wollen benschen!* [Gentlemen! Let us give thanks!]" and all further argument was cut short.

Jacob breathed heavily. The air in the room seemed oppressive and heavy with superstition; he yearned for the fresh air surrounding the school—yes, he yearned for his schoolmates, for the Christians; his confined spirit sought for those who understood it, as the solitary prisoner longs to speak with people, even though they were his enemies.

The evening and night were dreadfully long to him, and the next day he hurried to school like a liberated bird. When he entered the classroom, he could have embraced his schoolmates in the joy of seeing them again. It did not occur to the inexperienced

---

[4] Child of the earth, peasant.

boy to doubt that the feelings with which he was filled were shared by the whole world. He encompassed them all with a cheery and affectionate look and cried, "Well, how were you while I was away?" But the boys had not changed in the few days that had intervened, and one of them replied, "Fine, thanks, Bendixen, but probably not as well as you, for you have been up with the Jewish priest and were patted and got cakes because you were so nicely in the synagogue." Uproarious laughter, much more the result, however, of youthful exuberance than of malice, followed these words. But Jacob's overflowing feelings contracted spasmodically and he suddenly recalled again that he was a Jew and these were Christians. An intense pain seized him; he dimly felt that he had left the shore where he belonged, and was being repulsed from the other shore, and was now drifting, derelict, out in the current.

"Now the Jew has gone crazy," said the other boys.

Chapter 12

WHEN JACOB WENT HOME FROM SCHOOL, to his uncle's house, it was as if he had to go to a prison, and when he thought about going back to school, the same feeling of loathing seized him. The weather was gray and unfriendly, and it seemed to him that even the heavens gathered oppressively over him and only arched from one prison to the other. Almost ill from psychological depression he came to his room and found unexpectedly a letter from his father. The letter dealt with Jacob's small affairs and concluded by saying that they hoped to see him at home soon, after the school examination was over. Home—the thought of seeing it again appeared at that moment in Jacob's fantasy with consoling strength; there was a peaceful haven where he could take refuge. His soul abandoned the disappointed hopes to turn to this new one with the same ease that the lottery player discards the old number and takes another.

He computed how many hours the long months contained; he deducted those that would be spent in sleep and rejoiced in being able to shorten the rest with reading. Every time a day had passed, he calculated how great a part of his term of imprisonment had now elapsed.

Then it came, the so long anticipated day of departure; Jacob rode with a farmer to the coastal town opposite Funen. When he had reached the first inn, he went ahead on foot, and when he had gone so far that he thought he was out of sight of any human eye, he sprang into a field, threw himself on the ground, rolled in the grass, and uttered inarticulate cries, cries of joy, over which a spectator who had known the cause, would have wept with pain. This child rejoiced like an animal at having escaped people.

In Nyborg his father was waiting for him and took him home. When the carriage stopped before the door, his mother ran out, clutched her son, and almost carried him in, weeping and hugging him. His uncle came over, and pulling Jacob by the ears in his usual manner, he said, "Oh, are you here? What do you want here?" but concluded this address by kissing the boy, while he pinched him still more strongly on the ears. Jacob almost melted away under all this affection.

A few days passed, and the profound impression that the reception had made on Jacob was obliterated by other feelings which forced themselves on him.

He had hurried to the spot in the garden to which were attached the fondest images of his childhood. There was the arbor where the family was accustomed to set up its *suko*[1] during the Feast of Booths. Here he had dreamed his fantasies, here he had imagined himself wandering with his people in the wildnerness, seeking shelter from the scorching sun under its booths, here he had in childish ambition imagined himself his people's leader, a divinely inspired Prophet. He found himself again on this spot and, stretched out on a bench, he closed his eyes to invite again the beloved dreams. But they did not come, or else they came and were not well received, for his ambition was now different—to receive a brilliant *examen artium* diploma, and with this tableau of the future, shades from Sinai Desert would not and could not be of help. Jacob left the spot with the same gentle pain with which one, when he wakes up, gives up the hope of being able to continue the pleasant dream from which he was awakened.

He recalled the peace that on Sabbath mornings had reigned over the garden, the reverence with which he had regarded every ripe berry as sanctified because on the Sabbath it is forbidden to pick the fruit of trees. He wanted to experience again this gentle feeling, and early on the first Sabbath after his arrival, he slipped out into the garden. But the garden and its fruits were no longer holy; he could not awaken the gentle memories to luxuriant life, because he no longer considered it a greater sin to pluck a cherry on Saturday than any other day. He even smiled

---

[1] Arbor, tabernacle.

at his former superstition, and he came back from the garden with a smile on his lips, but with dejection in his heart.

He had made an effort to subject himself to the ceremonies and bring them into harmony with reflection. That he should wash his hands before a meal, he found hygienic; that bread was broken while a blessing was recited, he found poetically beautiful; that one put on one's hat when grace was said and God was invoked and supposedly present, he also found beautiful—after all, the grandees of Spain covered their heads in the presence of their king.

But one morning his father, with a serious expression, took him aside and said, "It seems to me, Jacob, that you are not putting on your *tefillin.*"

"No, father, I'm not," answered Jacob, with secret fear of the scene that would now follow.

"Did you forget them in Copenhagen? If so, I can lend you some for the time being," his father persisted.

"You must not get angry, father," replied Jacob in an uncertain voice, "but I pray to God in the morning without *tefillin.*"

"What?" shouted his father in a tone equally hurt and indignant, "you don't put on *tefillin* any more? Jacob, my son, that you should cause me that grief!"

"Father!" he said, "I cannot feel convinced that it is worshipping God to wrap a black leather strap seven times around your arm and another leather strap around your head. God, I am sure, looks only at your heart; if it is good and innocent, then *tefillin* are not needed."

"Leather straps, Jacob! Do you see in *tefillin* only leather? Is the synagogue only a collection of stones to you? Is it the leather that we worship, or God's holy words which are attached to it? Isn't it written in our loftiest prayer, *Schema Jisroel,* that we are to place these words on our head, on our heart, and on our hands?"

"Yes, it is, Father, but it is, I am sure, meant figuratively. I place God's words, but not the parchment on which they are written, on my heart."

"And your *arbakanfos*, Jacob?" asked his father, as if he wanted to empty the cup of sorrow to the bottom. "Have you also taken off your *arbakanfos*?"

"Yes," he whispered, uneasy at the expression on his father's face.

His father straightened up from his bowed position and, extending his hand, he said, "The Jew Philip, son of Rabbi Bendix, has a son no longer. The son he had will let himself *schmatte*[2]. At the Jew Philip's grave no one will say *Kaddish*. No one will pray that his dust may rest in peace. His lineage shall be forgotten by the Jewish nation, and before God's throne he shall accuse himself because he brought a son into the world."

Then he left the room.

Jacob stood a moment as if shattered by these terrible words and by the awe-inspiring bearing with which his otherwise so gentle father had pronounced the anathema over himself. But in the next instant he remembered the occasion, the circumstance which in his eyes was so insignificant, that had caused such an invocation, and this appeared almost comical to him. It was impossible for him to recall quite vividly the enormous importance he himself, scarcely three years ago, had attached to the *tefillin* and *arbakanfos* as Judaism's symbols.

But he was not given the opportunity of long reflections, for his father and his uncle entered the room, the first with an air of resignation and pain, the latter with an expression of violent emotion.

"You don't put on your *tefillin* any longer," began his uncle immediately, "and don't wear your *arbakanfos*, either! You are a delightful boy; you are a joy to us. You probably also eat *chaser*[3]— does it taste good? . . . Answer me, boy, have you eaten *terefo*?"

Jacob's knees trembled, but he answered, "Yes."

A violent blow from his uncle's hand instantly followed this confession. Jacob reeled and almost lost consciousness; it took him a moment to regain his senses.

---

[2] Be baptized.

[3] Pork.

This was the first time in his life that he had received bodily punishment. His eyes roamed the room as if after long habit seeking a weapon. But in the next instant he had reached a kind of decision; he left the room, the house, the town, and wandered down the highway. With clenched teeth, unable to bring forth any definite thought, he kept walking.

During the first moments after he had gone, his father and his uncle were too furious to heed his departure. After several minutes had passed, his uncle went to the window and looked down the street. When he did not see Jacob, he turned to Philip and said, "It was a good thing that he ran off; otherwise I would perhaps have beaten him to a pulp."

"Where did he go, I wonder?" asked Philip.

"He has probably run down to the beach and doesn't dare come back before we send for him. But as far as I am concerned, he can run to the end of the world; he is going to let himself *schmatte* some time, anyway."

"You hit him hard," began Philip after a short pause.

"Should I have maybe taken him on my lap and patted him on the head and said, 'God will bless you, my boy! You abandon the faith of your father, you eat *terefo*, on *Pesach* [Passover] you eat *hometzdik* [leavened food], about which it is written in the Torah that a Jew who does that shall be accursed in all eternity; but in spite of that you are my own little Jacob!' Ought I to have said that, eh?"

Philip covered his face with his hands.

"What am I to do with the boy? How am I to defend it before God if he persists as he has begun!" he said a little later.

"He is *barmitzvo*! You have no responsibility when good words and punishment are fruitless."

"Where is he, I wonder?"

"Oh, he is probably, as I said, at the beach or out in the garden. I will have Benjamin go down and look for him."

He called Benjamin, but the latter related that a little while before he had seen Jacob go out of the town's East Gate. Now the mother entered. "Where is Jacob?" she asked. "Is it true that he left because you beat him?"

Philip and Isak looked at each other.

"That damned rascal!" cried the uncle. "He is going to get as much thrashing as his hide can hold."

"Stop it with your hot temper," said Philip. "You may push the boy out into bad company. People may also hear that he is running loose, and why. What will my family say to that? It is best to get him back and quietly send him to Copenhagen. Let him then, in God's name, look out for himself. I wash my hands of him; I have given him a Jewish upbringing."

"But it was your idea with the damned university studies!" cried Isak, going to the door. "Benjamin! Run over and have my carriage hitched up; have it brought up to the door immediately."

Jacob had already gone several miles when his father and uncle came dashing up and overtook him. When they came up beside him, his father said gently, "Jacob, climb up, come back with us."

He answered, "You said I am no longer your son; let me go and look after myself."

His uncle cried, "Now don't be childish, Jacob. Come back with us; everything will be forgotten."

Jacob said, "It's easy for you to forget! You hit me, Isak Bamberger."

"I was too hot-tempered, Jacob; come back with us."

"No, just show me the kindness of letting me never see you again; you have hit me."

"Boy! Your old uncle has asked you for forgiveness; is that not enough for your obstinate temper?" cried his uncle.

Jacob had a feeling that he now could give in with honor, but a mixture of defiance and vanity forced him to continue on his way again; however, his father then said, "Will you then never see your mother again? Nor me, either? Then at least let us say good-by, my son."

Jacob burst into tears and climbed up.

They came home, and nothing more was said about the reason for the quarrel; but no dissension in a family is worse than the one the origin of which cannot be discussed.

Jacob quickly noted that he was like a stranger in the house. Food and drink and every comfort was gladly granted him and he was like a cherished guest, but nothing more; for he stood outside the familiar relationship that embraced his father, mother, and uncle. What a painful feeling, that one alone, that when he entered the living room their conversation ceased!

Jacob saw that his father was sorrowing, and knew that, even if he wanted to, he could not dispel that sorrow; for he had already eaten of the forbidden foods and even if he put on the *tefillin* again, they would not believe that it was sincerely meant.

He could still find acceptance with his mother; in a mother's heart affection for the child always prevails. One evening, when he was sitting with her in the twilight, he ventured to speak to her about the unfriendly relationship between his father and himself.

"Your father," said his mother sadly, "will not stop being an affectionate father; everything in his power he will do for you. But at the sight of you he will always become sad, for he knows that when he and I are gathered to the Lord, we will look for you in vain."

"Don't cry, Jacob," she said when he burst into tears, "I will go first, and I will pray for you in the presence of the good God."

Jacob's tears flowed more strongly. A little later his father came in, and Jacob noticed that his mother's hand, which had entwined itself in his hair, involuntarily drew back at his father's entrance. He dried his tears, and an unutterably bitter feeling crept into his heart.

When the hour of his departure came, they all felt that a stone had been lifted from their hearts. Parting was painful, but living together was burdensome to them.

When Jacob stood on the ship taking him back toward Sealand's coast, he felt he was more homeless than the seagulls sailing around the ship in the gale.

Part Two

Chapter 1

ON THE EVENING OF THE 28TH of October 182-, the home of the wealthy wholesale dealer Israelsen in Copenhagen was festively lit. His son had passed his university admittance examinations, and in honor of this event, a splendid evening celebration was taking place. In the heavy silver candelabras wax candles were burning, and the light sparkled back from the massive silver table ware and crystal covering the table. Besides the wholesaler's family, the company consisted of a few Christians, among them a couple who had the same day been admitted to the university, as well as an older Jewish university student and finally Jacob Bendixen.

When everyone had taken his place at the table, and Jewish hospitality had manifested itself in the multitude of dishes served and in the zealous entreaties to the guests to help themselves and to consider themselves at home, the wholesaler raised his filled glass and said, "Let us drink a toast to my son in honor of the fact that today he has happily passed his university entrance examinations." Everybody joined in the "Hurrah!" which the young Mr. Israelsen himself led.

A little while afterward, one of the guests, Wilhelm Fangel, rose and said, "If I may be permitted, I would like to propose a toast to one of us young university students present, one who has richly deserved it, since he passed his entrance examinations with highest honors—Jacob Bendixen. *Skaal!*"

It was the first time that Jacob had received a personal honor from anyone. That same day his name had indeed been read out with distinction in the university church by the *Rector magnificus*, but that was a distinction which in accordance with the dictates of the law simply followed from his examination grade, a distinction which would have existed as his acquired property, even if the *Rector magnificus* had not, in his cold tone, recited the usual formula. Here, on the other hand, it was a personal, voluntary homage, and the pride and ambition lying in his character awoke at this moment for the first time to enjoyment. Rising to clink with all the glasses extended at the same time toward him, he cast a quick glance at Fangel's face, a glance with an expression as if he would immediately take care that he never forgot this man.

"Highest honors?" asked the wholesaler when they had sat down, "what does that mean?"

"That means," replied one of the guests, "that Bendixen has been admitted to the university with distinction, that he received a mark even higher than the top grade."

"Aron," said the wholesaler, gravely addressing his son, "why didn't you also get high honors? Haven't I spent just as much money on you as Bendixen's father has on him? Why shouldn't I get just as much enjoyment from my money?"

"Well," answered the son, wagging his head crossly, "Bendixen has also done nothing but study."

"And what have you had to do, other than study, you lazy rascal?" cried his father.

"I have not been lazy," replied the son, sullen and extremely embarrassed at the lack of constraint with which his father gave vent to his anger.

Wilhelm Fangel intervened, "You are doing your son an injustice, sir; he has certainly also been very diligent, but the Lord does distribute talents differently."

"That's true, Mr. Fangel," said the father, mollified. "You are a sensible young man. But tell me, what does this distinction really consist of?"

"The one who receives more than six grades of *prae* and none of *haud*, *non*, or zero is solemnly named by the rector of the university as the best student."

"And were there others besides Bendixen who were so distinguished today?"

"No, he was the only one."

Wholesaler Israelsen's eyes sparkled, and he said, "He was the only one who was singled out for distinction, and he is a Jew!"

He rose and said to Bendixen, "Now I'll drink to you! If only you were my son!"

"My young friends!" he added after a pause, turning to the Christian students, "it is a sign of honor when an old Jew gets up for a young one. You have seen that I got up for Bendixen. My son is a blockhead."

In spite of the wholesaler's clumsiness, there was something moving in his behavior, and Jacob almost had tears in his eyes. Wilhelm Fangel sprang up and cried, "Sir! Here you are *Rector magnificus*! You hand out honors and reprimands! Long live the rector, Wholesaler Israelsen!"

The entire company at the table joined in, "Three cheers for him!" and clinked glasses amid general merriment.

"Have you been to the theater recently?" the wholesaler's oldest daughter Rose asked her table partner, one of the students.

"No, unfortunately not; I haven't had time on account of the examination."

"Haven't you seen *Blanca*?"

"No, I haven't, Miss Israelsen."

"Heavens, it is supposed to be so marvelous."

"Then you have not seen it, either?"

"No, I must tell you that I have only a quarter of a seat in the theater, so I'll be lucky if I get to see precisely this play."

"A quarter of a seat!" cried the student, measuring the young lady's ample figure with his eyes. "Yes, in that case it may be rather difficult."

"Yes, that is, we four sisters take turns in using one seat. It is also a shame, father, that you cannot subscribe to another seat for us," she said, with a reproachful look at her father.

"The one seat damned well costs enough money," answered the wholesaler, "let me see, four marks and nine months . . . how much is four times nine?" he turned to his youngest son to drill him in mental arithmetic.

"Four times nine, father? . . . two marks four!"

Some laughed, but the father turned with a satisfied smile to his neighbor and whispered, "What a business head there is on that boy! With God's help, he will be a source of satisfaction to me; he won't study at the university and waste the Lord's time and my money. He will get distinction as a businessman, but not before the debtors' court. But nobody is eating or drinking. Help yourselves to everything, please! Bendixen, eat, drink! A lively student must also eat and drink. You must come and visit me again."

Bendixen thanked him heartily for this invitation.

"How is your father?" the wholesaler went on. "I remember him well; I was many times in your grandfather's house."

"Thanks, he is well!"

"And your mother? Isn't she a daughter of old Rabbi Nathan and Gidel, a sister of Philip Hertz's wife?" asked the wholesaler further.

"My mother is dead," replied Jacob.

The wholesaler's expression changed from cheeriness to the deepest sympathy. He covered his head and softly mumbled the formula, "*Boruch dayon emmes!* (Blessed be the just judge!)," and the whole family looked at Jacob commiseratingly.

"When did she die, poor fellow?" asked the wholesaler.

"Three months ago," replied Jacob, clenching his lips to keep from bursting out crying.

"Poor young man! What did she die of?"

Jacob could not stand it any longer. Fortunately one of the guests pushed his chair away from the table, and the wholesaler was thus reminded that it was time to leave the table. He got up and said, "I hope you enjoyed your meal," and everybody shook each other's hand and went into another room.

Jacob was ill at ease; the wholesaler's son, the student, was annoyed; and the wholesaler himself was depressed. A Jew feels himself personally affected at hearing of the death of a Jew. He regards himself and his people as God's chosen. But there is nonetheless a terrible enemy whom God, in accordance with the world order, cannot avert—that is death. This enemy has been inside the congregation and has taken its victim; the angel of death has been in the Jew's circle, perhaps has moved over his head! When will his own fatherless children be subjected to the terrible *kria*?[1] When will he himself be brought into contact with that dark power and be taken out to *kever ovos*,[2] to that mysterious life that rustles around out there? For there is a life out there—hasn't one heard the departed praying together in the mortuary when a pious man's funeral was approaching? Hasn't there been a noise like angry voices when a *kall*[3] is to rest among the devout? Yes, there is a life out there, and it is this mysterious life in death that the Jew regards with shrinking awe. But the Christians believe that, too! For is it the still, motionless dead that they fear at night in the cemetery? Isn't it death's life stirring in their ghosts?

The party broke up soon after, and when he had gone several streets, Jacob was alone with the Jewish student who almost the entire time had been a silent participant in the celebration. His name was Martin Levy.

"Wholesaler Israelsen is a bit crude, but his food is excellently cooked," remarked Levy.

"Oh, I think he is a good-natured man," replied Jacob.

"Did you notice his wife? She did not utter a single word the whole evening. When she finished eating, she sat and twiddled her thumbs with an almost human look."

"She is probably not accustomed to being in the company of Christians."

"And what four Graces of daughters! Each one fatter than the other!"

"Mr. Levy," Jacob burst out, "I do not like to speak ill of the man at whose table I have eaten."

"Ah, I don't mean it so badly. You well know that we Jews always have to *ruddle*[4] a little at each other. Besides, I sat without saying anything the entire evening, and therefore I really ought to have some compensation."

---

[1] Rending of garments [as a sign of mourning].

[2] Grave of his fathers, cemetery.

[3] One who has not lived piously [i.e., *chalal?*].

[4] Slander, run down.

"You really were very quiet—why was that?"

"Yes, but first, tell me—are you on some friendlier footing with Israelsen's family? And are you such an ardent Jew that you always stand up for Jews?"

"Neither! That's the first time I have been in Israelsen's house—I don't know myself why I happened to be invited; I knew the son only casually. And as far as Jews are concerned, I could wish that I fit in better with them than I do."

"That's just what I wanted to know, so as not to offend you again accidentally. You see, I was sitting the whole time on pins and needles, because I didn't know at what moment the Christian students would be offended by a little scene. You saw yourself how the father treated the son, you also heard the little business head. But particularly I was afraid that the wholesaler at the end of the meal would put his hat on and shout, '*Rebbosai, wir wollen benschen.*' It is really remarkable that he did not do that. What do such Jews want with Christians in their homes? In that situation, Judaism is absolutely incommensurable with Christianity. In such a mixed company I don't feel comfortable. The parts of the group are rigorously separated; there is no common spirit uniting it and in which one can move. If one is understood by one part, he is incomprehensible to the other. No, I want to be among either all Jews or all Christians; in either place I feel comfortable. We Jewish university students are amphibians who can live both with Jews and with Christians."

Youth always imagines that the experience it has had is a discovery that nobody else knows. Jacob was surprised to hear another speak of Jews and Christians in the same direction in which he himself had thought and felt so much. It took him a little while to reply. "Amphibians, you say, are what we Jewish students are? It seems to me that we are just the opposite of amphibians, that we have left the element where we belonged, and have ventured into one that does not accord with our nature."

"Oh, that's imagination!" cried Levy. "That's only until one gets accustomed to life in both circles. When one has an easy temperament and now and then closes his ears, it is actually pleasant to move in this way alternately in two opposing elements; now one is a bird, now a fish, according to one's fancy."

"You certainly do have a fortunate temperament," said Jacob.

"Oh, yes; come visit me some time, and I'm sure we will have a good time together."

"Drop in on me, too; here is where I live."

"Agreed! Tomorrow I'll come and smoke my morning pipe with you, before I go to the hospital. Well, good night then; thanks for this evening."

"Good night, Levy, and thanks!"

A few days later, very early in the morning, one of Jacob's cousins burst into his room without taking the time to knock or greet him. He shouted breathlessly, "You are to come over to father! The rof [5] has sent for him and you."

"What am I supposed to do at the rof's?" asked Jacob. "I don't have any business with the rof."

"Chutzpo!"[6] cried the cousin. "You don't have any business with the rof? But he has business with you! He wants to see you."

Jacob felt inwardly flattered at this invitation, which showed what attention had been aroused among the Jews by the fact that a Jewish child from the provinces had turned in such a brilliant examination, but in youthful arrogance, or to tease his cousin, he said only, "Very well, I will come."

"And this evening you are supposed to go to Wholesaler Bernbaum's. They sent us word, since they didn't know where you lived."

"I am supposed to go?" asked Jacob.

"What gavo[7] has gotten into you since you've become a bit of a student! Who wouldn't jump at a chance to accept an invitation from the rich Bernbaum! But go or don't go, a'ch mein Dago!"[8]

---

[5] Rabbi.

[6] Arrogance.

[7] Conceit.

[8] "Also my sorrow!" "What do I care?"

With these words the cousin ran out. When he got home to his father, he stuck his head in at the door and called, "Now the *gavostinker*[9] is coming right away!" after which he continued his way to his shop.

When Jacob arrived at his Uncle Marcus's, his aunt was in the act of pressing a large shirt-front frill; she tied this around Jacob and stuck his uncle's large diamond stickpin in it. All the way to the door she followed him, brushing the smallest speck of dust off his clothes.

Marcus strode in front with an unaccustomed proud air; he shared with his nephew the honor of being called to the *rof's*, and in his thoughts he appropriated the lion's share.

"How the other Jews will stare on Friday evening when they hear that I have been invited to the *rof's*!" he said to himself.

Jacob also walked along silently, thinking of what the *rof* would probably say to him; the closer they got to their destination, the more he felt himself moved by an apprehensive awe. In spite of what he called his better understanding, it was as if his conscience were beginning to prepare itself for interrogation and judgment over the ceremonies he had transgressed.

When they had climbed the rickety stairs in the ancient house, they were received in the anteroom by the *knelgabbe*,[10] who quietly led them into the room where the *rof* was sitting and reading his *Chumash*.[11]

It took a long time for the *rof* to look up, and in the reverent silence that reigned Jacob summoned his courage so that he could calmly regard his rabbi.

Over the pale face with the white beard, over the old man's entire appearance, over all his surroundings, no matter how old-fashioned and faded they were, there rested a peace that instinctively aroused in Jacob a profound, melancholy yearning, like a single, solitary light on land when there is a storm at sea.

---

[9] "To stink of pride" is a Jewish idiom.

[10] The *rof's* servant, a learned and pious man who ranks high, like the king's valet.

[11] The Pentateuch—the Five Books of Moses—which is printed; the Torah is written on parchment.

Here, he could see, doubt had never reached; here reigned an eternal Sabbath; alone in the company of his God, separated by ceremonies from the entire Christian world, this man lived in a spiritual Canaan.

"If only one could be a Jew like him!" said Jacob with a soft sigh.

Finally the *knelgabbe* ventured to approach the *rof* and whisper in his ear that the invited guests had arrived. The old man bowed reverently over the book before he turned from it, and then said to his guests in a friendly way, "*Boruch habo*, welcome." When they had stepped closer and had received the laying on of hands and the blessing, he invited them to take a seat and contemplated Jacob. But it was apparent that he was now embarrassed for a topic of conversation with the latter. He had not given any thought as to what he really would see in the young Jew whom the Christians had honored, and now that this person stood before him, a feeling came over him that this youth from his people was filled with a foreign element which he neither grasped nor esteemed. The old man continued to stare at Jacob; Jacob looked back at him expectantly; his uncle was sitting on pins and needles; the *knelgabbe* was standing in reverent silence by the door. Finally the *rof* got up, got a large red apple and presented it to Jacob, saying, "Don't forget to put on your *tefillin*."

He went back to his *Chumash*, and the audience was over.

The entire episode had, in all its quietness, been so peculiar that it made an almost fairy-tale-like impression on Jacob. When the rabbi had fixed his clear, devout eyes on him, it seemed to him that the *rof* had seen into his heart. But as this gaze continued and the expression of the eyes became more and more incomprehensible, it seemed as if the rabbi and he were gliding away from each other, drifting apart at an ever growing distance. When the door had closed after them, and the *knelgabbe*, who accompanied them to the stairway, had said his last "*Seid moichel*"[12] and had silently gone back, he felt as though he and Judaism had had a confrontation, and after a fruitless attempt

---

[12] "Pardon"; "farewell."

at mutual understanding had gone their separate ways without having achieved any object.

He was interrupted in his dreamy thoughts by his uncle, who with hardly suppressed anger said, "That was quite a way to talk to the *rof*!"

Jacob replied meekly, "But I didn't say a word, Uncle!"

"That was just the trouble!" cried his uncle, "one does not sit like that and stare his *rof* in the face without saying a word."

"But what should I have said to him, Uncle? Just tell me that!" said Jacob, annoyed.

At these words Marcus stopped furiously and turned to him, putting his hands on his hips. "Am I supposed to teach you what you should say to your *rof*? Is that why your father let you study at the university and spent money on you? Eh? Answer me!"

"No, that's certainly not why my father let me study," replied Jacob, walking on.

"Jacob, Jacob!" said his uncle, overtaking him again, "you are making a fool of me to boot. You don't care about either *rof* or uncle, perhaps not about father, either. You have become a *goy*, you will end up by letting yourself *schmatte* . . . but after all, why am I getting angry here? You are not my son, thank God!"

"Listen, Uncle!" said Jacob, "I don't want to quarrel with you. I have lived in your house, and you have treated me with love; therefore I make allowance for your words. But now be fair and tell me—what was I supposed to talk to the *rof* about? Should I not have waited until he addressed me?"

"That's all the same now!" replied his uncle. "But you have become a *goy*! I have noticed that, but I didn't want to say anything. What business is that of mine? You are *barmitzvo*[13] and I have no power over you. But I advise you for your own good, turn back while there is still time! Things do not go well with anyone who abandons the God of Israel, believe me! Don't do any *chilul Shem*.[14] Now this evening you are to visit for the first time the rich Bernbaum's cultivated and devout family—watch

[13] See Part 1, Chapter 9 [pp. 76–78].

[14] Literally, "profanation of the Name"—"do not give any offence."

your step! Quarrel? Why should we quarrel? You are my brother's son; you are welcome in my house as always. Will you come in with me?"

"No, thanks, Uncle; I am afraid that Aunt will also scold me when she hears about the visit. There, take your stickpin, and thanks very much for the loan."

"The poor stickpin!" said his uncle, looking at it, "when it was stuck in your shirt-frill, nobody thought of the visit turning out like that!"

"Well, Uncle, it really can't complain; it came along to be seen, not to talk."

"*Azusponim!* [impudent fellow]" said his uncle, unable to suppress a smile, going into the house.

In the evening Jacob, quite uneasy and anxious, set out for the distinguished family's house.

When he entered the reception room, where there was a rather large gathering, the hostess rose and came to meet him, saying "Welcome, Mr. Bendixen! I am glad to see you in my house; it stands open for any scholar, young or old. You will meet several here, to whom later I will have the pleasure of introducing you. Please take a seat; we are having a reading."

Jacob bowed, took a chair, and sat down at the table. Around it sat the hostess, her four daughters and two sons, as well as a young Jewish student who dined in the house once a week, and the wholesaler's office clerk, who was the reader. The wholesaler was sitting by the tiled stove asleep. Further away, at the window, were a couple of Jewish students; Levy also appeared later.

"Where was it that we left off?" asked the hostess.

"At 'Ha'," replied the office clerk, "I made a mark with my fingernail over the 'Ha'."

"Who says that 'Ha'?"

"Noureddin."

"Oh, I remember; read on."

The office clerk read *Aladdin* with a tone as if it had been his employer's ledger, and with a strong Jewish accent. But Jacob was so completely absorbed in his feelings as a guest and in his respect for the hospitable house that he instinctively tried to find everything beautiful; soon he was following the reading with the same interest with which one hears a beautiful melody, even when it is poorly performed. The students at the window were putting their heads together and laughing.

The reading proceeded for a time undisturbed, until the place where Noureddin calls out with new copper lamps to exchange for old ones. Here the reader wanted to introduce some variety into his monotonous presentation, and the words "Who will sell old copper lamps for new?" he tried to the best of his ability to reproduce with the same intonation that peddlers use to hawk peat in the street.

At this noise the wholesaler awoke, rubbed his eyes, and said, "That was a strange way to do business! What kind of crazy book is that, you have gotten hold of?"

The hostess angrily said, "Don't disturb us in our esthetic enjoyment . . . read on."

The reading got under way again; it rolled on like wheels over cobblestones.

The wholesaler made several efforts to fall asleep again, but when he couldn't succeed, he straightened up in his chair and looked at his wife. After some moments of silence he said, "What do you think, Rebecca—Refoel Liebmann was run over today. It must be a dreadful house with the many small children."

"God have mercy!" cried the lady, "where did it happen?"

"On Knippelsbro; I heard it at the Exchange, but I didn't have the heart to tell you immediately."

The lady said nothing, and it was apparent from her glances that her thoughts were more with the poor unfortunate family than with the reading. She did not regain her good humor until she had whispered something to her daughter, and the latter had gone out, doubtless to take care of having something sent to Refoel Liebmann's family. Then she again enjoyed the reading.

"Shouldn't we have tea soon?" asked the wholesaler a little later.

The lady said, "We'll be through soon. Aron, hurry up a little more."

One of the students said under his breath, "Getty-up!" The reading now indeed changed from a steady trot to a gallop. When the reader came to the last word, he stopped as suddenly as if the carriage shaft had struck a tree. One almost felt the jolt.

Tea and other refreshments were now passed around to the company.

The lady said, "That is certainly a delightful work! Classic!"

"I beg your pardon, Madame!" said one of the students, a law student, eagerly coming up to the table. "There are, I am sure, significant errors in it. If it had not become the fashion to find *Aladdin* classic and divine, reasonable people could still gain a hearing. I shall only call your attention to some few things, and you will certainly agree with me. What I first and foremost demand of a poet is truth and naturalness. By that I mean that, for example, a sailor should talk like a sailor and not like a professor, a shepherd like a shepherd and not like a wholesaler or a shipowner—isn't that right?"

"Yes, that is quite correct!" said the lady.

"Well, then I also demand that the Oriental should talk like an Oriental and have Oriental manners. He should not . . . oh, may I borrow the book . . . Aladdin should not talk about 'tearing trousers in two at the knee', which is not Oriental, since in the Orient they don't wear trousers; likewise he should not play various games which are Copenhagen games and not Oriental ones. Still more unreasonable is the fact that he 'measures young women over the chest' in a strange house, for such things are not permitted in Oriental harems. All such things the poet could have avoided by going to the trouble of reading a little about the Orient, about which various travel descriptions give sufficient information. Furthermore, it is thoughtless to have a poor tailor's boy's favorite dish be pheasants. . . ."

"Yes, but in the Orient, Mr. Isaksen!" said the lady.

"Well, all right, let's skip that about the pheasants, but meat broth, which Aladdin has the spirit of the lamp bring, that they don't have in the Orient."

"Are you absolutely certain of that, Isaksen?" asked Levy; "the whole human race, after all, comes from Asia Minor; who knows if meat broth has gone the same way?"

"I have no desire to joke now," said Isaksen sullenly; "I am perfectly serious about what I am saying here; it annoys me that such mistakes, which are glaringly obvious to the healthy human understanding, have been able to go on so long uncriticized. One cannot for a single moment abandon oneself to the illusion in this work; every moment one's intellect is unpleasantly affected. Mustapha, Morgiane, Noureddin, Aladdin, etc. constantly fall out of their roles as Orientals and speak like Copenhageners. For example, on page 66 the word 'knacker' is used in Ispahan! . . . Here, on page 100, Morgiane speaks of 'Siberia' . . . on page 186, 'tea urns' and 'cookie pans' in Ispahan are mentioned; . . . on page 324 the *elves* sing *psalms* and pray to *Allah* to reward Fatime. That is disgusting. There is in particular a place about which just a few days ago I debated with one of my acquaintances; that's page 48—the poet has the spirit of the lamp say,

> A new *Prometheus* will yet again restore
> The noble light to humankind today;
> Another Odin once more through the mountain bore,
> And will steal the mead and Gunnlöd betray.

This familiarity of the spirit of the lamp with Greek and Nordic mythology may, I am sure, be *juridically* defended—for the spirit of the lamp, no branch of knowledge need be unknown. But taken *poetically*, the spirit of the lamp is Oriental; an Oriental spirit and fragrance should be diffused over the fairy tale of the lamp. Here it is *Oehlenschläger* flaunting his knowledge of mythology and again absolutely tearing us out of the illusion. And then into the bargain he takes pieces of Greek and Nordic mythology in one mouthful, so that it is infuriating—what do you say, Mr. Bendixen? Am I not right?"

Jacob answered hesitatingly, "I really have not seen those errors you name before, just as I did not know that there were spots on the sun before astronomers told me there were."

"Are you studying astronomy?" asked the lady quickly.

A couple of the students started to laugh. The lady turned to them with tears in her eyes and said, "Goodness, what did I just say, since you are laughing at me?"

The two students got red in the face and assured her that it was not at her they had laughed.

The lady turned from them with relief and said to Isaksen, "It may very well be that in *Aladdin* there are all the errors you have named. Aron also reads so wrongly that one doesn't hear the errors. Aron! You ought to try for more taste. But all the same it is my opinion of Oehlenschläger, that he is a gifted man. He is sometimes a little overwrought and unnatural, and his forte may not be the Persian myths; he ought to stick to the Danish and Roman ones."

"Yes," said Isaksen, "there is, for example, the myth of Amor and Psyche; I'd like to see him treat that."

"Amor and Pysike?" said the lady. "It seems to me that somebody talked about that here the other day?"

"I beg your pardon, Madame!" interposed Isaksen. "It's not 'Pysike', but 'Psyche'."

"It's dreadful, the way you are badgering me this evening!" said the lady angrily. "It's spelled 'P-s-y' and it's not pronounced 'Pys'?"

"No, it's pronounced 'Psy', Madame."

"Don't come and try to teach me that!" cried the lady. "My common sense you won't argue me out of! It is pronounced 'Pys'—isn't that so, Aron?"

"Yes it is; indeed, I always read it as 'Pys'," said Aron.

"I assure you, it's pronounced 'Psy', Madame!"

"You are rude, Mr. Isaksen; it is not nice of you, here in my own home. You think, just because you are a university student, that you have absorbed all the learning in the world! Well, really!"

"And you, Mrs. Bernbaum, probably think, because you have a bit more money than my parents, that you can treat me like that!" said Isaksen, taking his hat. "I am sure that I will not burden you again! But even if it were the last word I ever say, it is still 'Psy'! Good night!"

There was no one present who could pick up the conversations's broken threads and erase the unpleasant impression which this scene had made. A few disconnected remarks about the wind and weather were exchanged, and the guests gradually slipped away.

When Levy and Bendixen had walked together some distance down the street, Bendixen said, "There was something strange about this soirée; it was almost like, one can imagine, Emperor Christoph and his Negroes holding court in Haiti. About them we read that one of them goes around with a pair of general's epaulettes on his otherwise naked body, another has a pair of cavalry boots and uniform jacket but no trousers, a third even makes do with a pair of spurs on his heels. Similarly, the people here have decorated themselves with esthetic refinement— Isaksen had prosaic intellect with all its naked dryness, the lady has sensitive foolishness, and her sons and daughters had, it appeared, nothing at all, not even a spur on their heel."

"That is a very good image!" said Levy laughingly, "it is a little crazy. But," he added more seriously, "refinement will also not be able to penetrate the family life of the Jews until we, who go in advance, ourselves form a family life."

"I wish," said Jacob, "that I had not been present. It has been depressing to me to see Jews behave like that. What must the Christians think of us, when they are witnesses to such scenes as that between the lady and the students."

"It was not particularly pleasant to me, either. . . ." Here Levy broke off suddenly with a burst of laughter. "Really, it is comical," he said, as Jacob looked at him with astonishment, "it is almost absurd to think that we immediately start to talk seriously and profoundly about our 'nation'! A pair of Christian students leaving a party would be talking about wine, a card game, or women, as is fitting and proper for sensible and upright young men."

"But still," he went on a little later, "that is a sign that basically there is some hope for the Jews. Individuals never stand isolated; they are the children of their time and their surroundings. It is precisely our worry about the Jews that shows that a new spirit is stirring in our people. Give it time! The Jews will catch up! Our present state of education is a building put up in haste; while the outside is being whitewashed, inside there is much still under construction. In twenty, thirty years, when the forces now stirring have fermented and clarified, we will surely force the Christians to respect us."

"God grant that!" said Jacob. "All that I wish for is to be able to acquire a universally respected position among them."

"That ambition is not one of the greatest," said Levy.

"And still it can be difficult enough to satisfy even that!" replied Jacob with a sigh.

"No, now we are getting too deep in the matter!" cried Levy; "this evening I damned well want to be cheerful and happy; come on, let's go to a coffee shop."

Chapter 2

ONE DAY LEVY CAME INTO Jacob's room like a man who
has put down a great burden and takes a deep breath.

"Oh, hello!" he cried, "Let me have a pipe! I have taken a
week's leave from the hospital to study some anatomy, but now I
want first to rest up this afternoon. So I am visiting you; first
we'll chat a little, and then we'll go out together, eh? But what
the devil kind of face is that you're putting on? Now, I have seen
you in a bad temper many times, but never so utterly
melancholy-morose as today. Your stomach must be out of order,
or else you're bilious; perhaps we even have a disease of the liver.
Or, let me see, we had yesterday an interesting case with a lesion
of the spinal cord. I would be extremely happy to be able to serve
you with my still fresh experience. Are you thirsty? Let me see
your tongue."

"Take a pipe, Levy, but don't joke; I really can't take joking
today."

"Has something really unpleasant befallen you? Has
something happened?"

"I can tell you, Levy, you will understand me. Yes, I just
want to speak out; it's getting too burdensome for me now."

"My God, what's wrong? Is it an unhappy love affair?"

"Yes, it is an unhappy love affair," said Jacob bitterly. "But
the unfortunate thing is that there is so much hatred in that
love. Oh, yes, it can very well be called an unhappy love affair!
My whole temperament, my spirit, my inclination belongs to the
Christians, and I could wish myself able to advance against
them at the head of an army, to bombard Copenhagen, in order to
gain their reciprocal love."

"That method has not yet occurred in my practice," remarked
Levy.

"Don't mock me, even if I make myself ridiculous in your eyes. I am too irritated to be able to weigh my words."

"But, in God's name, what have they done to you? And who is it who has wounded you so deeply?"

"It's not a new wound inflicted on me; it's an old one that has reopened. Yes, this wound is old; I think I got it at birth. It is the anti-Semitism which I suffered under elsewhere, and with which I am now again confronted. What the schoolboys began, the university students have continued. In between course lecture periods they tease each other and have fun—that's as it should be. Now today they hit upon the idea of throwing paper wads at each other, and although I did not take part in the fun, I was hit in the head by many of them. At first I thought it was accidental, but then I heard first one and then another say, 'Give it to the Jew!' I pretended not to hear it, and quietly put up with everything. But finally a piece of wood hit me in the back. So I got up, picked up the piece of wood and threw it as hard as I could in among them; it struck one in the head so that he had to leave. Now I have taken an uncontrollable dislike to attending courses. Even access to the university they block for me, for the Jew. How have I deserved this persecution? Aren't they adults, haven't they enough intelligence to recognize that knowledge is our common mother, that we are brothers?"

"Yes, but brothers hit each other in the head with blocks of wood."

"Don't joke, Levy!" said Jacob. "If you can't understand my feelings and share my indignation, then say so, and I won't say any more."

"Frankly speaking, I don't understand that you will allow yourself to be shut out of courses by a few thoughtless boys, instead of going up there and looking them defiantly in the eye."

"Oh, Levy, you don't understand that this has a far deeper meaning for me. Maybe you go so far as to think that all of my pain is caused by the wood that hit me in the back. No, what has happened is undoubtedly a trifle, but it reminds me of all the misery weighing on me and on you, too, Levy—Jew! Why didn't you become a *Schächter*[1] like your father? Why didn't I remain behind my father's counter? Why has our spirit left the home where there were loving arms, and sought *Wahlverwandtschaft* with the Christian spirit which contemptuously repulses us? We are and will remain Jews, just as the Negro slave is and will remain black, even if they 'emancipate' him. Like him, we are emancipated to understand a freedom and equality that is poisoned for us. Will they ever forget the Jew over the person? Won't the *Jew* always stand before their thoughts as a barrier? In a social gathering they don't say 'the Lutheran Petersen', 'the Lutheran Jensen', etc., but they say 'the Jew Bendixen', even if they don't say it aloud. If they want to be really nice, they say 'member of the Mosaical faith' or 'your nation'. If I am sitting and dining among them, and, for example, ham is served, my neighbor never forgets, when he passes me the dish, to ask, 'Do you eat this?' 'May I offer you some of this?' . . . Jew! Jew! Ought one not to think that we bear this word branded on our foreheads, since they never fail to remember it!"

"What you say is true, but I am accustomed to such things, or I am not as sensitive as you in this respect, probably—it doesn't bother me much. If somebody offers me ham, I eat it, no matter how much doubt he expresses about my capacity for it."

Jacob, tired and angry, was silent, and there was a pause in the conversation.

"Listen, Bendixen!" Levy cried suddenly, and a tremor in his facial muscles showed that at this moment he was moved by a profound feeling. "I realize that there is a great difference between us. I am poor; with me the consideration of my future, of a living, has overcome the irritability that has also been in my soul, though less than in your case. I am also an easy, careless nature, but you are more impatient, dreamy; and, moreover, you are rich. With you, the worry about making a living will not stifle the other worries. You must make a decision, an energetic decision; you cannot move in both regions, as I can, so you must

---

[1] Butcher for the Jews. A position which is much higher among the Jews than among the Christians, since the *Schächter* must be a very holy man.

choose *either* the one *or* the other. Become a Jew, attach yourself
to the Jews, study Jewish theology and become a rabbi."

"That is impossible!" Jacob burst out quickly. "Doesn't my
conviction reject the greater part of the Jewish ceremonies?
Should I build my entire future on hypocrisy and deceitfulness?
Furthermore, I *cannot* attach myself to the Jews. The first
condition for a happy life together is similarity in education.
And you might just as well advise me to live in a little
provincial town among shoemakers and tailors—however warm
and good-natured they might be. My blood loves the Jews, but my
intellect cannot live among them. It is a Christian intellect, and
it seeks its like with instinctive fierceness."

"Then become a Christian! Be baptized!"

"Levy! You cannot mean that seriously. Be baptized! Deny
my past, my childhood, my entire being. . . . Be baptized! Give up
the battle like a coward—for I feel, and I have never felt more
clearly than at this very moment, that it is a battle and a higher
battle than for my insignificant person. It is one for my people,
my poor cowed people, my dead mother's race. If we, who in
education have gone in advance of our people, abandoned it, only
the dregs would in the end be left and the Christians'
ascendancy would be complete, and their persecution would be
vindicated. No, I will fight the Christians, so that they must in
me simply acknowledge the human being in spite of the Jew—let
me perish in the battle, I dedicate myself to it. Besides," he went
on after a pause in a deepening voice, staring into space, "besides,
I do not acknowledge the Christian religion. Judaism is indeed in
the process of disintegrating under its contact with civilization,
and the disintegration is affecting the minds going in advance; a
worm is gnawing on our existence, and we are being torn apart
because we are caught in the middle of the transition. But
present-day Christianity is also tottering, faith has vanished
from their minds, and they are seeking anxiously, almost
desperately, for a new Christianity. The worm is gnawing the
whole race, despair is hovering over it. When they sing their
most joyful songs, I seem to hear a secret consuming pain
through the tones. They don't know about it, the jubilation rises,
and the despair in the same measure raises its demonic-mocking

voice. When I on such an occasion sit among them, I imagine with silent horror that Samson is shaking the pillars of the edifice, and we all are about to be buried."

Levy looked at him silently.

Jacob went on, "And it has been my consolation in the long oppression that misery is brooding over us all."

"Bendixen! Bendixen!" said Levy, "There is something terrible in your nature."

"Oh, at this moment I truly feel how I hate them! Now just let me speak straight out—I have considered it an honor, a condescension, when one of them crossed the street at my side! Is there enough hatred in the world to make up for this humiliation!"

"And I have heard Christian students reproach you with being proud, aloof, stand-offish!" cried Levy.

"Because in my humiliation I was afraid of approaching them! Because I was waiting for a friendly gesture on their part with the same timid yearning the slave has, waiting for a friendly glance from his master."

"But can't you see that there must also be a fault on your part, when people who have wanted to approach you, have not been able to do it?"

"I am the oppressed one; it is up to them to approach me."

"But do you think that every Christian always carries around the memory of the Jews' oppression in the same way you always keep it in your irritable nature?"

Jacob said nothing.

"Don't be unjust," resumed Levy. "I suggested to you one of two alternatives before; I see that there must be a third. You can certainly be like me and associate with the Christians. Only control the irritability of your nature. Why won't you try to associate with people who obviously like you? There is, for example, Wilhelm Fangel; he always speaks of you with the greatest good will, he is almost in love with you. Why don't you meet him halfway? You want to carry on the battle for the Jews, you say. How do you want to carry it on? Is there any other weapon than self-control? Is there any other means than your drawing closer to the Christians and the Christians' drawing closer to you? We Jewish students should carry on the battle, that's true. We should go in advance among the Christians and by our personality teach them to acknowledge the good in the Jews. Well then, let's go . . . take your hat, and we will go out to the surgical academy; there we'll meet Fangel and several others. I'll be your doctor and even your pharmacist and nurse; I will not only prescribe the medicine, but will prepare it myself and give it to you. Come on!"

Jacob hesitated.

"Bendixen!" said Levy, "Now it's my turn to be serious. Today I am opening for you the door to people. Maybe we two will never again meet each other in the same frame of mind as today; maybe I will never again feel the interest in helping you as at this moment. Take advantage of the moment, or the door will slam shut."

Jacob took his hat and went with him.

Chapter 3

AMONG THE STUDENTS OF THE UNIVERSITY of Copenhagen, the medical students are the jolliest and the ones who harbor the fewest prejudices. They see in the person only the more or less good person, perhaps even only the more or less good cadaver. Since a Jewish case of typhus is treated with the same medicaments as a Christian one, since a Jewish bone is no more difficult to saw off than a Christian one, since finally muscles and nerves are arranged in the same order on a Jew as on a Christian, they don't see the slightest grounds for making a difference between Christian and Jew. The nature of their studies brings them closer together than other students; for that reason, and also because they become familiar with seeing life and death, pain and healing, balance each other, and a pill, an enema tip the balance, there is more youthful recklessness, more social fun among them than among the others.

Among these men Jacob soon felt at ease, and at the frequent gatherings at the maternity hospital and the hospital, where scientific debates alternated with the most light-hearted joking, he began to take part in the student life which had always seemed so glorious to him. It was the sociability more than the merriment that was so refreshing to him; it was the feeling of for once being among *comrades* that was so salutary for him.

In this way he spent his first year as a student; he took his second examination, and after this it was natural that the career course of study he chose was medicine. With the increased cheerfulness that entered his temperament, much of its irritability vanished, and he began to think that there was no peculiar curse hovering over him, or at least that the curse that had drawn close to him in his childhood and youth had receded like a storm cloud. Jacob was now twenty years old, and after having heard him discussed so long, at least a few feminine readers probably want to know how he looked. Well, he looked like a Jew who has learned something—that is to say that intelligence had ennobled the expression in the Jewish physiognomy, which is repellent to many. For knowledge goes its purifying way through the soul, and the soul works and works so long until it has made its abode fit it, until it, so to speak, has the face made over into its signboard.

Jacob is now twenty years old, and the story has thus once more in haste sprung over a few years of his life. Why not? No person's life is in reality an unbroken series of events deserving of note. One must from time to time give the hero time to catch his breath.

However, just as one receives from an absent friend a single letter which orients one about his travels, so we take a single episode from this time which may orient us about the years skipped over.

AN EXCURSION IN THE WOODS

"How fresh and pleasant the rain that fell last night has made the air!" said one of the interns who one morning were standing at the window and looking out into the courtyard, while they waited for the clinic's professor.

"I'd like to take a hike in the woods today," said another, looking up toward the dark blue sky. "Is there anybody who would like to go along?"

"Yes, let's all make an excursion to the woods today!" cried the first.

"I can't; I've got to teach."—"I've got to go to my tutor."—"I'm invited out."—resounded regretfully from several sides.

"I think, by God, here is a rebellion against the constitution," said Levy. "I think that the hospital will be reasonable. You've got to go to your tutor, you've got to teach, you've got to God knows what . . . all of this, precisely why you ought to go to the woods, you are adducing as reasons not to go out there. May I ask that the idea of the hospital not be violated and that the excursion to the woods take place."

"Since the matter has already been broached, it must not be dropped!" cried Fangel. "For the sake of the honor of the hospital, at least a carriageful must drive out. First the volunteers must step forward as if for a storm on a fortress (and there may very well be a *storm*); the rest will be selected by lot. Who will volunteer to go along? Step forward!"

They all stepped forward.

"I like that," Fangel went on. "And now deputations must be sent to the maternity hospital and to the General Hospital."

Levy said, "We ought to do like Saul, who slaughtered his ox and sent the bloody pieces around in the land with orders to march out against the enemy and with the message 'Thus it will be done with every one who does not follow Saul and Samuel'."

"Bravo!" shouted Fangel. "Gröndal, slaughter Levy and roam with the bloody pieces around in Israel."

"Alas, " replied Levy, "they are right when they say that our age is the wrong world. However, I bow to the spirit of our time and stretch my neck for Gröndal and Fangel."

"Well answered to a feeble joke!" cried Fangel. "The woods excursion begins well. *Allons!* Let's quickly have those conveyed into the hereafter, who want to be off, so that the excursion won't be delayed."

"But where is Bendixen?" asked one. "We must have him along. He is as good as a thermometer or a safety valve. When the rest of us are happy, he gets serious, and if we are serious, he gets light-headed and wild. On such an occasion, he is to be compared with the wooden disk in Watt's steam engine which brings water into the boiler when there is too little, and stops when there is too much."

"There is the thermometer, safety valve, wooden disk, etc.!" shouted Fangel, pointing toward the door, which Bendixen opened at that moment.

"Bendixen! are you going with us to the woods today?"

"Yes, of course. Is somebody going out there?"

"All of us."

"That's splendid. At what time?"

"At four o'clock we are gathering here and then going out and taking a carriage."

At that moment the professor arrived and duties began.

"Ha, how glorious it is to be free, to have escaped the town, where breathing is oppressed by walls and moats and philistines and towering buildings! I drink in the fresh air as the thirsty person drinks in the dew and does not think he can be refreshed. If only one could just one moment dissolve oneself into air and lose oneself in a whirlwind or even better in a waterspout: on light wings bore down into the sea and again dart up, all the way up toward the sun!—It is a sad lot that man has; even in death one does not become free, but is stuck down into a tightly closed prison, into the ground. It would be better if bodies were still burned, and the ashes, like the late Pugachev's, scattered to the winds."

This long outburst came from Bendixen when the carriage rolled out on the coast road and the Sound with the white sailboats lay stretched out before the eye.

Gröndal, his neighbor in the carriage, responded to his outpourings of the heart, "I also would rather see bodies burned. Then people would not be so set on getting their dead intact into the ground, and then one would surely now and then get a decent cadaver."

"Ah, you never think about anything except the cadaver!" cried Bendixen. "I think that if you ever meet a woman with a really interesting incurable disease, you'll marry her just to keep the body."

"You may very well be right," replied Gröndal.

König, who was sitting behind them, broke into the conversation. "It is a well-known fact," he said, "and it can be logically proven, that Gröndal cannot enter the kingdom of heaven."

"How is that?" asked Jacob.

"Oh, yes, for even if God wanted to be truly merciful toward him, He still would not put him in heaven, since heaven would be no paradise for Gröndal, because there are no bodies there. Gröndal's paradise would be hell, where he can observe any conceivable muscle contraction in the various kinds of fire in which the sinners are roasted."

"That is a most highly illogical proof," said Gröndal. "If patients bring their bodies along to hell, why shouldn't they then also bring them along to paradise?"

"Listen to him!" cried König. "He has even abolished the expression *people* and uses instead *patients*."

"Does any person come to the other world other than as a patient? Doesn't everybody in the end suffer from the most incurable, the most acute, of all diseases—death? Anyway, it's damned immaterial to me where the puff ends up that I intend to give off when I die."

"So you don't even believe in a soul and the soul's immortality!" cried König.

"Bah!" replied Gröndal, mightily exhaling the smoke from his cigar, and his face assumed a more noble, thoughtful air. "Your immortality is too massive for me. Whatever I accomplish down here in thought or act, in battle with the world and with myself, is my immortal portion. When the ink has run out of the pen, it can write no more. But what it has written, and what stands for eternity, is not ink and pen; it is the spirit that was in what was written."

Several more took the floor in this debate, and, as is usual on such occasions, everybody came out with his own opinion concerning immortality and life on the other side.

Finally Bendixen, staring thoughtfully out at the horizon where sky and sea touched, burst out, "It is strange that everybody arranges immortality and life on the other side to suit himself, and how we argue to get each other to prescribe the same rules to the Lord. As if life in the hereafter were decided by a majority resolution! Immortality—what else is it than the poetry of the entire human life, the source from which every poetic feeling streams. When poetry dies in me, my soul dies, even if my body lives on for a time. There is no immortality except for him who believes in it, and he who believes in it needs none; his life has been beautiful enough, he has received his reward for his faith. I believe in eternal poetry and eternal life."

"You are no Jew, Bendixen," said Gröndal.

"That may very well be, but I am no Christian, either!"

"Bendixen! Have you seen little Clara since, the one who was discharged last week?" called someone from the rear seat.

"No, I haven't," answered Bendixen in an annoyed tone.

"But she always cast her languishing eyes on you. You surely know where she lives, but you want to keep her for yourself."

"Oh, I'm not fond of languishing eyes. They promise more than they keep—and more than they can fulfill."

"What kind of nonsense is that! Don't pretend to be some paragon of virtue."

"I don't pretend to be any paragon of virtue. I appeal to you yourself. Such a glance, such a sunstroke that strikes the soul, doesn't it daze the soul in an instant with the dim presentiment of a nameless, unknown bliss? And does one find it, when the fulfillment comes? Have you found it?"

"One goes on and continues to seek; life is a continuous struggle and striving!" someone answered cheerfully.

"I don't care for the heartache that the brief coquettish flashes from pretty eyes arouse. I would rather avoid the fleeting blaze of the eternally unsatisfied yearning."

"Heartache! Bendixen is hysterical!" somebody shouted, laughing.

Jacob said nothing, and the conversation went on in a new direction. A short time later the carriage drove in at Klampenborg.

The establishment got its hands full with the noisy guests who demanded service, shouted and laughed, asked about all possible things and, when they got an answer, had forgotten what they had asked about. After long consideration and consultation that grew ever more serious, finally each one reached a decision and ordered what he wished, and in calm anticipation they strolled around in scattered groups.

König and Jacob had by chance come over to the dining room window, and Jacob was looking at some forget-me-nots standing in pots.

"May I take one of these flowers?" he said to the serving girl who was standing inside the window.

"Yes, by all means," replied the pretty girl pleasantly.

"What is that?" asked König, stepping closer. "Oh, forget-me-nots! Miss, will you give me one to remember you by?"

"Yes, I'll be happy to," she said laughingly, plucking a couple of flowers and handing them to him.

Jacob in a flash noted something that aroused in him a feeling of abasement, pain, and resentment.

"When I asked for these flowers," he said to himself, "it was not for the sake of the flowers; the pretty girl gave them a glow, and I asked for them on her account. But I said, 'May I take them?' But he, the lucky man, born in the Christian race, imbued without knowing it with romanticism's fragrance, immediately finds the right words and says, 'Will you give them to me?' Oh, how lucky these Christians are!"

They went off. König stuck the blossoms in his buttonhole and within half an hour had lost them; Jacob carefully placed his in his wallet. But when he came back among the others, there was within him a restless longing, a resigned resentment at his fate; he almost regarded the others as formed of better stuff than himself.

Someone asked, "Shall we do something until the food is ready?"

"Let's play robbers!" cried Jacob happily.

"Play robbers?" some of them said mockingly. "Yes, if there were a convent here nearby."

Jacob was ashamed to admit that he had never played, and that he wanted to take advantage of the opportunity to get acquainted with this bliss.

They could not reach any decision, and continued to stroll around until the meal was served.

A table was set out in the garden, on that lovely spot from where one looks out on the blue sea and the fresh woods. The sun was low in the sky, a mild cool breeze fluttered through the trees, and in the distance a few fishing boats glided along with red sails. A white tablecloth was spread over the table, the dishes steamed, the wine sparkled in the glasses, all faces beamed with youthful zest for life. Jacob surveyed the whole scene, the feeling of the beauty and pleasantness of the moment caused his heart to swell, youth's rich, healthy life glowed in his veins, while the still, consuming void gathered closer to his heart; he seized his glass and cried, "The first glass I sacrifice to the subterranean gods, to pain and sorrow and tear-bringing death. They lie in wait for us mortals with sinister looks when day's bright spirits are with us, knowing well that there will come a night and a darkness when the work is theirs. I defy you, you dark powers, for the light in my soul shall not be extinguished. But if I can buy your friendship with a glass of wine, then I will nonetheless do it—there, swallow this!"

And with these words he threw the wine on the ground, and the whole company jubilantly followed his example.

Fangel filled his glass and said, "I am no Bendixen, and I cannot begin my speech on stilts and finish in my stocking feet; therefore I am content to say that this, my second glass, I'll be damned if I don't sacrifice to myself. While the subterranean gods lap their part off the ground, I'll drink like a human being from my glass and I'll drink it bottoms up. *Skaal!*"

"Me too! Me too!" they all shouted, and the glasses were drained to the bottom.

"How's the steak?" asked Gröndal, glancing down in his neighbor's plate; "I'd like to know whether I committed an error by ordering turtle soup."

"The steak is tough," groaned the one questioned, resting his teeth for a moment.

"Then I'm relieved," said Gröndal, emptying his glass. "Incidentally, I would like to remark that a while ago there was talk of heartache at the sight of feminine eyes. That has also occurred in my practice. When I was about twenty, there was a pair of eyes which, when they looked at me, brought my heart into a strange, longing movement, quite in accordance with Bendixen's diagnosis. I did not understand it until, about a year afterward, I heard that she had drowned herself. It is exactly eight years ago this evening. Those eyes were pretty, and I'll drink a glass in memory of each of them."

Gröndal rapidly emptied two glasses.

"Ah, Gröndal," whispered König, "that's why you always run out to see when a drowned woman is being looked for in the daily newspaper. I thought it was only for the sake of the cadaver."

After a pause, Jacob said, "Sometimes one hears something for the first time, and still it seems as if one had heard the same thing before, in a strangely dim past. I remember with certainty that an incident like the one Gröndal just related has been before me in vague outline, as if my soul had had a presentiment that it would some day get to hear it. It was one evening on the main street. I was walking deep in thought, when a young lady came past me. Through her veil she sent me one of those glances we have discussed. I trembled inside; it was as if this sparkling of her eyes had warmed me up and I was suddenly standing in the cold again. An officer followed the lady briskly, spoke to her, and in the square she took his arm. I turned back with an inexpressibly bitter feeling in my heart. It seemed to me that the officer had seduced an innocent girl whom I loved. I made fun of my foolishness myself, but I could not get rid of this feeling. I have hated all officers since that evening."

"*All* officers! That's going too far!" said one of the company. "Although, who can tell how many of them have been guilty of the same thing as this one!"

"Yes, all officers," Jacob went on vehemently, "that is, all the young officers. Those are men who spend most of their time chasing women and with lewd thoughts, so that they in the end cannot regard any woman with respect, completely unlike the knights, whose place they have taken."

Levy bent toward Jacob and whispered to him, "And who form a corps which no Jew can enter, isn't that right?"

Jacob flushed and said nothing.

"Let's have a song!" some of them cried.

"Let the song go around!" cried others; "One after the other will strike up a familiar song, and everybody will join in on the chorus."

This was agreed upon. It was still in that good old time, the time of clubs, esthetics, and political childhood. No one then was yet liberal, illiberal, constitutional, or servile; the people had not yet eaten of journalism's tree of knowledge and seen that they were naked. It was in that good old time when Rahbek & Colleagues' convivial dithyrambs lived in the hearts of the people and resounded from their lips. Then there was yet no need of choral societies; song came with the wine just as easily as does a political speech nowadays. Various songs resounded now, interrupted by joking and laughter, out over the still Sound. When it was Jacob's turn, it sounded as though he felt some misgivings, but then he briskly raised his head and struck up one of Wilhelm Müller's *Deutsche Griechenlieder*. They are forgotten by the present generation like the furious struggle for freedom that gave rise to them. Perhaps few of those now alive recall the deep pain and the ardent enthusiasm for the Hellenic past and Hellenic freedom that breathed in many of these songs. Jacob sang one of them with his pleasant voice, and when he finished the company sat silent and serious.

"Look," he said after a pause, "now the sun is going down, and the same red beams that embellish our pleasure are perhaps shining on the corpses of Greeks and down into the prison to German students who wanted to be free. Let us at least remember them, before we lose ourselves in intoxication."

"That was contrary to the agreement!" cried one, "We were supposed to sing a song in which we could all join in the chorus."

"It's not my fault," replied Jacob, "why don't you join in? Curiously enough," he went on, "I, a son of the enslaved nation, am supposed to remind you about freedom! Although, rightly considered, it is as it should be; the Jews stand in much closer contact with freedom than you do."

"Utter nonsense! Now solid proof of that, Bendixen," they cried.

"All right; look: the Jews are freedom's filter. When you people suck in the delicious smoke, the tobacco juice sinks down to them. When the people in Germany and Denmark want to have freedom, they smash in the Jews' windows. As soon as there is freedom in the air, there is a twinge in the Jew's arms and legs, just as a change in the weather makes itself felt in a rheumatism patient. I ought therefore *ex officio* to speak to you about freedom. The small detail that I have come to love it instead of fearing it has nothing to do with the matter."

"For that proof I'll drink a glass of wine," said Gröndal, "and for the Greeks and Missolonghi I am prepared to drink with all of you together; here I throw down my gauntlet, figuratively speaking, of course."

"Yes, hurrah for Hellas and Hellenic freedom!" shouted Fangel. "To be sure, I know the land only from the punishments I got for Homer in school, but it may be for precisely that reason that I cherish an otherwise inexplicable tenderness for this land. And look here! Hurrah for Father Homer! *Pontos Oinoeis!* Isn't he right—doesn't the sea at this moment look like the finest Bordeaux wine? Oh, if only I were way out there! If only I could swim in that lovely St. Julien!"

"I protest against the external use of wine," said Gröndal. "But since we are drinking to Hellenic freedom, let us then also empty a glass for Danish freedom; that is after all, when you come to think of it, just as near and dear to us."

"Oh, yes," said Jacob, whose blood had begun to stir a bit, and who could no longer control himself, "I'll also drink to that; after all, I do love Denmark best."

"May the devil thank you for that!" cried Gröndal. "I would certainly think that it was your fatherland just as well as mine. Weren't you born and bred on Funen? Do you deny that?"

"No," answered Jacob, "but Denmark simply cannot be my fatherland as fully as it is yours, since I am not treated as its son as fully as you. Do you really think that any Jew who has come to know human rights and worth can with indifference regard the inequality that the state sets up between him and his Christian fellow citizens? The Jew is reproached that he has no fatherland—why is he not given one?"

"But the difference is really most insignificant," somebody objected, "there are very few things here in which Jews are discriminated against."

"Freedom cannot be divided; the slightest thing lacking changes it to oppression."

"Damned if I know anything in which Jews are discriminated against," cried König. "Do you receive worse examination grades because you are a Jew?"

"Anything, you say! I won't talk about opinion, although it perhaps is the most important and has greater effect than laws and decrees. But can a Jew become a civil servant? Can he become

so much as a watchman? Can he become an officer in the army?
In the civil guards when he is in line for captain, he has to
retire! I said I wouldn't talk about opinion, but I will
nevertheless cite some characteristic features. There are entire
guilds—for example, the ironmongers' guild—that exclude Jews,
and do not accept Jewish boys as apprentices. In the Volunteer
Corps no Jew can stand the persecution. When a playwright
knows nothing else to write about, he puts a Jew in a play and
gets a clown to play the role. They never get the ethos right; not
even the pronunciation is genuine, but the riffraff laughs, and
the riffraff on such an evening is the greatest part of the public."

"You are too hard, Bendixen!" cried Fangel. "In the theater I
have laughed myself silly over a Jew, but I'll be damned if I
despise the Jews."

"It is already harsh enough," remarked Jacob coldly, "that
anybody needs to say, 'I don't despise the Jews'."

"What do you want then, Bendixen?" shouted Fangel. "Do
you want us to yell 'Hurrah for the Jews!'? . . . then hurrah for
the Jews!"

"Hurrah for the Jews!" roared the whole company.

"I want," cried Jacob, ignoring the toast, "I want you to tell
me why I, as I stand here, am not just as good, just as fully
entitled to every freedom, to every trust, to every office, as you. I
want," he added in a tone halfway between bitterness and humor,
"I want you to tell me why I just as well as any of you cannot be a
watchman"

"You *shall* be a watchman! Bendixen shall be a watchman!"
they roared exultantly. "Hurrah for Watchman Bendixen!"

Jacob was exhausted by his own vehemence; he felt a certain
shamefulness over the recklessness with which he had abandoned
himself to his feelings. Gröndal had in the meantime gotten up
and gone to the kitchen to make a punch "according to his own
recipe" and now led the serving girl with the flaming punchbowl
out in triumph.

The fiery fluid was received with a tattoo hammered out on
the table so that the glasses and bottles rattled, and amid cheers
the liquid fire was poured into the glasses.

Next to being drunk among sober people there is nothing worse than being sober among drunk or half-drunk people. One stands with one's soul outside a circle of revelers whose merriment one does not grasp, because one with cold good sense demands a reason for their jubilation, which has no other reason except that they are jubilant. That cold good sense is more and more annoyed on behalf of human dignity, and one loses all his pleasure without the slightest use, because one with all his sobriety still cannot dilute the intoxication of the others. Jacob felt this unpleasantness and thought of leaving the company without saying good-by, but suddenly he seized his glass and emptied it, then another and another glass of the sweet, treacherous drink, and after a few moments had elapsed he felt he had caught up with the others.

The coachman drove cautiously homeward when the company, late at night, was safely loaded into the carriage. The gentle motion in combination with the pleasant coolness of the air soon lulled them all to peaceful sleep. When the coachman drove through the city gate, he poked the one sitting nearest and asked him where to drive them. Gröndal, who was the one nudged and who lived at the maternity hospital, answered, "To the maternity hospital."

"The drunken ass imagines he's pregnant," grumbled the coachman, elbowing another passenger and repeating his question.

"To the hospital!" groaned the one asked.

"He has more sense, in any case, for they are certainly dead drunk; but damned if they need to be hospitalized for that disease!" growled the coachman, jabbing at a third, who, annoyed at the rough touch, cried, "Go to hell!"

"But I can't drive around the streets with them until they sleep it off; that could take until tomorrow evening," said the coachman anxiously, pulling up. "Good Lord! If people are going to get drunk out, they certainly ought to give the coachman their address in advance."

When the carriage stopped, Gröndal half awoke, and thinking that the coachman was pulling up outside the maternity hospital, he said, "Call the senior midwife and tell her it's me."

"Oh, sure!" said the coachman, "He is not even satisfied with an ordinary midwife. He has really hung one on. Listen, you people, where do you want to go now?" he called out impatiently.

"To the hospital! To the hospital!" resounded snufflingly from various sides.

"If you're determined to go out there, you'll damned well go there," said the coachman indignantly, whipping up his horses until he stopped outside the wrought-iron gate, which opened hospitably to his passengers.

Chapter 4

ONE WINTER AFTERNOON JACOB was sitting in König's room. They were studying botany together, and König had painstakingly collected a herbarium which he liked to see used—and thus appreciated—by his colleagues. They had just entered on a lively debate about a rare plant, of which König had no specimen, when a message came from a woman in the neighborhood. The doctor must definitely come over; her husband had fallen in the street and had broken his leg.

"The blessed Copenhagen streets!" said König when, after the messenger's departure, he had thrown off his dressing gown and had hastily gotten dressed, "but they do provide a good intern with a little practice in the wintertime. Do stay here until I return, Bendixen; the whole thing will undoubtedly be taken care of quickly."

Since the door to the family's living room—König lived with his family—was ajar, Jacob became an involuntary witness to the following conversation:

The mother: "Don't sit there the whole time looking for sleighs, Louise! You won't get your dress finished. If we have a problem later, we'll have to sew at night, and God knows I won't have that."

Louise: "I can't help it, Mother. When the sleigh bells ring, I can't control my eyes. Do you know what I think? I sit imagining what if it were an elegant gentleman coming for me in a splendid sleigh? I know very well that no one is coming, but I still can't help looking to see if the fairy tale might not after all happen."

The mother: "You're being foolish. You'd better think of the fact that without a dress, you can't go to the dance."

"Oh, yes, the dance!" cried Louise, springing up and dancing around the room.

The mother: "But do be sensible, Louise! Does a grown girl act like that?"

Henriette (the older daughter): "But where are we going to get partners? Just think, there are already eighteen ladies invited. When there are ladies extra, the gentlemen are so arrogant."

Louise: "Oh, we two will be sure to get our dances as the daughters of the house."

The mother: "I must say, that is a hospitable thought toward the guests, my girl! But there are, I am sure, enough gentlemen. There are your two brothers, and the two lieutenants, and Gröndal, and Bendixen. . . ."

Louise: "Is the Jew included?"

The mother: "I thought so, since you complain about the shortage of dancing partners, but he can easily be crossed off the list."

Jacob heard no more. The young girl's remark had gone through him like a knife-thrust. He had attached himself to this girl with a certain affection; her cheerful, lively nature had interested him. She had often talked in a friendly, even warm, fashion with him, and now she was spurning him when he was compared with others, and only because he was a Jew. He was not hardened enough to receive calmly a thrust from that quarter. Without thinking, he got up and left.

Somewhat later König came home and, thinking that Bendixen had gone in to the family, he opened the door and looked for him.

"Where's Bendixen?" he asked when he did not find him in the living room.

"Bendixen? He hasn't been here."

"Certainly, he has been here! I asked him to stay and wait for me earlier, when I went out."

"Heavens! Then he may have heard what I said!" cried Louise, turning blood-red. "It seemed to me that someone a little while ago closed the door, but I thought I was mistaken."

"What did you say? And how could you talk unguardedly when the door to my room was standing open and there was somebody inside?"

"We heard you go out and didn't think there was anybody there."

"But what did you say, then, Louise, that you are afraid he heard?"

"Mother was talking about inviting him to the dance, and then I asked, 'Is the Jew to be included?' and Mother answered, 'He can easily be left out'."

"Well! That was damned well enough for Bendixen! How the devil can a girl who lays claim to being called cultivated forget herself to that degree, even in thought!" cried König furiously. "Bendixen is my friend; any other title my esteemed sister does not need to confer on him. But you will have to apologize to him, and if you won't, then I will do it in your presence."

"Ludvig!" said Louise, turning to her brother with a certain dignity, "you will surely think it over before you disgrace your sister. Besides, it will perhaps excuse me a little if I tell you the real reason for what I said. It was a kind of coquetry, or whatever you want to call it. Henriette teases me all the time about him, and now I wanted to affect a greater indifference to him than I actually harbor, and didn't know any easier way to do it. I hope that this admission is atonement enough for my unwitting offence, and that you now will take care of smoothing over the matter without humiliation to me."

"Yes, it's all very well that you make yourself faultless and push everything onto me," growled König, "but I demand now as justice that he be invited to the dance."

With that he went in search of Bendixen.

In the meantime Jacob's irritated mood had had time to subside and make way for chagrin and shame. His thoughts were approximately these: "What right did I have to hear these words! They were surely not meant to be heard by me; if they had known I was there, they would not have said them. . . . But why, after all, can this girl not think of me as anything else than *the Jew Bendixen*!. . . Bah! When all is said and done, I am indeed the Jew Bendixen. . . . In what a light I will now be regarded by the family! . . . I wish to God that that damned silly girl had closed the door before she talked. . . ."

While he paced back and forth with these thoughts, there was a knock at the door, and König entered. Each was too embarrassed to notice the other's embarrassment at this *vis-à-vis*. Mechanically they shook hands. Jacob in his mind groped with convulsive eagerness for the presence of mind that he felt was necessary, and succeeded half-unconsciously in producing the words, "I'm sorry that I ran off; I had forgotten a letter that had to be taken to the post office."

Poor König almost gave a start of joy at hearing these words. Involuntarily he cried, "Thank God!" but caught himself immediately, and the fear that he could have betrayed something by this outburst outweighed his joy. But Jacob found nothing strange in this exclamation; he had just said "Thank God!" to himself at the felicitous words that had escaped him.

In a relieved, warm mood the two friends sat down to chat; never had Jacob stuffed a pipe for König with so much politeness and eagerness, and never had König so busily assisted him in order to have the inconvenience himself. The conversation went with great liveliness from one subject to another, perhaps also because one was too afraid to let the other reflect on what might seem strange about their first exchange, and for the same reason they took leave of each other as late as possible. Reflection was the unpleasant consultant to which the friends reciprocally feared entrusting each other; they seemed to feel comfortable only when they were together and made sure that this guest did not appear.

Finally König found a way out. He anticipated the invitation to the dance, and when Jacob had accepted it with profuse thanks, both had a kind of strongpoint insuring that nothing disturbing had come into the friendship.

"You do dance?" asked König.

"Yes, in school I learned to dance, but I have never yet been to a real ball."

"Oh," cried König, "what is a ball other than dancing?"

With that he said good-by and left.

THE BALL

When, with a slight shiver of cold and nervousness, one steps into a ballroom before the ball has begun, one sees distinctly the particolored groups of ladies; one sees the walls, the mirrors, the chandelier; one has an eye for the lowered blinds, perhaps one even counts the squares in the ceiling. One meets one's friends and acquaintances, one hardly recognizes them; they speak another language than the customary one and their thoughts are elsewhere; one feels alone and is very shy. Then one believes that the peering and whispering ladies are secretly making fun of one, and dares not approach them, while in fact they wish for nothing more fervently. The modern age with all its etiquette and formality stretches its scepter over the room; the people move, not like human beings with red, warm blood in their hearts, but like statues.

Then the first stroke of the violins is heard, and a ray of life flashes over all the faces. They approach each other, arrange themselves in a row; an isolated happy smile breaks forth here and there like a warm glint of sun.

Suddenly the music swells in all its fullness, and closely entwined couples whirl around the room with radiant faces.

Where is the room now with its squares in the ceiling, with its chandelier and blinds? It has become a temple, an Ionic temple where Aphrodite sits enthroned and where her winged son amuses himself by discharging his arrows. He cannot bring himself to shoot hard into the bared bosoms, but into the heart that believes itself covered by a white silk vest and black coat he sends his cruelest arrows.

In the middle of the modern Christian city rises now, proud and smiling, the Ionic temple where the Olympic gods reign, where humans worship beauty and forget their catechism—for that reason the Christian priests have always thundered against dancing.

To be sure, not all are devout. There are some who walk around with a fine black coat, a stiff satin neckcloth, and a monocle in one eye. They find a lady's foot too large and the host's lemonade too sweet and several violin strokes half a tone too high; they dance only a little, but eat all the more. There are others who go around, very nervous to look at. They are afraid of falling in love, for what does one see at a ball? A pretty face, a pretty figure, a pair of pretty feet;

but domesticity, the beautiful domesticity and femininity which alone can make a man happy and bring him coffee in bed—that one does not see. These people are either theological students or batallion surgeons, and they have been abandoned on Mount Ida.

But when a person with a fresh and healthy heart for the first time steps into the ballroom, the gods smile as in their days of bliss, when sacrifices were offered on the Cyprian mountain; over his mind they cast forgetfulness of all earthly things, and they let half-forgotten, never-heard myths resound in his ear.

For a moment Jacob listened while the music exulted, beautiful women flashed by him, and he himself held a lovely girl in his arms. His soul stood still as if trying to recollect something and hold fast to itself. Then he suddenly recognized the scene. Here were the blue eyes and the fair locks from his mother's songs; the fairy tales had become real, he held one of the figures in his arms. The hair was no longer golden yellow—it had become somewhat darker, but that had come with the years.

It was Fangel's sister Thora. She had recently come home from Holstein, and Jacob had seen her for the first time this evening, when Wilhelm had introduced him. She was standing at that time in a circle of ladies, and not a word was said—a deep bow, an almost imperceptible nod were the whole introduction. As her glance glided over Jacob's figure, it had seemed to him as if there were something ambiguous in her eyes; she did not look at him, and nevertheless she saw him. There was in this glance an expression that for an instant set his fantasy in uneasy motion. Now on the other hand, when, happy as a child, she now looked out over the rows of dancers, now fleetingly looked at him as if she were waiting for him to speak, there was no trace of that glassy stare, and he wondered that he could have found such an expression. She was so pretty, there rested such a charm over her, there was such an elegance and harmony spread over her entire being that he almost did not have the heart to touch her, and, lost in rapturous feelings, he could not find words.

Finally he said, "So now I see you, the Miss Thora about whom I've heard so often."

"Yes," she said gaily, "here you see the famous Trondheim church, etc."

"And if someone asks, 'Has rumor lied?' I'll answer, 'No'," rejoined Jacob.

"He's not so stupid after all, once his tongue is loosened," thought Thora.

"Thora," he went on thoughtfully, "that's a pretty name. From my earliest youth I was taught to love that name."

"My German cousin also found something fascinating about it; he said it was the feminine form of Thor."

"Yes, in Danish! For there it is Sif with the golden hair and the gentle glance, who was a deity's wife!"

Thora seemed to hear the words less than the tone in which they were uttered, for she was silent and measured him with a furtive glance, as if she had been mistaken before. But Jacob was almost annoyed at himself over what he had said; he had felt something far deeper and more beautiful.

When another partner led Thora to the next dance and began a conversation, she involuntarily turned her head as if she were looking for something; her glance met that of Bendixen, far away in the ballroom. She blushed and lowered her eyes.

"May I have the pleasure of presenting my two friends to each other?" said König, leading a young officer toward Jacob. "Lieutenant Engberg—Intern Bendixen."

"I believe Mr. Bendixen and I are old acquaintances from Funen," said the lieutenant; "perhaps you don't remember me any longer?"

But Jacob had already recognized him; it was his first enemy's face. It was the boy whom he in deadly fury had fought on the beach. This meeting here, on this evening! It made an impression on him like that made on a summer day by a dark cloud blotting out the sun and reminding man of the night.

And the lieutenant was handsome and had an engaging, elegant appearance.

From that moment on, Jacob felt an involuntary dread of something evil threatening him, an ardent, indefinite lust for battle against an indefinite enemy. And from these dark feelings, his whole soul surged back in a fervent, enraptured bliss as he found himself at Thora's side.

They were standing by the window, a little apart from the rows of dancers. He said, "What strange bliss a person can enjoy. It is as if I seized happiness itself with my own hands, and as if I were alarmed by its too great nearness. I almost think that the human organism is too weak to tolerate happiness so close. One is most comfortable feeling like the sailor, when the offshore wind carries the fragrance out to him from the distant Spice Islands."

"You are very fond of dancing," said Thora.

"Dancing? No, one doesn't dance at a ball!"

"What? You aren't dancing?" she cried, laughing. "Haven't you this very minute been dancing with me?"

"Yes, I am dancing with *you*!"

Thora felt that this was no ordinary ballroom compliment; his voice was too heartfelt and energetic for that.

He went on, after a moment's silence, "It is told in old fairy tales that if one at midnight wants to dig up buried treasure from the earth, one must not speak. But if one wants to obtain life's treasure, one must speak—if only I had the magic word!"

"Oh, as far as I can tell, you won't be at a loss for it!" she said as lightly and gaily as possible.

"Yes," he said, turning pale, "if I had the word that breaks down the walls of prejudice, the magic word that spreads forgetfulness over much . . . in music I seem to be close to it . . . it's our turn, Miss!"

After midnight he was standing in a circle of his friends; they were clinking foaming glasses of champagne while the sound of muffled music came from the ballroom. A stream of blood gushed over his glass as he was putting it to his lips. Frightened, they rushed to help him, thinking a vein had burst; however, the blood was quickly stanched, but his formal suit was spotted. He had to go home, with all his uneasy annoyance at not being able to be near her, not saying good-by to her, but with the impression of the beauty of the ball pure and radiant, without having seen the smiling eyes become dull, the cheeks pale, and the dusty figures sleepily illuminated by the burned-down candles.

Chapter 5

WHEN HE AWOKE THE NEXT MORNING, his first sensation was a vague irritation, a deep feeling of shame, as if he had in some way made himself ridiculous. With painful uneasiness he went through everything he had said, every situation he had been in, and although every detail passed the examination without reproach, the collected whole produced again the painful sensation.

He said, "I was intoxicated! I was not myself! . . . What could that girl have thought of me? . . . Oh, maybe she won't recognize me, if she sees me . . . and I won't recognize her, either—she was, after all, in an evening dress!"

Nevertheless, he thought he could not put off an errand, undoubtedly a very necessary errand, to Wilhelm Fangel, and a little later in the day he went to see him. When Thora saw him, an expression of glad recognition flickered across her face, and at the same instant all his uneasiness vanished; an infinite happiness filled his being. The lady of the house was highly pleased that her daughter had had so many dances. She said to Jacob, "Today you must put up with disorder. You probably know how it looks in a house when daughters come home from a dance in the morning. But do us the pleasure of coming here again tomorrow evening."

Jacob went home as happy and light as a bird; but at home it occurred to him, "God knows whether they haven't told her how I behaved yesterday evening? Might there not be a little mockery in her inviting me to come back so soon?"

But nonetheless he went, and then repeated his visits as often as possible. All his misgivings were nothing more than expressions of the feeble struggle put up by that poor old honorable creature Good Sense against Love. Good Sense has an inkling that Love will crush it completely to death; it resists, but all its efforts only make victory easier for the craftily smiling Eros.

Without noticing this, he immersed himself more and more in this one feeling. Every word by her or about her increased in importance, the slightest alteration in her expressions could put him into a stifling fear, trifles which he never before had noticed among people could evoke the most painful reflections.

A time began in which his entire earlier life appeared dead to him, nothing he had earlier striven for or aspired to had any worth in his eyes; it was as if he had begun a new life, one that concerned only this girl.

It is perhaps a more accurate than pretty image to say that a person in love resembles an alcoholic. Just as the latter, depressed and weak after a binge, strengthens himself by drinking again, the lover seeks relief from his agitation and his apprehensions by hastening to his beloved. If this method of treatment did not exist, there would be neither so many drunkards nor so many in love.

Other young people also frequented the house, and at times Jacob found himself in a state in which it seemed to him that he hated this girl with all his heart. The feeling that controlled him, that irresistibly drew him to her, seemed then to him like a dark and hostile power; he toiled in the chains he wore, as if others had laid them on him.

However painful his state was, he nonetheless separated himself from his social friends in order to abandon himself to it. His thoughts were like those plans which one makes on a sleepless winter night, and about which one is almost embarrassed in the light of day and out among people.

. . . A tiger of the wilderness a travelling merchant has sold them. They have given it milk and fine bread instead of warm blood; they have stroked its skin with their soft hands, while sharp thorns have wounded its brothers. When the storm brings it a memory of the forest, it would gladly escape for a moment— it can not, it has become accustomed to their milk and fine bread and silky soft hands.

. . . Pinchas, son of the High Priest Eleazar, son of Aron, Moses' brother, took a sword and ran through a Jew who loved a heathen girl, him and her with the same sword.

. . . It is written that enemies shall inherit the ancestral gates of him who belongs to the heathens and lives with them. That is a terrible curse! But to see her belong to another!. . .

. . . How can it be that on a woman's lips a smile can reside that confuses my brain? The lips are, after all, considered sensibly, only flesh and blood, and the smile is perhaps only a mechanical movement. Yes, that I can say to myself here at home, but when I see the smile, my reason is gone, I am dizzy, I am as if drunk with bliss.

. . . He wears a red uniform with epaulettes, a plume in his hat, and a sword at his side, and I—am a Jew!

. . . The Gemoro[1] says that one must learn to ride, fence, and swim. I have acquired these skills. I am a knight disguised in Jewish costume—the misfortune is only that I cannot throw off the disguise.

. . . It burns my bowels like Deianira's robe smeared with Nessus's blood.

. . . As a child I was close to killing him in honorable combat. That was an anticipated anger. Now he is doing me the evil for which then I wanted to take his life.

. . . Was it an accident that she at that very moment walked beside me out the door, and that she took my arm before I dared offer it to her? Did she know that *he* was coming with us? . . . I could ask her about it . . . but if I then heard that the uncertain hope was a delusion . . . Oh, this state is terrible! I can doubt

---

[1] Part of the Talmud.

that there is a God, if he permits a person to be tormented in this way.

. . . What if she were a coquette and were playing with me! What if I were being consumed only to satisfy her vanity! Don't play a comedy with me, Christian girl! The poison fang has not yet been extracted!

. . . I wish to God that she had died in Holstein! . . . Oh, no! Then I would not have gotten to see her.

. . . It is said that many Jews have success with Christian girls, but in secret. Should I ever permit the *Jew* to be trampled underfoot while the *man's* lips are being kissed! Should I in complete secrecy permit myself to be declared a human being! No, no! I have that great advantage over the Christian: When one of them possesses a woman, he fears that she *secretly* can be untrue to him. But I would be sure of a woman's love if she dared to be mine in the light of day.

After Jacob had spent some time in this way, he was surprised one day by Levy's visit. It was, however, not actually the visit that struck Jacob; for Levy had already visited him several times, but had been quickly driven away by his sullen and taciturn mood. It was rather the resolution with which Levy seemingly had come, namely to stay. He took a pipe, sat down and expelled long clouds of smoke which were penetrated only by isolated short remarks and equally short answers.

Finally Levy said, "I come at an inopportune moment, I see that very well; but the purpose of my visit must excuse me. I have received a curious disease to treat and don't dare to act on my own. And now I am doing you the honor of wanting to consult you."

"What kind of disease is it, then?" asked Jacob.

"The matter is, briefly told, this: I had a patient who was suffering from an obstruction. I prescribed the usual remedies in the usual doses. Now the person has swallowed a whole bottle of medicine at one time, so that he has gotten a chronic colic."

"And you're asking me about this!" cried Jacob, bursting into laughter. "I'm supposed to give my learned opinion about this!"

"Yes, for 'you are the man, King!' as the prophet Nathan said to King David—you are the patient!"

"I!" cried Bendixen. "Are you crazy, Levy?"

"Yes, you! I prescribed for you a teaspoonful of Christian every other day, and you emptied a whole bottle."

"And that vile metaphor—," cried Jacob almost beside himself, "you dare to apply to—," the word died on his lips; he could not bring himself to utter his beloved's name while the frightful metaphor was present. "What gives you the right. . . ."

"Easy, easy, Bendixen! I imagined that you would lose your temper—people in love are always hot-tempered. But remember that it is a friend talking to you, that he is not speaking in his own interest, but for your sake. If you are so unreasonable as not to want to tolerate my sympathy because it inhibits your affections, just say one word and I'll go."

Jacob did not have the courage to utter such a word; Levy went on, "I have used an unpleasant metaphor, but that does no harm. Perhaps, on the contrary, it is beneficial to present crude, material reality against ideal images and daydreams. Be reasonable, don't moon around about a pretty face. The whole world knows that you visit the Fangels almost daily and make a fool of yourself with your love pangs."

Jacob was almost crushed with shame and could hardly bring forth the words, "Has *she* said that I am making myself ridiculous?"

Now it was Levy who did not have the heart to be consistent and attain his object at the expense of truth. He replied good-naturedly, "I am not saying that; I am only saying what I think is so."

But with these words Levy lost all the conquered terrain. He had not reckoned on the fact that a lover does not recognize any other judge than the beloved, that the entire rest of the world is irrelevant to him and so to speak does not even exist for him. Jacob breathed again, and even prepared now for the first time to combat Levy. He asked, "What do you have against the girl?"

"Against the girl? Nothing! She is a quite splendid girl—for a Christian."

"But what if she loved me, even though I was a Jew?"

"She can't! At least she cannot want to marry you."

"I beg you, Levy, don't insult the lady we are discussing by assuming that she should be able to love me without wanting to marry me."

"She can't, any more than a Brahmin girl can marry a Pariah. Or yes, she can, but *he* cannot, for what kind of marriage would one be in which the wife thought she belonged to a better caste than her husband?"

"That difference is nullified by love!"

"Yes, if they lived in a desert, if there were no family and friends and acquaintances of the Brahmin girl who thought they would stain their honor by extending their hand to the Pariah. Remember, my friend, one does not marry only the girl, but her entire social circle, at least her family. And the girl herself—let her as a lover forget that you are a Jew; as a wife, when the burning love has cooled a little, she will perhaps sometime remember it. Just imagine that sometime in anger she let you hear that."

Jacob trembled, but said nothing.

"But a cultured girl will never do that," he said after some hesitation. "No! She will never do that!"

"And then there are the secular laws! Who will perform the marriage? A Christian minister. In which religion will your children be brought up? In the Christian. As children they will absorb antipathy against Jews and learn to despise their father. Imagine your own child whom you are holding on your lap and examining on what he has learned in school suddenly interrupting you with the question 'Dad, wasn't it the Jews who crucified Christ? Those vile Jews! If I only had my hands on a Jew, I would kill him!'"

"Levy, those are terrible words you are using!"

"And note," Levy continued, "that marriage is something higher than the mere cohabitation of two people who bring children into the world. There is a religious element in marriage that has its spirit in which man and wife should fuse together in a higher unity. But there is something hostile between Christianity and Judaism; like Atreus's and Thyestes's flames they can burn close together without becoming one. I don't know where this dark, indescribable enmity comes from. Would it be the curse uttered by the one who died on Golgotha; is it his blood that is between us? . . . I don't know, I don't know the origin, but I ask you, have you never in your life noticed anything of the curse that rests on us, or have you now suddenly forgotten it?"

"Blood between us? Levy, do you believe there is such an avenging power in spilled human blood?"

"What's wrong with you? You look as if your hair were standing on end! Don't be frightened; I didn't mean it so literally."

"But you, Levy, yourself? Have you never thought of getting married?" said Jacob, evidently with his thoughts elsewhere.

"Who, me? When I get a good practice I'm sure that a good match in one or another Jewish family will present itself. I'll have a good living, and lead a productive life, and I'll be content with that."

"Yes, you, Levy—you are lucky!" said Jacob. He continued staring into space; suddenly, as if in a prophetic ecstasy, he cried, "I know it! It is a calamity; there has been a secret curse pronounced! But I defy it! Let the cup be filled with the deadliest poison—I will empty it!"

"Then shall we go play a round of billiards?" asked Levy.

This altered direction of thought was so violent that it manifested itself mechanically on Jacob and spun him completely around.

"Yes, you are staring at me. I only mean that, if you are absolutely determined to be crazy, then you need to be it in only one way. You don't need to shun the world; that only makes you still more insane from love. As far as I am concerned, I wash my hands of the matter."

"Well," he went on, when Jacob without saying anything turned toward the window and stared out, "can you make up your mind?"

"Yes," said Jacob, breathing deeply.

And as he was going, he clenched his hand tightly as if to hold fast to a decision that wanted to escape.

FRAGMENTS OF THORA'S LETTER TO HOLSTEIN

——You can well believe, dear Wilhelmine, that I was courted at this ball! There was a *Kammerjunker* Hvidborn and a Lieutenant Engberg; they were so eager to court me that they often got in each other's way, and then they looked like two roosters who wanted to fight over a grain of barley. It's the funniest thing I know, to see and hear two such gentlemen outdoing each other with compliments. And there was also at this ball a remarkable person. I don't mean exactly that he attracted much attention on account of looks or elegance; no, the remarkable thing is that he looked almost completely like the other young gentlemen, and that I was afterward told that it was a Jew. You can imagine my surprise when I called to mind your *Haus- und Schutzjude* over there, this dirty, shabby, money-grubbing person who had all of a thief's characteristics except that he would steal indirectly and always gave a little in exchange for what he stole. And this young man is a Jew! It almost seems impossible to me. At the very thought that he could cheat anyone, I think I am committing a grievous sin. No, the name 'Jew' certainly has, as far as he is concerned, no other significance than a kind of nickname, like that which is given to soldiers to designate the district in which they were born.

——This person perhaps seems to me to stand much higher than he actually does, precisely because I involuntarily apply such a low standard. Just think, he not only is supposed to be an outstanding student, but he sings, too, and his voice is so soft and pleasant! I always think of your *Hausjude* . . . oh, let him some time sit at your piano and sing a romanza!

——Jew . . . Something dark, like hatred or contempt, envelops this word; but every time I look closely at it, it disappears like a shadow. There is really no conceivable reason to hate and despise a person because he is of another faith. And still, every time this word occurs to me, it is again enveloped. The reason must lie in the fact that there is something alien, romantic about this nation; it comes from the Orient, it is so strangely foreign right in our midst . . . or I don't know myself what it is. But I do know this—that I must not really know them. It must also be wrong to judge them all according to the specimens I have seen in Holstein; it is perhaps as if one would judge Danish women by the fisherwomen who sit along Gammelstrand. I rather imagine these people as living proudly enclosed in their homes like Rebecca in *Ivanhoe*, hiding behind a dirty appearance when they venture out, and only sending one single loyal representative out into the world to assert their honor and glory and then to return and collect his reward. It may well be that this is mistaken, but any other idea affects me unpleasantly.

——Saladin was after all a great king and a valiant, magnanimous warrior; the Saracens were just as chivalrous as the Christian Crusaders. I have read that in history and in Walter Scott. The Jews are really their fellow countrymen; they are also Orientals. And they themselves have had great heroes in the time of the Maccabees. And in fact Christ himself and the Apostles were Jews.

——He has something peculiarly expressive in his face. He is the only one out of all the young people who come here whose soul one seems to see. When Lieutenant Engberg comes, his uniform immediately catches my eye; with *Kammerjunker* Hvidborn I immediately notice his waistcoat and gloves; on the other hand, I have never yet remembered to see how *he* is dressed. I don't even know whether he has large or small feet—though he must have small ones, otherwise it would have offended me. His face is his whole person. The other day he was in a bad humor, and then he suddenly happened to smile. Without thinking, I turned to the window; it seemed to me that the sun had suddenly broken through the clouds. It is certainly remarkable to find such characteristics in a Jew.

——It is so clear to me now that, when the others talk, it is only in order to utter words. When he speaks, it is in order to express a thought. He is almost too rich in ideas; he clutches every question in such a way that I am almost sorry for the poor, defenseless question. And then his thought process is so peculiar, so surprising. He takes almost every matter from the opposite side from the one from which I regard it, and still he often comes to the same result. I believe that we think differently, but feel the same way.

——My sister teased me the other day and said that Bendixen was in love with me. She did not mean that, of course, but nevertheless it hurt me in a way; I almost cried. I can assure you that it has never occurred to me that *he* could fall in love with me; about all the others I have thought that, in my vanity. I have really never thought about it, but it seems to me as if I took it for granted that he already had chosen himself a lovely girl of his race, the best of its daughters, with whom he some day would withdraw and, hidden from the whole world, be happy. For that reason my sister's words surprised me, and also because I felt—it is all right to write this; I don't have to send the letter, after all—that I would have liked to be this girl of his race. But if he loves me, he will overlook this difference.

——He loves me! He loves me! Now it is morning, and I have sat here the whole night in front of the candle with my arms around my knees, and I have thought of nothing else than the words he spoke to me: "Thora, I have always loved you; my dead mother sang about you!" And every time I repeated these words to myself, I have almost laughed aloud with happiness, with joy. What peculiar words; "I have always loved you; my dead mother sang about you!" There was a peculiar power in their sound and in his voice; never has such an enchanting, overpowering feeling penetrated my heart through my ear. I felt faint, I came to only when I felt myself clasped tightly to his breast. How happy he looked! His lips trembled, his cheeks were quite pale; but in his eyes there was a look of pride, as if he had conquered the world . . . I was quite proud of myself.

17 February 1830

Dear Wilhelmine,

Now I will write you a proper letter. I have begun so
many, but those you won't get.

I am engaged! Yes, my girl, I did not adhere to what
we often talked about—that I would never get married.
That's the way things go in the world! He is a student and
his name is Bendixen, and he is handsome and charming,
believe me! What a blissful life we have been leading
recently! Someone has recently died in my mother's
family, a distant relative, and so for people's sake we
have to live quietly and withdrawn. But what happy and
loving days with him and my family! And you have no
idea how an engaged girl rises in honor and esteem with
her family; it is as if one celebrates a birthday every day.
Hurry up, my girl, and get engaged; that is the best advice
your friend can give you. Incidentally, it is very lucky with
the death and that we are living so quietly during this
time, for my fiancé has this funny idea that he doesn't like
to be congratulated. When some of the few who come
here have congratulated him, he has looked really afraid,
and we have heartily laughed at him for it. Then he
laughs along with us himself and explains that it comes
from a Latin proverb which says that the gods are envious,
and therefore he is afraid of being congratulated too
much. And then he looks at me, as if he were afraid that
the envious gods would take me away from him. But that
is a whim, an eccentricity, I won't be persuaded otherwise.
All men are peculiar, and since he therefore *must* be
peculiar, it is best that he is as harmless as possible. But
he is so loving and so good! And father and mother also
like him, and my brother is an old friend of his, so I am
the happiest girl on earth. Believe me, I was quite afraid
that father would have something against the match. You
know father; he is good and affectionate to us children,
but he has his own opinions, and when there is someone
visiting us, he sometimes sits perfectly still and listens,
and then he gets up suddenly with a little smile and goes
into his study. I was afraid he would have something
against Bendixen. But the day Bendixen went in to
father . . . oh, I'll never forget that day! I was standing in
the living room, which is next to the study, and was so cold
I was shivering; it was as if judgment were being passed
on me. The door opened suddenly and I heard father say

in the door, 'You are a good young man; that is enough.
Well, there she stands! Take her in God's name!'—Then
he embraced me and kissed me and said, "Now I'll just
go in and get mother, excuse my absence!" Oh, how kind
he is, my old, sweet father! Yes, my dear Wilhelmine, I
am happy! That you will be just as happy soon, you poor
little thing, wishes for you

                            Your friend,
                            Thora Fangel

Chapter 6

LOVE'S RICH, WONDERFUL SPRING! You possess a bliss that no one sympathizes with, except those who experience you . . . and that is precisely a sign that in you resides true happiness. You are still and silent like the glances that are exchanged between lovers; your language is a Masonic language—words that for the uninitiated sound meaningless and disconnected, or which he even angrily turns away from, possessfulness and intoxicating fragrance for him for whom they are intended. You are a true spring; without desire or lust the soul is rocked in bliss, lets itself without care be carried by the happy currents fluttering around it. There are those who gloat over never having experienced you, but secretly there is in their nature a sensation as if it concealed a bud that had withered before it blossomed.

It is short, this time of Paradise. Sometimes it lasts only until the man's eyes are opened and he finds that his beloved's body is beautiful and desirable to look at; then come the senses with their longing and hope, yearning and aspiration and struggle, when the dust is shaken from Psyche's wings. Or life's angel expels him, like the progenitor, to eat his bread in the sweat of his brow; when Amor has to carry burdens, he becomes pale and loses his wings. Then there may come still evenings, he has free time after the day's work, he plays in the setting sun's rays, rises again on his wings, but on his lips there is a melancholy smile, he remembers the coming day, and he sinks gently down again. Or in whatever other form the cherub comes—he will surely come and close Paradise. But at least one has been there, the heart has become rich and preserves its treasure in its memory.

It was a harsh winter evening. According to the almanac, spring was approaching, and winter seemed, in anticipation of its impending downfall, to make one more violent effort to sustain its power. The snow was swirled in large flakes by a sharp east wind, street lamps threatened to go out, here and there shutters were torn loose and clattered against the dimly lit windows. Jacob was almost alone on the street; immersed in his thoughts, he paid no heed to the weather, but strode briskly ahead to his new family's residence. There, for the first time since the period of mourning, was to be one of the usual soirées.

He had already reached the street, when two gentlemen went past him. A disjointed fragment of their conversation reached his ear through the noise of the wind. Just as they with bowed heads and long strides approached, one of them shouted in a surprised tone, "It's a damned shame! That lovely girl! . . ." The rest was lost in the distance that was speedily put between him and the speakers.

A searing stab went through Jacob. To be sure, those words need not have referred to him, but they had reached him at a moment when they came like a voice from an invisible power following his thoughts.

As long as he had had only one thought, one goal—Thora's love—his way had gone up a mountain that hid the prospect from him. But now that the goal was attained, now that he was standing on the peak of his wishes, the prospect widened to include completely new objects. Now that he stood with Thora in his arms, he thought of how this was regarded by others.

Here now was the answer he had agonized over giving himself; now it was spoken: people could call it a sin that this pretty girl was engaged to a Jew. . . .

When he entered the brightly lit reception room where the family was assembled, the ladies for the first time after the period of mourning in their complete finery, the house seemed quite strange to him, and he felt almost fear at being there. Thora, in a light-colored silk dress, looked very fine and distinguished, and her greeting, less spontaneous than usual because she was afraid of getting her dress wrinkled, seemed to him to be almost the splendid lady's condescension to him.

The wholesaler wanted, contrary to his custom, to spend the whole evening with his family, and his wife's and children's behavior toward him demonstrated an increased affection and attentiveness, as if in gratitude for his decision. He was an aging, somewhat portly man, with an intelligent and friendly face, with an affable and distinguished deportment. His earliest youth he had spent in a house where chivalrous memories from Caroline Mathilde's time still radiated, and himself had experienced the enthusiasm ignited over Europe by the first French Revolution. He had become a chivalrous democrat, a citizen without fear and without prejudices. He placed his pride in being independent of any great man, in wearing his hat just as high as the king himself—as he was accustomed to saying— but no less in a certain chivalrous courtesy toward the fair sex, in still being able to perform the first dance in his house; and it was a real pleasure to see the aging man lead his lady with youthful liveliness and courtly dignity. There was only one thing his family complained about, and that was that he liked to go to the club every evening to talk politics with his friends from the 90's and have a game of cards—for that robbed them of his company. The lady could not get it into her head that politics and cards could not be just as good at home, and that the poor wine he paid for out, tasted better to him than the good wine from his own cellar; "but men are like that."

Although Jacob cherished an almost filial veneration for this man, he was still so unaccustomed to his company that it caused him a certain inconvenience. The others' joy, which he could not share, made them at that moment still more alien to him.

Shortly after his arrival, a carriage drove in at the gate, and the circle was swelled by two young ladies, friends of Thora, that is to say, the older one was actually the friend of Thora's sister.

Immediately at the first glance, when Thora received her with the utmost affection, Jacob had something against the younger one. She was very blond, her face was round and red-cheeked, her nose small and turned up, her upper lip curved upward as if in scorn, her eyes lively and audacious—in short, there was in this face something cheerful, inconsiderate, roguish, and mocking, which all together formed the indescribable expression in accordance with which a Jew would immediately judge, "She is a *rischainto*"[1]—a feeling which perhaps is nothing other than a suspicion that for such a fair-skinned person the Jew's dark physiognomy is very striking and therefore invites ridicule. Jacob felt this so keenly that he was seized with apprehension for the consequences of this friend's acquaintance with Thora.

When a girl has become engaged, her attentiveness toward her girl friends at first increases. It is as if she wants to show them that she is by no means so enthralled by love that she would to the slightest degree forget them. Since they now really have lost interest for her, the feigned interest seems in a quite natural way to be greater than the real interest was. Thora and Miss Sophie had a very great deal to tell each other, even before the ladies took their seats. Miss Sophie cast an expert eye on Jacob and whispered, "Your fiancé is handsome! What lovely dark eyes he has!" whereupon Thora likewise looked at him and blushingly lowered her eyes. Jacob had closely followed these glances; he saw Thora's blushes and weighed with stifling fear how much probability there was that Miss Sophie had evoked it with a more or less fine allusion to the fact that he was a Jew.

Finally the ladies took their seats, but during the general conversation that now got under way, Thora and Miss Sophie spoke to each other several times in whispers. He would have gladly given years of his life to be able to join the conversation and prevent these confidential exchanges; but all his thoughts revolved constantly around the same point, and he was scarcely capable of replying to the questions that were from time to time addressed to him.

The family noted the alteration that this evening had taken place in Bendixen. He, who in the family circle was customarily so cheerful, so cordial—indeed, so charming—now sat, gloomy and preoccupied, his glance wandering restlessly around, and even if he was not downright discourteous to the feminine guests, there was definitely a lack of attentiveness and affability in his behavior that had a disturbing effect on the conviviality.

---

[1] Feminine of *roscho*, anti-Semite.

Lieutenant Engberg arrived. He was immediately in deep conversation with the ladies; it seemed that he was bringing extraordinary news, for they enquired and listened with signs of the greatest interest. It also seemed that his conversation was very witty, for they broke into loud laughter several times, and presumably they reciprocated by discoursing wittily—at least Lieutenant Engberg laughed. Jacob alone sat as if he were quite outside the company; several times he did try to enter into the tone of the conversation, but every abortive attempt only made the repetition more difficult.

Thora saw that there was something wrong, but did not grasp the reason. She said to herself, "He surely cannot possibly be angry because I don't caress him in the presence of strangers? Can he be jealous? Yes, show me! I'll soon break you of that habit!" And then she again followed the conversation, apparently with great interest.

More strangers arrived gradually, but the larger number of guests only increased Jacob's strange uneasiness. It was obvious that he several times made a violent effort, but each time immediately thereafter something inexplicable seemed to appear to him, and he again became preoccupied, gloomy, and forbidding.

Late in the evening, when the guests had departed, the wholesaler was pacing with long strides up and down in the bedroom. Finally he stopped before his wife and said, "Mother, did you notice Bendixen's behavior this evening?"

"Yes, I thought he was a little sullen," replied the lady, unhooking her dress.

"I was annoyed with him the entire evening! What conduct of a young person toward ladies! I like him very much; he is a fine and honest fellow, and I will certainly be the last to reproach him for being a Jew. But this behavior this evening comes, I nevertheless believe, directly from the fact that he is a Jew. A Jew is not brought up chivalrously. But when he is engaged to a Christian girl, he really ought to improve a little."

The lady replied, "I think that he was only annoyed because he could not be alone among us. But you are very right, for it is all very well that he likes us, but one must see people, and he must not think that he can lord it over the house."

After a pause, the wholesaler said, "It's a ticklish business to tackle. I can't take it upon myself to be his teacher, and we don't dare to talk to Thora about it except with the greatest caution."

The couple talked a little more about this subject, and agreed that the matter should be treated with all possible delicacy, and that they would therefore not be too hasty but would wait for a suitable occasion.

Chapter 7

THE OPPORTUNITY DID NOT COME so easily, and now so many days passed that they almost forgot to watch for it. Whether it happened by chance or as a result of premeditation on Jacob's part—the family did not take that into consideration—for several days he came only at a time when no outsiders were there. And then he was again affectionate and charming, although he bore the signs of suffering.

On Saturday evening Thora said to him, "You are coming tomorrow morning, aren't you?" Jacob paled, and on his face was an expression as if he were with an effort conquering a painful sensation. "Are you ill?" cried Thora. "Oh, no," he said, passing his hand over his forehead, "it's only a slight indisposition; it will soon pass." "Oh, no, you are ill," insisted Thora with anxious solicitude, "you haven't looked well now for several days. You'd better stay home tomorrow! I will get Mother to pay you a little visit with me."

Thora did not notice that the suffering expression on Jacob's face disappeared at these words; she interpreted his silence as confirmation and did not rest until he had consented to being driven home.

But the next day Jacob was perfectly well, and when Thora on the following Saturday asked him to come Sunday morning, he promised to appear.

Contrary to all expectations, he found her alone.

She was almost amazed at the expression of childlike joy with which he looked around, regarding now her, now the room, as if they were meeting after a long separation. There was something in his bearing that touched her, without her being able to explain to herself what it was.

She sat at his side and brushed the hair from his forehead
and looked into his eyes, which with inexpressible tenderness
regarded her. Although she felt that she loved him, it
nevertheless seemed to her now, as she saw this expression in his
eyes and heard this soft voice, that she did not love him enough,
that she was not grateful enough for all this love. On her side,
the conversation was only a few words. He talked a great deal,
but in that subdued tone in which strong passion often speaks, as
if it were afraid of giving itself too free a rein; but the words were
very clear, very definite, very strong, sometimes intertwining
into images that betrayed his soul's southern home.

She bent over him, still more warmly and lovingly, and as
she sat in this way, Jacob suddenly seemed again to notice in her
eyes that staring, dual, deep glance, and even more strongly than
the first time. Now, too, it caused the blood to rush with violent
force toward his heart.

He was silent, and she clung to him more tightly.

Her mother and sister came home and interrupted this *tête-
à-tête*. Jacob went to meet his future mother-in-law with the
greatest cordiality, helped her and her daughter out of their
wraps, and asked, "Where have you been so early, dear lady, and
in such finery?"

"We went to church together to hear Mynster preach,"
answered the lady. "Thora, do you have a cup of coffee for me? It
is frightfully cold today."

A little later he left, but he had to promise to come back
early in the evening.

When he had gone, the lady, setting the empty coffee cup
rather violently on the table, said, "It is just dreadful with that
man! Goodness, I don't think he even likes for us to go to church!
I wonder if he wants the whole house to convert? . . . What a face
he made when I said we were coming from church! Merciful God!
Can't he be as tolerant as we are!"

Thora was hurt by these words and burst into tears.

"Oh, don't cry, my girl!" said her mother. "The whole thing
is not that bad. Your father and I have spoken about him, and we
agreed that you can very well change him for the better. An
engaged girl has a great deal of power over her fiancé. If you

behave sensibly, you can very well accustom him to being a little more chivalrous, as your father says, and cure him of all those moods. Goodness knows he is certainly fond of you; you can wrap him around your finger."

Thora stopped crying, because her thoughts fixed themselves attentively on what her mother was saying.

The evening came; there were outsiders present, and over Jacob's bearing there again was spread an inexplicable cloud. He was not discourteous or sullen; there was nothing he could actually be reproached for. If anyone had not seen him in his brighter moments, he would perhaps not have found his behavior at all striking. It was only that he was quiet; a certain uneasiness, almost fear, showed itself in his looks. And that disturbed the family who wanted the future son-in-law to be cheerful and make the house lively and cause people to say, "God knows, that is a charming man Miss Thora has gotten engaged to!"

Among the visitors he was moved by the same feelings as on the earlier evening, but something else was added. When Thora had come to meet him in the entrance hall, she had patted him on the cheek and said, "Let me see now that you are really cheerful this evening."

From where did this request originate? Had there been talk about him in the family, perhaps argument, reproaches?

When Jacob later in the evening spoke with the lady of the house, there was a coldness in her tone that he had never before noticed, and when he addressed the wholesaler, the latter answered him politely but—almost too politely. Jacob turned away, his lips trembled, and he had tears in his eyes. From this moment he became even quieter and more reticent, so that it even seemed to arouse the attention of the guests.

Now Thora herself felt that her fiancé's behavior was rather strange, and when he had gone, she reflected seriously on how she should go about changing him.

Chapter 8

THE FOLLOWING MORNING JACOB SAT preparing his coffee with that profound seriousness with which one often seems to attend to mechanical tasks while not at all thinking about them.

"It's after all a good thing," he said, turning off the tap of the urn, "that Levy is away. I am almost afraid that he will come home soon—although he is indeed the only person I can talk to."

Jacob sank into deep thought, to be interrupted by someone knocking, and the door opened slowly, as if the person entering had not expected to find it open.

It was Levy.

"Levy!" cried Jacob in surprise, going to meet him. "Welcome! That's very odd; I was just thinking of you!"

"Sh!" said Levy, stopping at the door with a solemn face. "Sh! Don't disturb my feelings; I am entering the abode of an engaged man. I am entering—that is what is most remarkable! You are at home, lucky man. You do not despise room, board, and cleanliness, notwithstanding the fact that you are living in and from love. . . . I congratulate you!"

"Thanks, thanks, Levy! But come away from the door! Come and sit down!"

"Done! Well, seriously speaking, how are you then? Yes, there's probably no reason to ask. With fever, naturally, with the fever of ecstasy. . . ."

Jacob strained his facial muscles and the nerves of his eyes to make bliss shine from his entire face and thus reply affirmatively to the question. With equally forced cheerfulness he pushed Levy down into the sofa, handed him a pipe, and said, "May I pour you a cup of coffee? You must have something for your congratulations, especially since you deliver them so nicely!"

Levy cast a quick glance at Jacob while he poured the coffee, then lit his pipe calmly and thoroughly and arranged himself in the most comfortable position on the sofa. When he had tasted the "aromatic beverage" and convinced himself that it was good, he said, "I will certainly drink your coffee, Bendixen, but you must nevertheless admit that it is no treat to offer when one presents his congratulations on such an occasion. I had expected to see champagne bottles lined up, twenty-seven champagne bottles to deliver the appropriate twenty-seven-gun salute. Or have you already delivered it?"

"No," answered Jacob, smiling.

"Merciful God!" Levy went on, "When I look around properly, what kind of a person are you, anyway! When one is mooning about in love's seventh heaven, when one walks on the ground only out of charity, so to speak, and therefore dances, floats away over the paving stones, how can one sit like this in his room and quite prosaically make his coffee out of a tin funnel-pot? Why doesn't one at least let the water boil over while he is immersed in his beloved's eyes, which are eternally floating in front of him? Why doesn't he forget his rye bread with butter? Why doesn't he in distraction eat his rye bread without butter, while he in his thoughts goes from arm to arm in his beloved's family, is caressed and patted by aunts and cousins, and moves among the family's friends and acquaintances, proud and admired as a very devil of a fellow? Amor! Is this your highly praised omnipotence, when—but Bendixen! You don't look at all enraptured; your eyes are no longer sparkling, your smile is losing itself like the trickling spring in the desert."

At the last, sparkling descriptions Jacob had indeed forgotten to pay heed to his face, and sat there listening with a gloomy and melancholy expression.

"You have only yourself to blame," said Levy. "Next time, don't try to dissimulate to me. Do you think I don't know you well enough to know that you aren't happy in the way you tried to show? What is wrong?" he asked seriously and

sympathetically. "Isn't the family behaving well toward you?
Are they making *risches?*"

"No! It would be ungrateful to the highest degree of me, if I
expressed even the slightest complaint or displeasure," replied
Jacob. "Oh," he continued, "when all is said and done, it's not
them, it's I myself who cause me harm and misfortune."

"I thought so!" said Levy to himself.

"It's myself tormenting me; I can't help myself. Oh, I can't
describe to you the dreadful condition I frequently find myself in.
It goes so far that I am embarrassed to go there, when there are
outsiders present. It seems to me almost indelicate toward the
family to show guests that it has a Jew for a son-in-law. But
when I nevertheless have to be there, I am afraid when two people
talk softly, when they look at each other, when they smile
without my knowing why they are smiling. I don't have eyes and
ears enough to keep watch on all of them; I'm being torn apart—
and maybe these glances and smiles are the most innocent in the
world! That may well be, but I am afraid; that's just how it is. If
I'm not there, I long to go there; I imagine that my presence
always does help to hold back the remarks, if I am very watchful.
And then, too, when I am away that fop, Lieutenant Engberg,
buzzes around my fiancée."

"Are you now, to make the misfortune complete, also
jealous?"

"No, but he courted the same girl as I did, and now that she
has chosen me it seems to me that honor requires that he
withdraw. It does take a certain nerve to visit the house as if
nothing had changed. It's as if he were expecting that his time
might still come."

"But isn't he a little related to them?"

"Yes, he is, slightly, but under such circumstances that
cannot have any bearing."

"Well, but all this is nonetheless really of minor importance,
if you only get on well with the family, and it, as you yourself
say, treats you with all possible delicacy."

"But have you never noticed that there is a delicacy that
wounds? The misfortune is, after all, precisely that delicacy is
needed. Their delicate silence has something painful for me, who

have become so accustomed to hearing certain words that I imagine them everywhere. If they only would once talk about Jews and make fun of them in my presence! That would be a kindness to me; that would show me that they completely forgot that I was a Jew. But not the slightest sound about Jews is heard, although on countless occasions it must have been on the tips of their tongues. The other day there was talk about a man whose name was Jacobsen. I read on all faces the eager desire to ask if he were a Jew, but I was present, and they were embarrassed and didn't say anything. It is continuously in their minds that I am a Jew; my presence constrains them, and with me they cannot speak with such an intimate lack of consideration as if I were a Christian. My greatest happiness would be to merge with them, disappear as an individual and live as a part of their family life, but every moment I am torn out of it with a sudden jolt, and I stand there among them as an outsider. Our blood will not mix in blood brotherhood; there stands between us a hidden, fatal power, and it separates us from each other."

Levy sat with his head bowed and was silent long after Jacob had finished. Finally he said, "If I had racked my brain, I could have said in advance precisely the same thing to you that you have now told me. The thing is that we are Jews, and practically the worst of the matter is the fact that we ourselves know that so well. For that reason I did my best—but that doesn't matter now. I am your doctor, and I will continue to be that, although you have not followed my instructions; but if you got a patient who had a cold and as a result of his indifference to your advice caught pneumonia, you wouldn't leave him lying helpless, either, simply because the pneumonia was his own fault. Will you accept a piece of advice?"

Jacob had thrown himself on the sofa and put his hands over his eyes, and did not reply.

Levy paced back and forth for some time, and then said, "You could ask why I come to you and force you to confide in me. I could ask myself about that, for I'm damned if I know. It sits here, inside my ribs, and wants out, and if I were not a confirmed enemy of the materialists who say that feeling has its seat in the heart, I would believe that I liked you a little. But I don't, for in that case I would naturally pace back and forth across the floor and wring my hands and say, 'What the devil did you also want to go and get engaged for! If you only had left those stupid tricks alone! If only you had stayed away from them!' but I don't do that; I am not your friend at all, I am nothing else than your family doctor, and you are ill. You are now lying there on the sofa, I am making a diagnosis of the disease and in my learned brain am running through all case histories of this type. Let me have a cigar . . . oh, here they are . . . when the cigar is smoked down, I think, we should be finished. Pay attention now and be astonished. The thorough examination reveals various conditions under which an engagement between a Jew and a Christian girl can be happy. In the first place a happy marriage can take place when a Jew from the Jewish quarter becomes engaged to a Christian lady who in rank stands approximately at the same level as a serving maid. By a happy marriage I mean one in which all the engagement's promises are fulfilled. While such a pair is engaged, there is, at least once a week, namely on Sunday, a cosy little fight up in the lady's garret room, and the whole thing generally ends with the lover strolling down the stairs while the beloved cries, 'Go to hell, you damned kike!' after which on Monday a warm reconcialition is celebrated. The lover's ear is no more wounded by such a term of address than is his lady's by the clout with which he in an impassioned moment regales her. When the couple is married, this life is continued, except that the passionate scenes can occur on any day whatever, regardless of whether weekday or Sunday, but that also the happy moments of reconciliation are more frequent. Grounds for disagreement are: lack of money, jealousy over all too demonstrable infidelity, and the like; exceedingly seldom, even during the honeymoon, will such a lover fly into a rage over a look, a gesture, still less over an *omitted* gesture. This is a happy married couple, with strong nerves and strong fists. Another case is that a rich Jewish good-for-nothing makes the acquaintance of a poor Christian girl and her coquettish mother. He presents them with gifts, goes with them to the shops, appraises shawls and dress materials, in short becomes so indispensable that they, in order to remain constantly together,

get engaged. During the engagement the lover adorns his beloved
for himself, after the wedding—for others, by which, however, I
don't mean that he didn't also adorn her for others during the
engagement. Finally, I have also imagined the case that a Jew
marries a Christian girl for the sake of money or other worldly
advantages. That is an arrangement, a piece of business as with
oranges—one accepts the fact that half of the goods are spoiled,
and sets that much higher a price on the other half. Now, at the
time you were enthralled by the strange exalted raptus called
love—I beg your pardon: at the time you went and fell in love—I
was afraid. I had no rubric ready where you could appropriately be
placed; I was afraid that you would get caught in a situation
where the soul would be crushed out of your body. But now I have
had my eyes opened to the possibility that a Jew like you, a nice
and honorable fellow—head up, there!—stumbles across a
Christian family which as far as possible is heartily tolerant
and tries to make up for what is lacking by constant
attentiveness, one which has the almost unbelievable quality
that there is no mob of relatives who on all occasions are more
solicitous about the family than the family itself. Here a
perfect—indeed, a romantic—happiness is possible, if only the
Jew with his wounded temperament doesn't act like the hedgehog
who raises his quills if either friend or foe approaches, and gets
the idea of becoming intolerant. Bendixen! Compare your
situation with those other kinds of engagements and praise your
God and Creator, and be sensible, be pleasant. Don't sin against
God's gifts! If the others have forgotten that you are a Jew, or
seem to forget it, then forget it yourself, or act as if you forget it.
And the girl does love you, there is no doubt about that; why
don't you talk to her, why don't you bring yourself to touch upon
these delicate feelings sometime, make her your confidante—
well! There we have the remedy! Talk to the girl, man! Then you
have an ally in the family itself, the most powerful ally, the only
one you really need! Now I have finished; *dixi*, I have spoken—
and my coffee has gotten cold."

Long before Levy had finished, Jacob had leapt up, cheerful
and happy. "You are right, Levy!" he cried when Levy ceased
speaking. "You are absolutely right! I have been blind, deaf . . . I

have been a—why don't you give me a good scolding? I have earned it! . . . Oh, I am alive again, I am newly born. . . ."

"Yes," Levy interrupted him, "I am also specializing in obstetrics."

"Oh, don't joke now! You have rescued me from all my cowardice and childishness! You are my benefactor, yes, truly my benefactor! How can I ever repay you!"

"I hope, never; God deliver me from becoming so crazy! But, since you mention reward—you are now making a good marriage; make me your family doctor—that's immediately a little practice. But that's right—you are yourself a doctor; I must therefore let you have my philanthropic efforts absolutely gratis. On the other hand, when you have had your wedding, and I come and congratulate you, you can offer champagne instead of coffee."

When Levy had gone, Jacob hurried to his fiancée. On the way, he said, "Yes, I will frankly confess to her all my childishnesses; she shall see into every fold of my heart. She will stand by me and as my good angel she will keep the evil thoughts away."

His heart was very light, his glance very cheerful when he climbed the stair.

Chapter 9

THERE WERE GUESTS. The moment was obviously not favorable for his purpose. But his mental energies were in such lively motion, his determination drove him ahead with such strength, that he did not hesitate to defy all hindrances.

The company was in lively and rather loud conversation when Jacob entered. There was a French lady and the family who had introduced her, besides Lieutenant Engberg and a couple of other young people.

When Jacob arrived, Thora remembered that she was supposed to be angry, but there was in his face such unaccustomed cheerfulness and cordialilty that she immediately again forgot this and received him with her most affectionate smile, and with a certain pride presented him to the French lady as her fiancé. The foreign lady presumably found in this attribute of his an invitation to bestow special attention on him; she managed immediately to draw him into the conversation, which lightly and vivaciously moved around the observations she had made in Copenhagen during her short stay.

They naturally spoke in French, and Jacob soon discovered that Lieutenant Engberg spoke the language far better than he. He promised himself that the latter would not have such an advantage for long, but this did not help him at the moment. He was not accustomed to feel himself inferior in any contest where he stood man against man; the lieutenant's superiority was painful to him, and there were moments when he was overcome by a jealous bitterness, especially since Thora also spoke beautiful French and their mutual proficiency brought about a livlier conversation between her and Engberg than between them and Jacob.

With uneasiness and annoyance he began to remember the purpose of his visit, and the company standing in the way of his precious concern began to be irksome to him. But he was not given time to reflect on this; the conversation's current swept him along with it. Almost against his will he talked a great deal, as if to make up for not speaking well; he took part in the others' laughter, although inside he almost had the urge to inflict injury.

Coffee and cakes were served. "Try this, Miss," said Thora in the middle of the lively conversation to the French lady, handing her the tray, "it is genuine Danish wheat cake; you won't find its equal in France. It is sent to us by my own aunt in the country . . . oh, that's right, Bendixen, now Auntie may come to town. Oh, I'm so looking forward to your meeting my sweet Aunt Mathilde!"

Without really taking note of this bit of news, Jacob replied, "I'll be happy to, especially if your aunt is as good as her wheat cake; I'll have another piece in honor of her safe arrival."

Jacob said *pièce* instead of *morceau*; *pièce* means, of course, a whole piece, a whole cake. The French lady exclaimed laughingly, "Indeed! You must mean well by her, or else you must be very hungry." At that moment Thora and the lieutenant joined in hearty laughter. It seemed to Jacob that the lieutenant made an effort to laugh, and that Thora on the other hand laughed without constraint. It should have been the other way around. He was so much the less inclined to excuse this involuntary outburst since he had not, after all, really shared in the others' cheerfulness. He thought he was the object of ridicule in this company, that he was being humiliated and made ridiculous, although the house itself ought to protect him. Nothing more was needed to erase the superficial cheeriness from his face and let despondency and humiliation shine through.

And so sudden was the alteration in his features that the two ladies instinctively stopped talking, while the lieutenant, seeing this shift of facial expression, again broke into loud laughter.

Jacob then turned to the lieutenant and said in a voice trembling with anger, "Lieutenant!"

The latter turned pale and became silent.

But the sudden stillness, in which Jacob could hear his own cry slowly die away, caused him to feel the blunder he had made. He groped in vain for ways to get the conversation going again; all his intellectual powers stood still on one point to discover such a way out. For a few seconds he suffered true torture; he felt frightfully alone, and nevertheless it was as if the eyes of the whole world were fixed on him. He suffered under the curse of having spent an isolated youth and of not having acquired society's polish along with the education of the intellect.

The sound of a stagecoach driving up and stopping outside the house broke the spell-like petrification which had settled over him and the company. They rushed to the window to see who it was; Jacob in his heart blessed the strangers who arrived so opportunely.

"Mother," cried Thora, "it's Auntie!"

"Yes, for heaven's sake, Auntie!" her sister joined in, running out of the room, clapping her hands, to receive the aunt.

The guests took their leave, and Jacob, who was ashamed and depressed, would also have liked to go if that had been proper.

When the aunt had embraced and kissed her sister and her nieces and enquired after the absent wholesaler's health, Jacob was presented to her as Thora's fiancé.

"Congratulations," said the aunt very coldly and courteously to the respectfully bowing Bendixen.

"But how did it happen that you came so unexpectedly, Mathilde dear?" asked Mrs. Fangel.

"Goodness, it is a happy occasion," replied Aunt Mathilde, "you know that after his sister's death, my husband lost all desire to remain at the parsonage, although it is a splendid living, and then he applied for the parish that is vacant here in town. The day before yesterday the letter arrived that he had gotten it. As soon as I heard that, I had no desire to be a village parson's wife a moment longer. I came into town, and now you have me until my husband comes. Heavens, how I have longed for Copenhagen."

"Oh, that's wonderful!" cried Thora's sister. "Then Uncle will be our parish minister! Then you can be married by Uncle, Thora!"

"Thora?" exclaimed the aunt with a sharp glance, "Is she to be married by a Christian minister?"

This utterance came so unawares and surprisingly that Jacob at first could not believe his ears, but then he assumed that it could not possibly be otherwise than that it was said in stupidity.

Questions and answers in the meantime criss-crossed uninterruptedly. While the aunt talked, Mrs. Fangel already had a new question on her lips:

"When is your husband coming? He will take over the position immediately?"

"Yes, he is only having an auction of our rubbish out there. Here in town we are to have new things from top to bottom."

"But doesn't Auntie want to go in and change?" asked Thora's sister. Thora had silently gone to the window; Jacob was standing almost unthinking at another window, tracing on the pane.

"Yes, I do, my girl! But let me first have a cup of hot coffee. . . . Ah, look there, the lieutenant!" she cried, catching sight of Engberg, who had stayed behind and now came up to her. "Yes, you should have a real scolding," she added half in an undertone, "to let my niece be taken away from you right under your nose like this."

Jacob heard these words, and here there was no mistaking and no doubt; the aunt seemed to him like a demon broken free in order to torment him.

Finally she went in to change. He was afire with yearning to go up to Thora, apologize to her for his behavior, and conclude an alliance with her that could make him secure against the dreadful aunt; but with a dejected air she too left the room and went into the bedroom to the others.

Some time passed, which he spent in choking fear for every word possibly exchanged inside there.

His glances undoubtedly expressed his mortal fear, for later Thora came up to him and tenderly pressed his hand, looking at him with tears in her eyes. For that moment, Jacob's pain was gone—only for a moment—for in the next moment he asked himself, "How long will she be able to preserve respect and love for the Jew who is persecuted under her own roof?"

At the table Jacob was seated beside the aunt, as if to insure that they got acquainted, but the first words the aunt addressed to him were, "Well, I am glad that you do eat with us!"

A little later she turned in a friendly way to him and asked concerning his birthplace, examinations, etc. When he had told her something about these, she pronounced, "But what does your family say about your engagement to a Christian girl?"

Jacob still had enough self-control to give an evasive reply, but he felt exactly as if he were lying on a torture rack. He would have given years of his life to be able to stop this tongue, to be able to keep it from sending out those poisonous words which the whole company absorbed. He felt a powerless fury boiling inside him, a burning hatred rising against all those who heard the words and especially against the one who sent them out.

But she had already, with the same naturalness and simplicity, glided over to another conversation with one of the company at the table, and seemed to have no idea at all of the pain she was causing, or the hate she was engendering.

Now Wilhelm also came home; at the sight of his aunt, with whom he had spent so many happy summer vacations, he flew to embrace her. Then he extended his hand to Jacob in a friendly fashion, as usual, but the latter was incapable of accepting a hand that had affectionately pressed that of the aunt; he replied to Wilhelm's greeting with a cold "Hello."

He felt all eyes resting on him, felt that they regarded him as a disturber of the family happiness, and a kind of joy exulted in him—he had managed to do something malicious to repay that which they had serenely allowed him to suffer.

When he went home, he was almost stunned; there were moments when he took the whole thing for a dream, but at the next moment the reality appeared before him again, clear and crushing. When he opened his door, he smiled bitterly at the thought of the friendly feelings with which he had last closed it.

Chapter 10

A FEW DAYS LATER, the post brought him a letter, and a warm joy, tinged with sadness, filled his heart when he recognized his father's hand.

He read:

> *Mein ben jochid* [1] *(lebe lang!)*
> I have duly received your letter from which it is learned that you *baavonosenu horabim*[2] have become engaged to the daughter of an *orel*.[3] Have you truly considerd what you have done? Hear your father's earnest words. You come from *koschre yehudim*,[4] our *ovos ovosenu*[5] have been *meschaduch* with *yehudim*,[6] they have never abandoned their fathers' God. But what do you intend to do? What would your mother, *oleho hascholom*,[7] she who rests in Eden and will be a *malitzo joscher baadenu*,[8] what would she certainly have said if she had lived to see that you would want to be *meschaduch* with *bnos Ches*?[9] You are not an *am hooretz*,[10] after all, you could choose a *kalo*[11] among the richest of your fellow Jews. Do you think you

---

[1] My only son.

[2] On account of our great sins.

[3] I.e., non-Jew.

[4] Pure and spotless Jews.

[5] Fathers' fathers.

[6] Intermarried with Jews.

[7] May peace reign over her.

[8] One who intercedes for our sins.

[9] Marry into Chet's children.

[10] Fool.

[11] Bride.

can be happy with a Christian girl? Do you think she will forget that you are a *bar jisroel*?[12] And your offspring, will you tell me what will become of them? Will you be able to be *megadel lethoro*?[13] My son, my son, you are blind, you are going toward ruin, you are bringing your father to tear out his hair and curse his birth. Like the poet, will I come to call my house *i kovod*?[14] But why am I speaking of myself? My head is turning grey and bending toward *kever ovos*,[15] and I long for it; since your mother's death I am alone, and now you are going to the *goyim*, never to return. But the blame is only mine; I myself sent you into temptation. And at your cradle I prayed to God to take all *masol*[16] from my head and place it on yours. I am only giving you my best *ezo*.[17] Your uncle and aunt and all our *mischpocho*[18] out here are angry and don't want to talk about you, and say that you will let yourself *schmatte*.[19] But I am after all your father. The Lord will forgive that I cannot pronounce *klolo*[20] over you. I reach out my hand to you; my son, bow your head and receive for the last time my blessing: *Jevorechecho Adonoi vejischmerecho, joer Adonoi ponov elecho vichunecko, jiso Adonoi ponov elecho vejosem lecho scholom.*[21]
Kan divre ovicho jedidecho.[22]

Just as he had finished reading this letter, there was a knock at the door, and an aging Jew entered and asked for alms. He could not have chosen a better moment than this, since his

---

[12] Son of Israel.

[13] Bring them up according to the Law.

[14] Honor has gone.

[15] The grave.

[16] Blessing.

[17] Advice.

[18] Family.

[19] Be baptized.

[20] Curse.

[21] May the Lord bless and hear you, his countenance shine over you and be merciful to you, may he lift up his countenance toward you and give you peace.

[22] Thus speaks your father who loves you.

father's letter had made Jews and everything belonging to Jews precious to Jacob. To see this Jew begging hurt him as if it had been one of his closest family, and he gave the supplicant a generous gift. The Jew thought it was a mistake, and hastened away with the words, "*Gott soll Euch benschen!* [God bless you!]"

These words and the accent in which they were spoken—they sounded to Jacob as church bells on Christmas morning must sound to a Christian; an immense, violent, painful longing seized him, he envied the poor Jew who was now going to Jews. The veins in his head swelled with impatience . . . home, home, to his father's arms! . . . and Thora?

Like a bird tied with a thread flying swiftly out into the air but being suddenly stopped and having to fly in a circle around a fixed point, Jacob's feelings stopped at this name and took another direction.

Thora . . . all the affectionate feelings his heart contained awoke with redoubled strength. His beloved's picture rose forth, clear and lovely, and filled his heart with love's bliss, until with a new movement of thought her surroundings suddenly came into view and cast their black, threatening shadow over the picture.

"What am I to do!" he finally said. ". . . It must go as God in Heaven wills!"

At the same time, the Fangel family was sitting, conversing intimately, at the dinner table. The wholesaler had gone to the club, Wilhelm was walking up and down, and went to the door several times as if he wanted to steal away, but, captivated by the contents of the conversation, decided to remain.

"He is basically a quite mannerly person," said Aunt Mathilde, when Mrs. Fangel had expressed her surprise that Bendixen had not been seen the whole day. "I had imagined him with a real Jewish street peddler face and I had decided secretly that he must not remain long in the house. I was already a little hard on him the other day, but now I'm almost sorry about it. You basically don't have bad taste, little Thora . . . if only we can cure him of being a Jew."

Thora said nothing; she had on the tip of her tongue "Mind your own business, little Auntie."

Mrs. Fangel said, "I have always liked him a lot; he is a solid, quiet, and upright person. The only thing I don't like about him is his sullenness lately. Before he became engaged, he was always so cheerful and friendly; when he looked at me with those big dark eyes, it was with such strange tenderness, as if he wanted to beg me not to refuse him Thora. He looked as if he could go through fire for me. Scarcely had he become engaged, when that was all over."

"Perhaps his family is against the match?" said the aunt.

"I really don't think so; he never speaks of it."

"Then that's exactly what I believe!" cried Aunt Mathilde, who always prided herself on her knowledge of human nature.

"No, I really don't think so," said Mrs. Fangel. "He has his own fortune, and if his family had been against the match and had any power over him, it would have prevented the engagement. His only real family is an old father who lives a long way from here."

"You could also try to find out what is wrong with him," said Thora's sister to Wilhelm. "The two of you have always been such good friends."

Wilhelm replied, "I never interfere in my sister's love affairs. My sister has gotten a fiancé; more I cannot do. Besides, you all saw how sulky he was to me, too, the other day."

"If I were to say my true opinion," said Mrs. Fangel, "I believe . . . yes, it is almost ridiculous—but you remember, Mille, don't you, that day we came from church—I almost believe that he doesn't like the fact that we are Christians."

The aunt burst out laughing and cried, "Do you think, then, that he wants us to become Jews?"

"No, certainly not . . . but it seems to me . . . yes, I don't really know myself . . . but I can't explain to myself that strange face in any other way."

"That is called proving in a circle," remarked Wilhelm, standing still and regarding his mother with a sarcastic expression.

After a moment's silence, the aunt said, "It will all improve; leave it to me! First, I will make him sick of being a Jew. If he genuinely loves Thora, then he will also love her faith, and on the day he is baptized, I will with all my heart give you my blessing on your marriage to your handsome fiancé," she added, going over to Thora and kissing her.

However much animosity Thora felt over her aunt's self-willed interference in her affairs, she was nonetheless touched by this proof of love on the part of her aunt, who was idolized in the family. She did not dare to make any objection or undertake any steps herself. She thought that it was probably best to let the matter take its course.

Chapter 11

THE MORE AUNT MATHILDE THOUGHT of this matter, the greater interest she took in it. She pictured to herself in advance the triumph she would enjoy when she had enriched her congregation with a new member, just as when she, out in her parsonage, had gotten a tardily hatched chick or kept one alive which all the others had given up. She determined to push the matter quietly and deliberately in order to reach her goal slowly but surely. All the threads were to be in her hand; she would control every word spoken to Jacob, and everything would be calculated to lead him toward the desired goal. Amid these calculations she came to be warmly fond of him, fond as of her own triumph, for he was essential to it.

She chose Wilhelm as her adjutant, as her confidant. She set forth for him how she had thought out first in all friendliness to impress upon Bendixen that he was a Jew, to point out the excellence of Christianity, and if he then denied this, to combat him most zealously, and in the end to win the most glorious victory. She asked Wilhelm if he didn't have some theological books where one could find some good proofs to use in the upcoming debate. "My husband and I have no children," she concluded, "If I succeed in getting this young Jew baptized, we will take him as our own child."

"Auntie," said Wilhelm, "you are definitely descended from the priest Thangbrand."

But she became annoyed over this remark and said, "I don't like for you to say that. I am not intolerant. It doesn't bother me at all that the person is a Jew; it's not for the sake of his eternal salvation, either, that I want to have him baptized. But since he has gotten engaged to a Christian girl, he ought also to belong to the Christians."

"Yes, Auntie," replied Wilhelm, "but I really don't think that your method will hold up. According to what I know of Bendixen, he won't believe that it is being done out of friendship when you speak to him about Judaism and Christianity. If he is to be made a Christian, then it should be done precisely by treating him as though nobody knew otherwise than that he was a Christian, and by being kind and good to him; then perhaps he would become Christian without himself realizing it."

"Yes, that's a right way!" cried the aunt, "Let him go on being a Jew until he became Christian of his own accord! Oh, yes, that's priceless!"

"That's the same thing the wind said when it wanted to force the wanderer to take his cloak off. As far as I am concerned, I don't want to get mixed up in the matter. Bendixen is a little sulky with me lately; he will surely get over it, and I am certainly going to steer clear of women's affairs."

It went approximately as Wilhelm had said—the aunt was not successful with her gentle remedies. Bendixen simply tried to avoid her; he came only to collect Thora for a stroll, to go to the theater, or for some other entertainment, and did not stay in the house for very long. Aunt Mathilde was in a bad mood for several days, and once she said, "You know, Thora, your fiancé ought rather to make a date with you in the street; then he wouldn't have to come up here at all."

"Yes," said Mrs. Fangel, "it really looks as though he hates us all."

Jacob got a hint of this from Thora, and the following days he addressed himself to Mrs. Fangel, invited her to go along for walks, took her to the theater, and collected her along with Thora, and when he was alone with the two of them he was so affectionate and warm that the earlier good relationship was resumed.

The aunt frequently made bitter remarks, but Mrs. Fangel defended Jacob.

"Such an engagement I have never seen before," said Aunt Mathilde, "it is as if it were secret and only the mother is supposed to know about it. He never comes when there are guests, and to the others of us he doesn't speak a word."

"But he doesn't have time; he is studying for his examination," said Mrs. Fangel apologetically. "It would be good if all young people were as studious as he is."

But one day an invitation came for Wilhelm and Mille from the State Counsellor with whose daughter Mille had gone to school. Toward spring the State Counsellor and his familly customarily gave a large party, and before Thora went to Holstein she had been invited every time along with her sister. This time she was not named in the invitation.

Mrs. Fangel looked thoughtfully at the note and said, "It's very strange that Thora is not invited."

"In that case her fiancé would also have had to be invited," said Aunt Mathilde, "and you know, don't you, that they didn't want to."

"I don't know that," said the lady.

"In the first place, he is after all a Jew . . . but it just occurs to me—has he been introduced into the house?"

"No," answered the lady, "he has always been so reserved, almost disdainful to our acquaintances; it is certainly his own fault."

"And yours!" cried the aunt." If he had been a lieutenant or a *kammerjunker*, you would also have been more eager to present him to the world than you are now."

"That is perhaps true," said the lady softly.

This matter was now much discussed. Mrs. Fangel declared that as things stood, Mille should not go, either, and Wilhelm declared that in that case, he would also remain at home and not go to the State Counsellor's. "That won't help," said Mrs. Fangel, "Mille shall not go to a place where her sister is not considered good enough."

There was silence. Wilhelm drummed on the window pane; the ladies sat down discouragedly and picked up their sewing.

Jacob arrived. He greeted Mrs. Fangel in a friendly fashion as usual, but she responded coldly to his greeting. Wilhelm took his hat and left, while Mille, with her handkerchief to her eyes, went up to her room.

When he was alone with Thora, he asked what was wrong.

"Ah," she said, "it's nothing more than childishness. Wilhelm and Mille were invited to the State Counsellor's, and because I wasn't invited along, they are now to remain at home. That's what she's crying about."

At these words, Jacob had instantly grasped how matters really stood. But the pain and embarrassment which this aroused in him was lessened by heartfelt gratitude at the delicate manner in which Thora related the matter to him. He took her in his arms, and at that moment he considered whether he should not now confess his weakness to her and ask her whether she could forgive him for it and whether she thought herself strong enough never to see the Jew in him. While he was still struggling with himself, Thora said, "You shouldn't take it so much to heart! I don't care at all about going to the State Counsellor's! If only I have you!"

After these words, it seemed to him a pity to express any doubt.

As he left, he said confidently to himself, "Just let them all be against me now; she will still with a loyal and loving heart stand by me."

Chapter 12

THE WHOLESALER WAS TOLD of the occurrence with the State Counsellor; he smiled and said nothing.

But from that time on, Mrs. Fangel often fell into deep thought, and once Thora surprised her as she sat weeping. With anxious foreboding, Thora went up to her and asked tenderly why she was crying, but her mother embraced and kissed her and said, "You can't help it, my dear child!"

When Jacob came, she received him as a guest to whom courtesy was due, but it was clear that it often cost her an effort. Mille was less restrained; she left the room as soon as she saw him, and slammed the door after her. The aunt received him with sarcastic remarks and hints, and when Jacob looked pleadingly at Mrs. Fangel, as if to remind her of the support she had earlier given him, she lowered her eyes or invented an errand to another room.

In this way he was then alone with the dangerous enemy, and unarmed, for he didn't dare respond to her for fear of a violent outburst, which in the sullen mood reigning in the family might result in the breaking of the engagement.

The house, once so lively, became still and gloomy, but for no one so deterring as for him. If on a spring day the gentle sunshine and the blue sky seemed to arouse a new life in his breast, and he, happy and full of longing, with rapid stride hastened to his fiancée, he had only to catch sight of the house from a distance, and it was as if the sunshine ceased, and he entered with an unsure and anxious look.

And it was not even so much the unfriendliness he himself was exposed to that filled him with apprehension—he had already begun to get accustomed to that—he suffered still more on Thora's account, for he had a feeling that love is a sunshine blossom; it can endure a violent storm, and after the storm it rises doubly beautiful, but when it must stand in the shadow, without sunshine and without dew, it bows its head and withers.

Under these circumstances it was a relief for all concerned when the wholesaler one day declared that the family should move out to their country house. His wife did object that it was still very early, and that no other families had gone out, but the wholesaler persisted in his demand, and they moved out.

With this alteration they at least had the advantage that they saw each other more seldom. But Jacob often had to think with bitter uneasiness of the fact that Thora was now all the more exposed to the aunt's influence. When he was sitting as best he could among his books this uneasiness would come over him, he would hurry out to the country, as anxious as if a threatening calamity were hovering over her head, and when he then arrived there the hostile atmosphere soon drove him back to town.

Chapter 13

LEVY AND JACOB CONTINUED TO MEET, but both avoided a conversation on this subject. Levy was undoubtedly able to judge from Jacob's appearance roughly how things had gone, and since he no longer had any advice to offer, it was painful to him to concern himself with Jacob's affairs, and the latter on his part feared to touch upon his unhappy circumstances. He dreaded facing them squarely.

One beautiful day at the end of July Levy accompanied him out of the city gate on the way to the country house. Levy walked along, looking around among the strollers, the passengers in the carriages, the riders, and those who were haggling with the coachmen over the fare per person. Finally he addressed Jacob, "You are boring today, although come to think of it, you've constantly been that lately. What a different, splendid fellow you were last year! At that time there was hope of making a real physician of you . . . oh, look there!"

A Jewish family had come up in a four-seated Holstein carriage, and since they filled only two seats, they were sitting patiently waiting for more passengers and passing the time by talking of their domestic affairs. From time to time the father called out to one of the children a friendly warning not to fall out of the carriage or to the horses an anxious "Whoa!" when they lifted their heads.

Levy pointed in their direction and said, laughing, "I would like to stand here; when the coachman climbs up, maybe the father will start to *bensche haderech*."[1]

---

[1] Bless the road; pray for a safe journey.

Jacob, whose thoughts at the sight of the Jewish family had taken a completely different direction, said with a sigh, "A week from today, my uncle's oldest daughter is to be married."

"Well, you don't need to sigh over that," said Levy, "you are, after all, provided for."

"But I would like to go to the wedding," said Jacob after a little reflection.

"Well, then, go!"

"Yes, but they haven't invited my fiancée."

"But you can't expect your engagement to a Christian girl to be officially recognized by Jews!" cried Levy. "Do you want your cake and eat it, too?"

"No, I'm sure I would be happy if I had the benefit of just one of them."

"It's absolutely dreadful the way you are constantly hanging your head. Heavens, man! Make an end of it! Screw up your courage and talk with your fiancée; she is still no more than a woman!"

"No more than a woman! Yes, you should only know what trouble one single woman can make!"

"What? Is your fiancée making trouble for you? Has it already come that far with love? *Ach Du grosser Gott Amour!*"

"Oh, no, the aunt!"

"The aunt? What aunt is that? When did she drop from the clouds? I thought that heaven had let a completely charming, auntless family fall into your hands."

"She's a parson's wife from the country. You have no idea what a *rischainte* she is!"

"A parson's wife! I'm damned if I don't believe it! They are the most intolerant people in the world, far worse than the Turks and even the parsons. Such a parson's wife manages the housekeeping, receives offerings and small tithes, and never sees a Jew bring a goose, much less a chicken. What thoughts must such a poor woman have about Jews! . . . Well, and your parson's wife?" he went on, when Jacob said nothing.

"She has caused me to regret the wish that I once expressed to you: that in the house they would let me hear that I was a Jew. That was challenging fate, and I have been punished. She talks of practically nothing else; she treats me as if it were her firm intention to force me out of the house."

"It's a pity that she didn't come before the engagement."

"Why so?"

"Why? You say yourself that she wants to have you out of the house."

"Oh, now don't talk like that, Levy!"

"But she will have to leave sometime, won't she? Or is she a widow, and does she want now to spend her pension in honor of your health here in town?"

"Her husband has gotten a congregation here in town; he is supposed to come when he has held an auction out there. The poor man presumably is completely under her thumb, since she goes away and leaves him to take care of everything. But what will it help that he comes and that she gets her own house—they will naturally still be as thick as thieves."

"Then meet her head-on; try to force her out of the house!"

"I can't do that; she dominates the whole house; if I antagonized her, I would antagonize the family along with her. Life in the family has become unendurable since she arrived."

"Listen, you know, Bendixen," said Levy after a pause, "get married, take the girl away from them, the sooner the better."

"I must have the family's permission, and until I pass my examination and get a practice, they naturally won't give it to me, especially under the relations now prevailing between us."

"But you have your own money, don't you? You don't need a practice."

"I don't have any more than what I myself can live off. What would become of a marriage in which I could not provide my wife with a tolerably comfortable life? And my fiancée has been brought up in wealth."

"But her father is rich—"

"Should I let my wife be supported by her father? Then we would really hear them scream at the Jew! Besides, he is a businessman, and a businessman is really never rich. A large dowry one time—that I could accept; but a yearly allowance— that would only make me as dependent on them as I already am, or even more so. Believe me, I have thought enough about all that; I don't really do anything else."

"Well, then, as I know, your own father is rich."

"Levy! You can't mean that! I should take from my father to support a Christian girl!"

"Then, by heaven, I know no other course than that you get baptized. When you stop to think, that's also the most natural thing—if you really love your fiancée with all your heart, then it is an easy matter to get baptized for her sake."

"Such theories drive me wild! The theory looks so good, and still I could instantly refute it with another theory that is equally untenable: A good man does not abandon his faith for any worldly happiness. But you know very well that I *cannot* get baptized, I, who still every morning and evening say my *Krischmo*.[2] I don't know—but I am fonder of Jews now than I was before. . . . I have often imagined that I was baptized, so vividly that I regarded myself as a Christian, and I cannot describe to you what a torment it was when I met a Jew on the street, and what an inexpressible relief it then was, when I said to myself, 'But you are not yet baptized.' Just then I started thinking of those baptized Jews here in town who on Friday evening, when the Jews went to the synagogue, went with them to the entrance and remained outside until they sang *L'cho dodi*,[3] and then went home weeping."

"Then I will discharge you as incurable and say good-by to you; I have to go to town."

"Oh, go along with me a little more, Levy; I am so dreadfully downcast. I wouldn't wish you in my place—although then you would better feel what I am suffering."

"Poor fellow!" said Levy, "I wish to God that I could discover a New Pitcairn Island to which you could carry off your fiancée and live in paradisiac peacefulness, isolated from the whole world."

---

[2] See footnote to Part 1, Chapter 2 [p. 10].

[3] *L'cho dodi likrahs kalo:* Up, my people, to go to meet the bride.

"Yes, if only such a forceful resolution were possible! If only I could gather all my sufferings together at one time for a battle with me, and venture everything to repulse them, even my life! That would always be better than being slowly tortured to death like this. The proverb is right: it is a slow death to be trampled to death by a goose. And I am being trampled like a worm and don't even dare to bite . . . how I hate that woman! If the thought of my fiancée were not always uppermost in my mind, I think I would have killed her long ago."

"Your position is a painful one, Bendixen; you're going around with a cavity in a tooth and want to be rid of it, but don't have the courage to have it pulled. And there are only two alternatives to choose between—you must either be baptized or break it off."

"The fact that I am placed between these two alternatives and cannot choose between them—that is precisely the trouble!" cried Jacob impatiently. "When a person is standing between fire and water and calls for help, it's easy to say, 'Jump into either the fire or the water'."

"Well, then, run away, man! Run from both the fire and the water!"

"There's just no getting anywhere with you today," said Jacob.

"Heavens, what am I supposed to do? There's no getting anywhere with your situation, or out of your dilemma—say that, rather. I would gladly jump into the fire or the water for you, damn it! You can be assured of that, but I can't see that it could be of much use to you. If I can be of help to you, just tell me, here I am, command me! If you don't know at the moment, and hit on it later, you have my address. Good-by! My regards to the parson's wife!"

As Levy was walking back, he said to himself, "Now I think I have put the poor man into such a frame of mind that he will go and do something stupid, and the stupidest thing he can do is at least smarter than to keep going the way he is going."

But Jacob did not do anything stupid that evening, as it turned out. The nearer he came to the country house, the more his fierceness diminished, and the dull, lethargic, but irritable mood again settled over him.

When Thora saw him coming, pale and exhausted by the long walk, heat, and emotion, she thought he was ill, and hurried anxiously for medicine. His appearance even aroused the anxiety of the other members of the family; they surrounded him and asked sympathetically about his health. When Thora came with the medicine, Aunt Mathilde tore it from her, to count the drops herself. Jacob felt strangely well for several moments; he had become so unaccustomed to friendliness that he forgot all ill will over these demonstrations of affection. He felt how greatly he could love all these people. When he and Thora returned from a short stroll in the garden, he was as newly born; for the first time he noticed the vines twining on the wall of the house. The table set for tea in the room facing the garden looked very cosy and inviting; he had never before seen it like that.

Aunt Mathilde met him at the door. "Well," she said, "you look as fresh as a daisy. Thank God! I was already afraid that you would die here. We poor people don't know a thing about how you should be buried."

Mille laughed loudly and went out.

So the truce was already expired.

Jacob was almost ashamed of the gentle feelings he had harbored a moment before; he reproached himself for cowardice. It was, after all, yearning for peace, he said to himself, that had had the greatest share in his happiness over the care they had shown him—"I made myself weaker than I was, only to enjoy their solicitude! Oh, how deeply they have degraded me! Now I understand how my whole race could become so cowed that, with a sickening slave mentality, it licked the hand that beat it!"

Chapter 14

"I'M FED UP WITH IT!" said the wholesaler at the dinner table. "I will have peace in the house. You poor thing," he said, turning to Thora and patting her on the cheek, "you aren't having a very happy engagement."

Thora began to cry.

"It can't go on like this!" he went on vehemently. "There has to be a change in things. I thought it would be fine when we came out here, but it is just as bad. If Bendixen doesn't behave well, I will point it out to him; if injustice is done to him, in the future I will take his side. There will be peace here in the house!"

The aunt took the floor: "The change that must take place here will certainly be either that Bendixen gets baptized or else that we all become Jews."

The wholesaler flushed to his eyebrows but he controlled himself and said, "I hope that my sister-in-law does not come to regret the zeal with which she concerns herself with this matter. If you have nothing against it, I myself will still take care of my family's affairs."

With these words he rose and left the room.

Aunt Mathilde sat for a time without saying anything. Then she turned to her sister and said, "That probably means that I had best leave the house? Now it has gone so far that he is sowing discord in the family. But I tell you this," she shouted, springing from her chair so that it fell over, "I tell you this, Thora—I will not allow myself to be forced out by your fiancé! I am staying! I am staying, until your father and your fiancé take me and throw me out the door! Then you can marry the Jew for all I care! Then I will have done all I can!"

A pause set in after this outburst. Aunt Mathilde held her handkerchief to her face and sobbed; the others sat with downcast eyes, each occupied with his own thoughts.

"There he comes!" said Mille, pointing at the window.

"Thora, you go out and meet him; it is wiser for him not to come in here," said Mrs. Fangel, going over to her sister.

Jacob had not been out there for a couple of days, and his longing for Thora had grown stronger than the ill feeling, mixed with fear, that he felt toward the family. Moreover, another feeling impelled him; it was self-reproach, an uneasiness, as if he were on the point of doing Thora an injustice by going to the Jewish wedding taking place that evening. From the moment that the *schammos*[1] had visited him and invited him with the old formula "*Ihr seid gepreit zu der Chuppo und zu dem Essen*,"[2] an irresistible longing, like homesickness, had taken possession of him. To excuse himself he told himself, "But I don't keep Thora from going to the Christian church, and she has her family, doesn't she; what do I have?" But still, his conscience was not completely at rest.

Only finding an opening was painful to him, a suitable way of saying it, but since she continued to walk silently at his side, and he in his embarrassment knew nothing else to talk about, he summoned up all his courage and said, "This evening there is a wedding at my uncle's; his daughter is getting married."

"Oh?" she said, "and are you invited?"

"Yes," he replied, and it pained him a moment that she so definitely assumed that she was not invited; the thought was present, then, that there was a barrier between them. "Yes, I am invited."

"You're going, then?"

"Yes, I did think I would—although. . . ."

"Go ahead, my dear!" she said. "I hope you have a good time."

The resigned tone in which she spoke pained him. He felt so grateful for the willlingness with which she wished him a

---

[1] Parish clerk.

[2] "You are invited to the wedding and to the meal."

pleasure that he searched his thoughts for something that might in return gladden and cheer her.

They had entered the woods and had reached a fringe that opened out on the Sound. There they sat down on a grassy bank.

The early afternoon sun shone warmly on the sea, which lay like a faithful dog at the foot of the land; out in the gulf, ships with shining white sails moved slowly, almost imperceptibly. The coast of the island of Ven looked like bluish vapor resting waveringly on the horizon. Under the trees it was cool; no sound was heard except isolated intermittent birdcalls, as if the birds felt too good to hold long conversations.

After a profound pause Jacob burst out, "How unnatural human relations seem, when one looks at nature! Over sheer trifles we human beings battle each other and make life unpleasant for ourselves, when we could be so happy! How pityingly must lofty nature smile when it looks at us. It is as if the scales were falling from my eyes; at this moment I regretfully feel how great a blame I, too, bear for the unfriendly relations between your family and me. Thora! I will go straight to your aunt and extend her my hand; if she gives me only one single good word, I will stay home from the wedding, I will belong only to all of you."

"Will you really do that for my sake!" cried Thora.

"Yes, dear Thora, and for my own sake! At this moment I am very happy; I see so clearly. It is unmanly of me that I have for so long been afraid to show myself weak and give in."

"Oh, thank God! Then everything will be fine! It has always been said that nothing would be in the way, if only you. . . ."

"If only I what?"

". . . Come over to our faith."

It is said that a person struck by a fatal shot keeps, for a moment, his calm appearance, and then collapses, as if death's thought were too great for him to grasp instantly. Jacob turned to Thora as if surprised, the happy smile still resting on his face; but an instant afterward, a deadly pallor spread over his features. He rose and went back with her through the woods and the garden.

"Are you angry?" she asked with trembling lips.

"Oh, no!" he replied, almost without knowing what he was saying, and continued walking.

He did not notice that they had entered the room facing the garden, where there were guests, including Lieutenant Engberg, until their voices aroused him. Then he hastily took his leave. Thora said in a half-choked voice, "Tomorrow morning at twelve I'm coming to town to take care of some errands; will you come over and come back with me?"

He replied, "Yes," and left the house.

When he had gone some distance, he stopped and leaned his head against a tree.

"So, then, the worm has gnawed the plant that I have cultivated, and under which I sought shade! . . . But she is not to blame; they have poisoned her ears. . . . Oh, if only I could tear her away from them! . . . But I love her so dearly . . . I left in too unfriendly a way," he continued, as he walked on. ". . . And nonetheless, how will I be able to see her again? . . . Oh, God! You have laid your hand on me, heavy but just."

Thora had gone out several paces with him. When he had left her, she looked after him for a moment with a bitter smile and then burst into tears. But a little afterward she dried her eyes, breathed on her handkerchief to hide the fact that she had wept, and went in to the company.

In Marcus's festively decorated living room the men were assembled for *Mincho* (afternoon prayer), which is recited before the wedding takes place; the women were in another room, busy with the bride.

The ceremony was about to begin, and Marcus delayed only in order to impress on his wife one more time all the precautionary measures.

"Is her hair done, the silver chain fastened around her, the veil wrapped around her head, so that she can't be recognized?" he asked, pulling his wife into a corner.

"Everything is in order," she replied impatiently, "if you will only begin the *Mincho*."

"My dear wife! Your carefreeness worries me. If only nobody makes a mistake! Keep in mind that one doesn't marry off a daughter every day."

At that moment his wife nudged him and winked toward the door.

"Jacob! My nephew!" he exclaimed in astonishment as he turned around. "There, you see," he said, turning briskly to his wife, "I thought so! He is after all a Jew at heart."

"How unwell he looks!" she said.

"*Och und Nebbisch!*[3] He certainly is not dancing on roses among the *goyim*! I tell you, it would have been more sensible of him to fall in love with our Mariane."

"Marcus! The sun is going down! Is there anything more you want from me!"

"Well, in God's name! If there is a mistake, on your head be it! . . . I wouldn't have wanted to do without his coming for anything."

He went over and greeted Jacob, and then gave the signal that the prayer should begin.

Everybody covered his head and turned to face the east with a low bow to the invisible deity. A deep silence reigned in the room while the men softly whispered the prayers and blessings. The setting afternoon sun shone on the windows opposite, so that they looked like colored glass panes in a church and cast a gentle glow over the little congregation.

When the *Mincho* was ended, the bridegroom's *schomer*[4] came to the women's room with the bridegroom's gifts for the bride—a pair of stockings, two pairs of shoes, a silk kerchief, and a prayer book. A little later came the bride's gifts for the bridegroom—a *tephilin* bag (a bag in wich he keeps the holy cases and leather straps), the *thallis* in which he wraps himself during prayers, and the *kittel* which he wears to pray on the High Holy Day of Atonement and in which he is buried.

---

[3] "Oh, the poor fellow!"

[4] Guardian, a friend or relative who sometimes sleeps at the bridegroom's the night before the wedding so that the evil spirit will not come and carry him off (cf. the Book of Tobit).

Now the trumpet blast sounded, and the door to the main room opened; the men in pairs accompanied the bridegroom and placed him under the *chuppa*,[5] whereupon the women marched in, in procession, with the bride and, while the trumpets blew a solemn march, led her three times around the bridegroom before placing her at his side.

The rabbi stepped in under the canopy, recited a solemn prayer, and blessed God, who has commanded systematic marriages; the bridegroom placed on the bride's finger the ring, which was immediately wrapped in a silk cloth (and must not be seen until the morning after the wedding). A glass of wine was brought in, the rabbi sanctified it with a short prayer and let the bride and the bridegroom drink from it, whereupon the glass was placed under the bridegroom's foot, and he crushed it underfoot as a sign that, just as this glass cannot be put together, the two should not be separated.

The deep reverent silence was broken by loud congratulations and the trumpets' fanfare; the newly joined families embraced each other and the young couple. It was a joyous group of jubilant, happy people.

At the lively meal, at which the older people relived their youth and in unrestrained merriment joked with the blushing bride and the happily smiling bridegroom, and the younger ones seemed to want, with high-pitched joy, to drown out their own longing, Jacob had been given the place opposite his uncle's youngest daughter, the one whom he had tutored as a child. She sat there, with her pale, fine features, and with her intelligent black eyes curiously and sympathetically fixed on him, as if she wanted to read in his face traces of the happiness the Christian girls had bestowed on him. He felt strange. The fatiguing walk in the warm weather and the suppressed pain had exhausted his strength and imparted to his soul a sickly supremacy; his body was in a state in which the senses only sluggishly and reluctantly perform their services, in which the eye sees as if through a fog and sound comes to the ear as if through an empty space. What he saw before him—all this joy and gladness, the

---

[5] A canopy under which the wedding ceremony is performed.

young girl with the intelligent, sympathetic glance—everything began to shape itself like something disquieting, spirit-like, like a magical picture his guardian angel was sorrowfully unrolling before him to show what it had in store for him. Every time his own situation came into his mind there was a stab like a white-hot knife through his breast; he felt like the woman in the fairy tale who as a girl for fear of giving birth had eaten magic grains, and in church saw the unborn generations coming toward her and with a reproving glance laying their lifeless hands on her breast, one after the other in long, immeasurable lines, until she from pain and mortal fear sank dead on the church floor. The sound of the company's jubilation seemed to him to recede, even the young girl in the end seemed a fading image of mist, while her black eyes still sought him, bidding him an eternal farewell. He swayed and held on to the table in order not to fall from his chair.

When he came to, he saw himself surrounded by the whole company; they all showed him the most affectionate solicitude. Almost crying, he thanked the Jews for their affection and hurried away in order not to disturb their joy.

When he stood in the street, in the still evening air, in the indistinct buzzing of passers-by and strollers, he was downhearted and depressed. It was as if he were homeless; wherever he directed his thoughts, he was met by horror and apprehension. Finally his thoughts stopped at Levy, and a ray of consolation flashed through his soul; he directed his steps toward the maternity hospital where Levy lived.

When he approached Levy's room, he heard loud-voiced conversation, but, as he recognized Levy's voice, he nonetheless entered.

In the middle of the large, green-painted room stood a table with a beer bottle and a chipped glass; on a corner of the table sat the host with his long pipe. Two of the guests, in dressing gowns, sat in the window with their backs to the street; others lay on the bed, smoking, or sat on the edge of the bed. Only two had condescended to sit on chairs, because there were no more chairs.

In spite of the nonchalant positions, the faces of those present bore the mark of energetic animation, as if something had occurred which interested them to an unusual degree.

"There's Bendixen!" shouted one, "That's something for him!"

"Bendixen!" cried König, sitting up on the bed, "Have you heard the news? There is a revolution in France! Charles X has been deposed. *Vive la république!* Look how he stands there in astonishment, like a statue!"

One of them added, "Gröndal has suggested that the whole clinic should emigrate to France and enlist in the republican army."

"Yes," said Gröndal, "I am fed up with the patchwork we have here. If an inmate of the 'rasp-house' prison now and again didn't stab one of the guards with one of those solid, broad knives they have out there, one would never get to see a decent wound. But there! And once one got over there, one could chop, stab, or shoot a wound to suit himself. I suppose that the Russians will now oppose the French, and there are no patients I like better than the Russians—you can trephine such a fellow and take away half his head, and he is just as lively for all that. Over at the General Hospital last year we had a Russian sailor who had been crushed by a dinghy that fell on his head. When I got hold of him, he was like mush. Three months later, I saw him on the market place beating up a farmer from Amager from whom he had stolen a cucumber."

"To be in Paris now!" said one. "How lively it must be there! The Jacobins put on their red caps, declare war on the kings of the earth—and perhaps of heaven, too—and hurl a million men against the enemy! Heavens! I imagine that the drums beat the call to arms the whole day and that the alarm signal is rung from the countless church towers, and that amid the noise the old regicides creep out and bask in the sunshine like snakes in the spring."

"Respect for regicides!" cried König. "I myself could have the desire to be a regicide—in a respectable way, of course, with due process, judgment, and execution. If only we had another king than white-haired Frederik! It's really a damned shame that we don't have a king for that purpose."

Gröndal said, "One makes the best of what one has. I vote for us to march immediately on Amalienborg. *Aux armes, citoyens!* . . ."

"I am to ask whether the doctor won't step downstairs; a new patient has arrived," said a midwifery student, coming in the door.

"I'm coming right away," said Gröndal, hurriedly putting on his slippers.

"I will go down and look at the new one," said one, going out.

Several followed, and soon afterward Levy was alone with Jacob.

"It is probably best to strike a light," said Levy. "How the days are getting shorter! A month ago, it was light until ten o'clock. So, now we can see what we are saying. . . . But what the devil has come over you? You look as proud and determined as—a king, I was about to say, if it didn't seem as though that kind of people were going out of style. Damned if that doesn't look good on you! It's been a long time since I saw a face like that on you!"

"It may very well be, because I finally want to *do* something! Levy, I'm going to France."

"To France?" cried Levy.

"Yes, I can't stand it here; I've got to get out of all this misery, I have to get out! It came like a revelation as I was standing among these healthy natures and thoroughly felt my own unmanliness and weakness."

"But what has happened?"

"Nothing except that today she, too, let me hear that I am a Jew, and demanded that I get baptized."

"Well, are you going to break off with her?"

"Oh, no, Levy! I know very well that it doesn't come from her herself! She gets no peace from the others; they are overwhelming her. And they have tormented me so that I often simply see red. I want to go to France; I want to win a position for myself and then take her there; there I can live with her in peace . . . there everybody has dark hair and dark eyes."

"And your fiancée? What do you think she will say to that?"

"If she really loves me, then she will wait for me . . ."

"And if she doesn't wait for you?"

"Then she doesn't love me, then it would go wrong even if I stayed here."

"Bendixen! Let's go to the woods on Sunday, then we can talk more about that theory."

"I am serious, Levy; if it is possible, I will leave tomorrow."

"Tomorrow evening I will come and find out whether you have left."

"Levy! Can you really, as a friend of mine, want to advise me to remain here and perish?"

"I am not advising anything. If I were in your place, I would perhaps do the same thing, and perhaps I wouldn't; I just don't know. But for the present I think that tomorrow, when you talk with your fiancée, there will be a great weeping and reconciliation scene, and on Sunday you will go to the woods, but maybe not with me."

"And I give you my word of honor that I'm leaving!"

"Sh! It's a good thing that no Christian heard that. As you know, it sounds odd when a Jew speaks of a word of honor. But all right, man, if you really want to leave, then . . . yes, then at least one loyal friend will see you off. And in that case on this last evening I will drink 'brotherhood' with you, my dear Bendixen."

Chapter 15

WHEN HE AWOKE, the decision of the previous evening lay heavy and oppressive on his breast. As soon as he thought of giving it up, he breathed more easily, but when he cast a glance at his circumstances, he soon felt once more the conviction that there was nothing else to do.

For a long time he paced up and down, repeating yet again all the reasons; then he went to get his passport before going to see Thora. With such an energetic step as this we sometimes strengthen ourselves when we feel ourselves weak.

The evening before, Lieutenant Engberg had closely observed Thora and Jacob when they came into the garden room as well as the way in which they parted. He now considered the time favorable for making a diversion; what he really desired was perhaps not completely clear to him, but he assumed that something would happen to his benefit.

People are generally far from as evil as their actions, or else one could not go unarmed in the street. When one, for example, wants to take another's sweetheart from him, one does not think of committing a theft, but says to oneself, "The poor girl is unhappy with that boor, who cannot appreciate her; with me she would be far happier. He will damned well console himself; in any case he is only getting what he deserves."

Lieutenant Engberg watched carefully when Thora came in the carriage with her father. When he could assume that her father had gone into his study, he went up.

She was sitting and waiting for Jacob; she was despondent and anxious over how they would meet after the previous day's scene.

When there was a knock and the lieutenant entered with a respectful bow, she felt almost relieved that it was not Jacob yet, and that she had been granted a reprieve; and there was perhaps a trace of this in her tone as she exclaimed, "Is that you, Lieutenant Engberg!"

The lieutenant interpreted this nuance in her tone to his advantage, and replied, "I knew that you would come into town this morning, and therefore could not deny myself the pleasure of inquiring after your health. You looked very unwell yesterday evening when I left you."

Was it that, amid the anxieties and unpleasantnesses, Thora's love had diminished or at least was not always ready at hand? Or is it true what they say—that the most faithful woman wants, through housewifely instinct, to have a lover in reserve? Or was there only in the lieutenant's soft tone something consoling for Thora in her apprehensions? Or. . . . Enough, instead of calling her father in, she was content with saying, "I am expecting my fiancé any minute; he will find it strange to see you here."

"Ah, it is only from fear of her fiancé that she is afraid of a *tête-à-tête*," thought the lieutenant. He replied, "I heard you yesterday setting the time for him at twelve o'clock, and it's only 11:30; in any case the occasion of my coming is of such nature that Mr. Bendixen might certainly be present. I only wanted to express my regret at having seen you unwell and my hope that it was only a passing indisposition, which your fiancé's affectionate care will soon dispel."

At these words Thora's eyes involuntarily filled with tears, and she held her handkerchief to her eyes, while she motioned with her hand for Engberg to go. Lieutenant Engberg seized her hand and kissed it.

At that moment Jacob Bendixen stood at the door.

All three remained several moments standing motionless. The lieutenant recovered himself first; he took his hat and went with a slight bow past Jacob out the door. Jacob stepped back a pace and the door closed between them and Thora.

"Just a moment, Lieutenant," said Jacob, following him, "what were you doing here?"

"When the head of the house demands an account of me, I will give it," replied Engberg, continuing on his way.

But Jacob laid his hand on his shoulder and said, "But perhaps you will give me an account of your visit to my fiancée—don't be in such a hurry, Lieutenant."

"Well," answered the lieutenant, turning toward Jacob and regarding him with a malicious glance, "I was trying to the best of my ability to console a poor young girl who has the misfortune of being bound to a boor."

Jacob trembled with fury, but he still kept sufficient control of himself to say in a fairly calm voice, "Permit me to tell you, Lieutenant, that you are a dishonorable fellow. I am ready to give you immediate satisfaction."

The lieutenant stepped back a pace, bowed deeply, and said, "Many thanks for the intended honor, but as an officer . . . you understand, don't you . . . to duel with a Jew. . . ."

Scarcely were these words uttered than the lieutenant felt himself seized by a hard hand and hurled through the large room toward the door. Here the lieutenant collected himself and made as if to stand his ground, but there was in Jacob's face, as he turned to face him, such a deadly furious, such an insanely impassioned expression that the lieutenant hastened out the door and disappeared.

Jacob remained standing several moments to regain his composure. He listened. It seemed to him that Thora must come out if she was innocent in this meeting—and he was convinced of this—but appearances were indeed against her, and she ought to give an explanation, and she ought to make the first step. . . .

She was sitting inside there, almost unconscious with shame and fear, expecting to see him open the door. . . .

He waited a few more moments—she did not come.

He opened the door to the corridor, slammed it hard, and went slowly down the stairs; at each step he expected to hear her call.

Outside the street door he stopped once again. Not a sound was heard; the large building was as if deserted. He already repented, he could have gone back, but pride drove him on.

For several hours he paced back and forth in his room, stopping at the slightest noise in the corridor to find out whether it weren't a message from Thora. Finally someone came to his door, knocked, and entered—Levy.

"What will you bet—nothing will come of the trip!" cried Levy at the door.

"That we will see about," said Jacob.

"Oh, I have thought it over more carefully; I'm damned if it will take very long for her to write, the family will give in, and it will begin all over."

"Yes, she may write!" said Jacob to himself. "She will certainly write to me and apologize, when she hears that I have gone away. Everything can be smoothed over precisely by my departure!"

In a firmer tone than before, he replied, "We will see whether I leave or not."

"In any case, I won't say good-by for longer than a week. It's a hell of a thing to say good-by for a long time. We won't say anything else than 'so long'."

"Shall I carry the gentleman's things? It is time," said the porter, who had just come in.

As he sat in the cabin, after Levy had left him, and with an almost unthinking gaze regarded his surroundings as something oddly alien, as something of no concern to him which would disappear of itself, he suddenly noticed by a lurching motion that the ship was under way. It was as if he only at that moment felt that he was parting from Thora. In desperate fear he dashed up on deck as if he wanted to leap ashore, but the ship was already a long way out.

The absolute impossibility appearing before him exercised an almost soothing influence on his mind. This great, calm expanse of water, in which only the keel's furrow evoked a momentary disturbance—it was as if put down by Fate itself: It must be thus!

The ship glided in its sure, rapid flight past large and small vessels. A fresh sea wind began to blow, a passenger struck a light and lit his cigar with such relish as if nothing more important existed, the sun broke through the clouds for a moment and shone on the disappearing city and the green land. The scene spontaneously revived Jacob, the blood flowed with pleasant warmth through his veins, he felt for a moment very light and free, and he inwardly cried, "Undaunted, now! I must go out in the wide, glorious world to battle for my whole existence. How many are there who at this moment would envy me!"

He wrote to Thora:

> I am writing this letter at sea, my beloved! Here the air is so fresh and strengthening out on the waves that cares and petty fear seem to be blown away from the mind, and it keeps only its warm hope of everything that is good and beautiful in life. Here I can tell you what at home never would pass over my lips—I can speak of the fact that I am a Jew. Yes, my beloved Thora, I am, and you know it, and you knew it before you loved me. It is no crime, even though in some people's eyes it is a defect, and I must confess to you that it has always seemed to me that no one could fail to see the defect. You cannot imagine with what dread and self-abasement I have always thought of it, and quite certainly I have thereby given rise to great misunderstanding. You don't know, either, with what strength I am bound to Judaism, how the mere thought of abandoning it causes me pain and horror. And nevertheless I really have abandoned it; it is not the religion that holds me—your race's God is, after all, the same as mine—it is my childhood, the memory of my people, of my parents, countless beautiful memories. I cannot renounce them, tear myself loose from them; I cannot cast them out of my soul—that would be as if I drove my mother out of my house to beg among strangers. But don't you believe that I can carry that love in my soul and still love you? Don't you really believe that there is a common love of God in which we can live, if only the world doesn't step in interferingly between us?
>
> When I came to you, it was to tell you good-by for a long time. I am leaving for France. In one way or another, with my knowledge or by acquiring new knowledge in a new sphere, with the exertion of all my powers, bringing to bear everything that I am capable of, I will endeavor to acquire a position in a foreign land, in a new home,

where you and I can live in freedom, and where no one hurls the difference in childhood or faith as a torch of discord between us. Will you wait for me for a time, until you learn of my death or my good fortune? Will you, my sincerely loved Thora?

An uncomfortable scene occurred the last time we saw each other. With me it left only regret over my vehemence; I do not blame you, but it made my departure doubly necessary—I think you yourself understand this. But let the memory of the apparently unkind parting disappear; hear my honorable, sincere words—they come from a soul that will love you forever. I think my soul would be lost if it loses you; it seems to me that hope for peace and happiness is linked only to you, just as humanity's hope for the light of day and warmth is linked to the sun.

Forgive me everything in which I have possibly in a despondent frame of mind offended you! Forgive me and keep your love for me, my beloved, my Thora! Oh, your name was in my childhood the name of God's message, and God has determined that I should love you, He has willed that with you I should belong to the world that is outside my childhood's still, narrow circle.

Just show your father this letter and gladden me with an answer! Write soon—oh, when I think of the joy of seeing a letter from you! It is like the first time I asked you for your love and listened for your answer.

Write soon and bless you! Yes, I bless you, and I transfer to you all the happiness which God otherwise may have intended for me. Those are words which possess power, although you don't know that. My father once gave me this blessing, and now I bestow on you my paternal heritage; with all my heart I give it to you, my beloved!

Part Three

Part Three

Chapter 1

THE COACH WITH JACOB rolled through the barrier into Paris.

In the streets, on the boulevards, his curious, inquisitive glances encountered strollers, merchants, porters, civic guards, but no rioters. The shops were open, customers went in and out; a detachment of national guards marched past with drums and the tricolor, but people passed without noticing them.

When he had found a hotel, he went out to look for the revolution, but it was nowhere to be found. Here and there lay piles of stones that had been used for barricades, but the pavers were already at work pounding them into the ground again; in one place he found a building riddled with bullets, but masons were already busy repairing it.

Jacob looked for the French people, that mighty people who recently in these very same streets had toppled a throne; he saw only passers-by like those in Copenhagen, calm peaceful strollers. He looked for the republican ranks who at the first glance would see in him one of their own and accept him as a brother; they were nowhere to be seen; to the passers-by he was just one more stroller. Nobody noticed him, nobody bothered about him, who had hazarded an entire life's happiness to hasten to them in order to acquire a new happiness himself.

He visited the Chamber of Deputies; they argued, vehemently and passionately—about a word, a letter in the charter; he attended the court's deliberations: they passed judgment on a thief who had disturbed the public security.

His head whirled; he began to feel as though he had sold his soul to the devil for a mirage.

He had wanted to hurl himself out into life's most violent turmoil, into battle and perils, in order to gain honors, fame . . . he went up to the office of the Minister of War to enlist as an officer, a non-commissioned officer in Algeria—as a non-Frenchman he could not even become a soldier!

He had hurried here with his blood storming, his muscles tensed for exertion, and suddenly he saw himself condemned to accomplish nothing,

With redoubled force his fearful, tormented thoughts turned back to Denmark and to those he had left there.

He had calculated the conditions in such a way that it seemed to him absolutely natural that he should soon receive letters. Levy, after all, knew where he had gone, and would have told Wilhelm Fangel; they would address the letter to the Danish ambassador.

He went up to the ambassador's hotel. The secretary told him politely that no such letter had been received. Jacob's bursting heart was still more strained by the effort to have to repay all the courtesy with which the secretary accompanied him to the stairway.

An instinct or a mania drove him to the post office. It was a kind of consolation to see letters, to convince himself that letters still existed in the world. How he envied a clerk one evening, who had picked up a whole packet of letters!

Should he turn back, of his own accord go home to Denmark, play a role like a truant schoolboy? . . . Or perhaps then a letter would come the day after he had left. . . . He had to stay, without acquaintances, friends, recommendations, alone with himself, his disappointed hopes, his mortal longings, his nagging memories.

He moved along in the countless multitude. Many an evening, when he unawares in his room talked aloud to himself, he was frightened by his own voice; he had not heard it the whole day.

It is hard being alone in a desert, but it is harder being alone in a large, crowded, noisy city. All the world's bliss is spread out before the eye: wealth is exhibited in all its tempting, ostentatious multiplicity, carriages roll past with magnificently dressed lovely women, friends stroll arm in arm, lovers exchange affectionate glances, two neighbors greet each other simply—to the stranger all this is dead; he is excluded from all of it; it is as if he did not at all belong to the human race. He stands hungry at a table where others are joyously having a meal; nothing is offered him, nor does he wish to dine with them—he wishes for nothing except to be able to hide himself in a desert or on the bottom of the deep river that runs through the busy town.

Suicide! . . . That thought rises perhaps in many brains under such a torment. Or drink, intoxication, stupor, oblivion to all cares. But Jacob was a Jew, and this people possesses a strangely stubborn patience. Perhaps it learned this patience at the time when the Egyptian Pharaoh had it baking bricks and obtaining the materials itself, and since then the Europeans have drilled it in patience. Nor does it get intoxicated; it is sensual, but like the Oriental peoples, like the hardened Arabs, whose meal is a handful of dates and a swallow from the spring, but whose tent is full of wives and slave girls.

As he was going one day through the *rue Montorgueil*—the street where one of Charles X's generals had to lay down his arms because of a hail of bullets and cobblestones from men, women, and children, and where the stones of the barricades have not yet quite laid themselves to rest like loyal cobblestones—his attention was attracted by a noise from the place where the street rises and is intersected by two other streets. The thought that the flames of the revolution were perhaps breaking out again aroused his spirits, and with hurried steps he approached the assembled crowd. In the middle of the crowd lay an overturned carriage, and the coachman was writhing on the ground under the blows raining down on him from a number of angry smock-clad men. Some of the bystanders were volubly retelling the cause of this scene: when the liveried coachman had come driving up, a crowd of men in workers' smocks who were standing around talking pointed at him and said something jeeringly about the aristocracy who kept carriages, and had forced him to drive up in between the remnants of the barricade. He had muttered a "*la canaille*," and this had given the signal for him to be jerked down from the box, at which the horses had jumped aside and overturned the carriage. Jacob thought he heard half-smothered screams from the interior of the carriage; he ran up, and when he had with difficulty forced open the coach door, he saw two ladies in an unenviable position, lying on top of each other and vainly attempting to get up. Seized with the eagerness which easily takes possession of a person whose forces have long rested, he shouted at the men in smocks, asking them if they wanted to allow their just wrath to be vented on defenseless women. It is one of the charming sides of the French people that even the lowliest seems to have an inherent feeling of chivalry and the ability to show it in an elegant way. The carriage was hastily righted, and the coachman escaped with the blows he had already received. The ladies could not get over their fright, in spite of the apologies which the men in smocks respectfully offered; they asked their rescuer to ride with them.

When the ladies had driven on a bit, their calm returned and the younger one poured out her gratitude. With the loquacity of a Parisienne, she did not allow Jacob to get a word in: "You have saved us from God knows what misfortune! You came like an angel from heaven. . . . What dreadful people. Did you see the one, what eyes! . . . His frightful beard was, incidentally, handsome, but it was so wild. . . . Thank God that you came! But it is Baron Descamps, it is his fault! . . . He is so solicitous of me; he doesn't want me to go to or from the theater in these uneasy times. . . . I am an actress, sir, leading lady at the Vaudeville Theater. . . . He's an old fool, the good Baron Descamps. . . . He courts me, sends me his carriage, I accept it . . . *voilà tout!*"

With these words she threw him a glance with her large black eyes.

"Léonie!" said the older lady in a reproachful tone.

"I speak my mind!" cried Léonie, "I have told him right to his face that he is an old fool. . . . Just think, sir, a man at least sixty . . . and then he wears a wig! . . . That doesn't matter; but this idea with the carriage, I won't forgive him for that. . . . Here's where I live, sir, *rue faubourg Poissonnière Nr. 3, Demoiselle Courtois.* . . . Please visit me. . . . You must come tomorrow morning, I insist. *Au revoir*, my lord knight!"

Chapter 2

"OH, THIS IS SPLENDID! Look how the houses fly past! . . . Oh, look how the horses pulling the omnibus are bounding; they want to race us—*à demain*, good horses! . . . Be careful—ah, thank God we made it! . . . Well, you certainly can drive!"

"Get along, get along, French horses! That's the way! Jump high, as merrily as you like! Get along, get along!"

"Get up, get up!" shouted Léonie, laughing loudly while she convulsively grasped him by the arm.

"Where shall we drive?" she asked, when they came in among several carriages and had to drive more slowly.

"I don't know! To the ends of the world! If the horses had wings, we would drive up into the air, up toward the sun like Phaëton . . . do you know the fable about Phaëton who fell?"

"Oh, have you also heard about the lovely phaeton? Yes, how sorry I was! They broke in at the Count's and took it out of the carriage house and used it for a barricade. Then a cannon ball went through it and splintered it into a thousand pieces . . . Oh!"

"What is it?"

"Didn't you see the little man in the light-colored coat? That's Mr. Arthur, the one who composed my Spanish bolero. . . . If only he doesn't look you up and want to duel with you, because we have been out driving together!"

"Don't you ever go for a drive with him?"

"He lisps so! And he smokes tobacco, too. . . . He has also courted Pauline. . . . Oh, now I know where we should drive! Out to St. Germain! Pauline is there today with her lover! . . . The poor girl, she has become so serious since she got acquainted with him. They go around and admire nature and belles-lettres, and I even think they have been to church. But then she naturally gets her revenge when he is not around. . . . I will introduce you to him. . . . By the way, what is your name, exactly?"

"Bendixen."

"Ben . . . Bennig . . . Don't you have another name? . . . But it occurs to me—when you stop to think, we got acquainted awfully fast. I saw you one single time . . . and already. . . . Shut up, I know what you're going to say. . . . Oh, a heavenly joke occurs to me . . . I will make you a prince! . . . Pauline is so proud because her lover is the son of a theater director; I'll overwhelm them, stun them, crush them with a prince."

"Is this castle St. Germain?"

"Yes, I think so. See, that little pavilion we are coming to— it's built on the spot where Louis XIV was born out in the open! Yes, we are all human. . . . At *Notre dame de la lorette*! There go Pauline and her little man. . . . Stop, let's get out!"

He started to help her out of the carriage. She stretched first one foot, then the other, as if she were afraid. He raised his burning gaze to her and said, "Jump down into my arms."

"All right, then, look out! . . . Hop! . . . Ow, you're squeezing me!" she cried, biting him on the cheek.

The other couple approached; Léonie assumed a solemn air and said, "My prince, permit me to present to you my friend Mademoiselle Pauline and her cousin, Mr. Albert. Mademoiselle, Mr. Albert—His Majesty the Prince of Ben . . . I beg your pardon, my prince, your name again will not come to my tongue."

"Bendixen."

"Prince de Ben-dik-senn—Those are some dreadfully barbaric names that these Russian princes have, but he is tremendously rich," she whispered to Pauline, who like Mr. Albert was standing in the deepest humility.

"My prince!" Léonie resumed, "Permit me to ask you whether you want to ride on a mule or on a dragoon horse. . . . You know, my prince, that we young ladies usually ride in St. Germain Park."

"Whatever it pleases Mademoiselle to choose!"

They went to the horse- and mule-renter, and when Jacob and
Léonie had mounted, Pauline said, "Albert! If the Prince of
Benedit, or whatever his name is, can ride a mule, so can you."

"I can't ride," replied Albert dejectedly.

"Will you pass up the opportunity to make such a
distinguished acquaintance?"

"I'm not ambitious."

"But I am!" cried Pauline with tears in her eyes. "I have
given in to you so long; now you are going to ride today—if not,
we are parted forever."

"Pauline, I don't know you any more! My reasonable, quiet
Pauline. . . ."

"I am not reasonable, I am not quiet, I want a mule—will you
or won't you?"

"Let us have two mules," said Mr. Albert to the renter,
sighing.

Léonie and Jacob had in the meantime galloped down through
the park, as fast as the animals could run.

Léonie's animal was a bolter, and Jacob said, "This is going to
be a real steeplechase; let's go—forward, get up, get up!"

Soon after, Léonie lost her handkerchief, then her little light
shawl, then her hat, and now she began to scream, "Stop him! . . .
Oh, I'll never ride again! . . . Save me . . . Oh!"

Léonie fell off; she rolled around in the leaves, and in the
first fright he stopped his animal and leaped off. When he
approached, Léonie sat up and received him with a merry laugh.
"Didn't I get off nicely? . . . That's what I always do, when I'm
tired of riding!"

Pauline and her cousin came up; Mr. Albert hastened to
dismount from his animal and asked solicitously about Léonie's
condition. Léonie seized both gentlemen by the arm; the animals
they left to fend for themselves; Pauline led the retreat on
muleback.

When they had reached the carriage, Léonie said, "Let's
drive back to Paris now and have supper at Philippe's. He has
the best *sole normande frite* in all Paris, and a red *Hermitage* for
six francs a bottle, that is like oil. When we have eaten, we'll

drive Pauline and her cousin home, and you . . . you, my prince, will be so good as to drive me home."

Chapter 3

"IT SEEMS TO ME THAT Baron Descamps does not like me."

This was said in a small, elegantly appointed room, something between a salon and a boudoir. Everything to be seen in it was small, quite as if exclusively meant for fine feminine figures, and finished with the greatest meticulousness: the round table covered with copper engravings and lithographs, stools and armchairs upholstered in red velvet, the sewing table, an opulent *chaise-longue*, and finally the rosewood bookcase with glass doors containing richly bound works of Corneille, Racine, Victor Hugo, etc.

Léonie was sitting at the window looking at a new dress; Jacob was sitting and thumbing through the copper engravings.

At his words she quickly raised her head and exclaimed laughingly, "He's good, the little man! How innocent he looks! Baron Descamps is courting me, you little one, and you are preferred over him—why wouldn't he scowl?"

"I am truly sorry about the poor baron, that he is not twenty years younger," said Jacob.

Léonie broke into even louder laughter. "How he can sit there, serious, and make fun of the baron! . . . Excellent! Splendid! You ought to be an actor!"

"But I mean that quite seriously," he said, sitting up in his chair.

Léonie's face suddenly clouded; she stared at him for several moments; then she said tenderly, almost pleadingly, "You aren't tired of me, are you? . . . Oh, now I remember, now it dawns on me . . . the last few days you have been so gloomy and dreamy; I have not seen a single one of the happy smiles that rewarded my love the first days. . . . What have I done? Don't you love me any longer?"

Jacob replied, "Léonie, I have never loved you."

At these words, Léonie's cheerfulness returned, she clapped her hands and cried, "Oh, he's coquettish, my little lover! . . . He's original! The others always say that they will love a poor girl forever; he says he has never loved her! . . . Oh, that's divine . . . for one single time, for variety!"

"Léonie," he went on, "try if for one single time you can find a string in your soul on which deeper tones can be struck. I have not deceived you, but nevertheless I have never loved you. My heart belongs to only one, a girl in the North; it will never have room for any other. Unfortunate conditions have separated us, and I have parted from her, I have gone alone and forsaken out into the world. Tortured and tormented to death, I found you; in your arms I sought to drink forgetfulness, to drown every memory of her whom I love. But the memories have only gathered strength through the few days' sleep into which I have lulled them; now they are again stronger than I, and with them repentance has come . . . oh, I seem to myself a miserable criminal!"

"Poor young man," said Léonie mockingly, "I have seduced you, I will have to offer my hand to you before the altar in order to restore your honor."

"I didn't think that you would understand me," he said.

She cried angrily, "You have deceived me! It is not even true that you have been in Paris only a short time. You have pretended that you spoke bad French, but now when you got excited you forgot yourself and then you spoke like a Frenchman."

Jacob replied, "The soul's passion can find the right words. It makes even the simplest man eloquent."

Léonie said nothing.

He continued, "When I was quite alone in this great city, your house hospitably opened its doors to me. When no person bothered with me, you received me in your arms, and I rested at your breast. You did not ask about fatherland, family, or faith, and although I cannot love you, I will be eternally grateful to you."

Léonie went up to him, suddenly attentive; she stared at him, as if she were beginning to understand him. Then she said, "You are suffering, my poor friend? The world has been hard to you! Only I have been compassionate and cared for the sufferer."

"Yes, I am suffering," he said, laying his hand on his forehead.

"Stay with me!" she cried. "Forget those who have driven you out! Stay with me . . . I will belong to you alone . . . I won't accept any gifts from Baron Descamps . . . I will leave the theater, I will work for you, take care of you, caress you, stay with me!"

"If only you could feel how warmly grateful I am to you! But it's impossible, I have to leave! Better again to go around alone in these streets than—"

Léonie was drained; she had experienced all possible emotions; now she sat down and wept.

Jacob went up to her and said, "It's said, and now I have to go. Good-by, Léonie! Regard me as a guest whom you have received and given what is better than shelter and food—your love. I am leaving; there will undoubtedly come another guest to whom you can show compassion."

He said this sincerely, and did not notice the slight mockery that lay in the words.

"Who would that be?" she said, lifting her tear-stained face to him, "The old, ugly Baron Descamps? I won't have anything to do with him . . . I hate him! I loathe him! Stay with me!" she cried, hugging him as he started to leave.

She fainted; he freed himself gently from her arms, called her maid, and left.

Immersed in himself and downcast, he walked mechanically through the streets. Sorrows and longings came flocking like old acquaintances and occupied their customary place; with every step he took he was greeted by a new memory, and although it caused him pain, he caressed it as if to atone for the neglect he had shown it.

The multitude of thoughts exhausted his soul; he walked listlessly and dreamily, unthinkingly reciting some verses which he had never before consciously noted:

> Do you to wear this dress desire?
> 'Twas Thora Hjortur's treasure.
> To choose it as festive attire
> Was in her youth her pleasure.
>
> Over these seams often would play
> Her gentle fingers so white,
> Now she slumbers in the dark clay;
> Another love is alight.

He continued to repeat it half aloud until he finally became confused in it and couldn't remember it any longer.

In this way, without himself noticing it, he came to the Palais Royal and entered the garden, where children and elderly people were enjoying the mild sunshine.

Suddenly he bumped into a man, and when he instinctively looked up to apologize, he recognized Baron Descamps at the side of an aging gentleman. He stopped in front of the baron; Léonie already seemed a memory to him, and the baron was a reminder of her.

"Not at all! No reason to apologize!" cried the baron, limping angrily. He started to continue on his way, but when he noticed Jacob's dejected appearance, a pleasant hope welled up within him. He stopped and said, "But what is wrong? You look as if a lover has been untrue to you!"

"That's not the case, however," replied Jacob, trying to smile.

"Then does Paris not please you?"

"Oh, Paris, if I were only away from here!"

"But you surely don't want to leave?" asked the baron eagerly.

"I would, gladly, if only I could."

"If I in some way can be of service to you. . . ."

"You can, Baron!" exclaimed Jacob, through whose mind an idea flashed. "You have influence, Baron, you are a member of the Chamber of Deputies; get me a place as an officer in Algeria."

"When do you want to leave?" asked the baron tensely.

"One hour after I get the appointment."

"Within twenty-four hours you shall have it! Here is my hand on it! . . . But now you shall first, upon my honor, have dinner with me and my friend here . . . Count Planhol—Mr. Bennigsen . . . come, let's go into Béfour's."

With these words he took Jacob's arm, and with a radiant face he stepped into the restaurant and ordered an equally resplendent dinner.

Chapter 4

A GALE WAS BLOWING on the Mediterranean. The frigate was tossed around as if the sea had given it to its waves for a plaything. Who would believe that it could be so harsh and cold on the Mediterranean Sea, on the sea which is wreathed with dates, palms, and orange groves!

Toward morning on the twelfth day after its departure, the frigate dropped anchor in the roadstead off Algiers. Some of the passengers, awakened by the sailors' rhythmic stamping around the capstan, went up on deck.

In the dim light of dawn, the land looked like an enormous white apparition that had risen from the dark blue sea. To the right of the ship, a promontory extended out into the sea, and on its summit, at some distance from each other, burned two signal torches on high poles; exactly between them the moon rose blood-red over the summit, so that for a moment it looked as though in Africa, the land of fairy tales, the moon, too, were standing on a pole. Intermittent gusts of wind swept from the land, now strong and cold, now gentle and mild and bearing the fragrance of unknown trees and flowers.

At daybreak it became lively in the harbor; the frigate was towed in. The sun cast its red rays on the white country houses winding in terraces up the hillsides, on the ruins of fortresses, and on the distant mountain tops. In the harbor a lively multitude moved—men in white turbans or red caps, Jews in black caftans and with long, matted beards, and talkative, inquisitive Franks. At the water's edge a solitary Turk was sitting on a carpet, smoking his pipe and staring with a serious gaze at those entering the harbor.

"Well, now I am in Africa," said Jacob when he had set foot on land, "now this is my fatherland!"

He had expected that in Africa there would immediately be a campaign against the enemy, that he would at once throw himself into numbing battle—and he was assigned to garrison duty. An insignificant numeral, an indifferent stroke of the pen of the secretary to the Minister of War had placed him in a regiment stationed in town. At this new setback it seemed to him as though his life's destiny were broken, the mechanism had gotten out of order, so that it no longer could function concurrently with happiness.

The French officers regarded him with resentment as a foreigner who because of connections had come among them, and wanted first to see proofs of his courage and ability before they drew closer to him. The only officer in the regiment who met him with affability and good will was a Pole by the name of Josinski. He was a young man, with a pale, melancholy face, but tall and strong, and the best horseman in the regiment. He and Jacob were often together, and then for the most part he talked about Poland.

"We Poles serve France recklessly in all her wars," he once said. "We are like the little Savoyards who go to Paris and slave to be able to support their poor parents. But we cannot even send our fatherland the fruits of our slavery. When death meets us on the battlefield, we only cast a pleading look at France not to forget Poland."

On another occasion he said, "You will rarely see a Pole happy. Our enormous national suffering has reached us in our mother's womb and given our soul a squeeze from which it cannot recover. . . . Oh, you don't know what it's like, not to have a fatherland! In a century we Poles will perhaps be like the Jews, who, scattered over the whole world, preserve the legend of their holy land, which a savior some day will lead them back to."

Jacob did not reply to this, and Josinski soon after began to talk about life in Algiers and the deadly boring garrison duty.

"I am not happy here, either," said Jacob. "I hurried here with a burning craving for action, for man's most violent turmoil, and now I am forced to lead the most lethargic life I have ever known. When I am not on duty, I sleep in order not to think, and the more I sleep, the sleepier I get."

"If one could even ride out to hunt in the mountains!" cried Josinski. "There is good hunting here! But one does run the risk, instead of bringing something home in one's game-bag, that one's own head will be taken home in a Bedouin's bag. And they call a country like this a conquest!"

One night the alarm drums sounded in the town, the garrison dashed to the *place d'armes*, people and cattle rushed in a confused mass into the gates. The Arabs had made a raid on the plain and plundered and murdered and spread terror right up to the city walls.

A small army sallied forth to punish the enemy, but the latter's light-armed bands disappeared as quickly as they had come, leaving behind smoking ruins and headless corpses to mark their way, while the French army in forced marches tried to overtake them.

From the mountains the wild Kabyles descended to help their fellow Muslims; the desert sent its Bedouins in their white, flowing burnouses. Reinforced by this assistance, the enemy had made as if to make a stand, and skirmishes had taken place the whole day between the French vanguard and individual enemy bands. A battle was anticipated the next day.

In the French camp everything was in the kind of lively motion which the enemy's nearness and the certainty of an impending battle induce in people's frames of mind. The soldiers sat or lay around the large bonfires that had been lit against the biting night wind blowing down from the Atlas Mountains. Some were drinking and making merry, others were talking softly with their comrades about beautiful France and the loved ones at home, still others—and these were especially the youngest soldiers—were talking loudly and uninterruptedly about all possible things; they were in a feverish excitement like lottery players the evening before the lots are drawn. The older soldiers who had often been under fire were telling about the enemy and his methods of warfare, and were giving good advice to their younger comrades; at a separate bonfire a soldier from the old times had gathered a group of listeners and was entertaining them with his reminiscences from the glorious time, when the man with the little hat on the evening before a battle would inform his soldiers that they would be victorious.

The officers strolled around in the camp, in cheerful, loud conversation as though on Paris's boulevards, as if the war had nothing to do with them, but only with the simple soldiers; and nevertheless the soldiers well knew that the next day their officers would go ahead of them in among their enemies.

Gradually the activity died down; the soldiers wrapped themselves in their grey cloaks and stretched out on the ground by the fire to sleep; in the camp was heard only the sentinels' signal cries from the outposts or a jackal's howling from the surrounding desert; at times resounded a wild cry, muffled by the distance, which showed that the enemy was alert.

"Have you ever been under fire before?" asked Josinski, sitting with Jacob in the latter's tent.

"No, I was just sitting and thinking of how strange it is that I have never heard a real cannon barrage, and that it nonetheless seems so familiar to me, so strangely familiar . . . I cannot really seize my own memory and convince myself that it is not a memory."

"It's probably a memory of the drills which you have imagined as actual battle. I could almost envy you: you still have in store experiencing the proud, wild terror that seizes one at the first salvos, when the cannons thunder, the bullets whistle, and the blood gushes; the bacchantic, bloodthirsty horror and the unmentionable feeling of one's manhood that fills one when every second can bring death and one throws oneself against the enemy. The first battle resembles the first love; one almost perishes in one's own feeling; later, through practice, one becomes calmer and more indifferent and looks better to those who notice one."

"I will not say anything about myself, but I hope that I won't show myself to be fainthearted. I have yearned for this moment."

An orderly stepped into the tent: "The general has received dispatches and a mail bag accompanied them; here is a letter for the lieutenant."

"Perhaps a letter from a faithful beauty in Paris," said the Pole with a roguish smile. "I will leave you alone."

The letter had a black seal and showed signs of having long wandered about to find the far-distant traveler's trail. It was from Benjamin, his father's shop apprentice, and informed him, after long preparatory circumlocutions, of his father's death. Then came a long accounting of the estate and a report on how the faithful Benjamin had invested the capital.

Death is a terrible reminder, and suddenly before Jacob's eyes every sorrow he had caused his father stood clear, all the memories from his childhood arose surely and powerfully, and the picture of his—still so young—misspent life unfolded before him. Then his thoughts, weighed down by remorse, turned back to his father's deathbed and to his previously departed mother. He saw her again, so gentle, so pale! He saw his father as his end approached, and he was alone! What was being alone in a foreign city, compared to being alone on one's deathbed! With infinite yearning his glazing eyes had sought his only son, and perhaps his last thought had dwelled on the crushing certainty that this son would not even say *Kaddish* over him when he lay in his grave.

"But I will after all say *Kaddish* for him!" cried Jacob, the tears rolling down his cheeks. "Just let them hear outside that I am a Jew! Yes, I am a Jew."

And he began, loudly and fervently, to recite the requiem: "*Jisgadal vejiskadisch schemei rabo.*"

"You shall have another *Kaddish*, Father!" he said when he had finished—and again he recited from the depths of his heart the Jewish formulaic benediction over the dead and over the God who sends death.

But the prayer was no more able than the tears to relieve Jacob's heart. It was too much to ask to be forgiven for, at one time, and there was an entire life to mourn. And there was not one single point in his future to pin his hope on; for even his love, even if the Christian girl were true to him, seemed to him at this moment hopeless and criminal.

In this way he spent the night; the grey dawn found him exhausted by sleeplessness and emotion, with his blood in feverish turmoil.

The drums and trumpets summoned the army to break camp; in long files the columns marched out to carry out the general's plan of attack. Mechanically and lethargically Jacob had mounted the horse that his orderly led out in front of his tent. With indifference, he saw the blue peaks of the mountains in the distance lit up by the morning sun, and without feelings of either fear or martial joy he heard the enemy's wild cries and signals and the earth thundering under the horses' hooves.

The colonel's orders led the regiment, after wheeling, down toward a level plain. Suddenly in front of this appeared a line of Bedouins who, shielded by a trench and a wild hedge, apparently intended to stop the French cavalrymen, and leveled their long flintlocks at them. More and more heads appeared in the long line, the white burnouses fluttering in the morning wind, the white hoods contrasting strangely with the brown faces and the black beards. Now the front rows stood erect in their white robes. Jacob reined his horse in. Jews were dressed the same way in the synagogue on the great Day of Atonement, dressed the same way when they were laid in their coffins. It was as if his father were there, clad in his shroud, as if all holy Jews were there, newly risen from the grave. At that moment sounded the signal to attack, but even if it had meant his soul's salvation, he could not have opened fire on these beings. The trumpets shrilled, rifles and pistols cracked, his subordinates flew to the right and left around him into the battle's smoke clouds; he remained stopped motionless.

Finally the realization of his position came over him, a thought of what his comrades, what the army would say of his behavior. He jammed the spurs into his horse's sides and forced it, without looking down in front of him, over the dead and dying, friends and enemies, in a wild dash after the regiment. But it had already repulsed the light-armed enemy and was recalled by the general from the fruitless pursuit.

It did not escape Jacob that he had sunk low in his comrades' esteem. Until then he had not enjoyed more respect than that which they thought they owed him as an officer; now he had their outright contempt. To be sure, it was not expressed in words, but he was all too accustomed to spotting the silent accusation to be deceived for a moment. There is in Danish a rather simple but expressive term for someone who is the object of contempt or derision: "He becomes 'flat'." It is indeed so—even the body seems to feel the humiliation; it shrinks together as if to make itself small, to hide itself.

In the afternoon, when the army had again made camp, Jacob was pacing back and forth in the most remote outskirts of the camp. He felt downcast, dishonored in the eyes of the world without being so in his conscience; but in vain he sought means to defend or excuse himself before the world. Under the vain effort he became desperate and embittered against himself and the whole world.

"It's a good thing, after all, that they don't know that I am a Jew!" he said. "Otherwise they would say, 'The Jew Bendixen is a coward'. Now I have at least the satisfaction that they simply say, 'The man, the officer Bendixen is a coward'."

A French officer came toward him, but went past him apparently without noticing him. Jacob's blood boiled; all his hatred concentrated itself in hatred of this one man.

"It seems that you don't see me, Mr. de Terry!" he cried.

The officer stopped, turned toward him, and answered with the most surprised look, "Ah, indeed, Mr. Bennigsen, you are right! I did not see you! I truly believe that you sometimes have the ability to make yourself invisible."

"How am I to understand that?" asked Jacob with trembling lips.

"However you please!" replied the officer with the most polite smile.

"So you will permit me in a moment to send one of my friends to you?"

"Mr. Bennigsen! I am at your service with the greatest pleasure."

Jacob sought out the Polish officer, who at first seemed to want to avoid a conversation with him, but when he heard that it was a matter of a duel, his face brightened and with a warm handshake he agreed to be a second.

At the appointed time the two adversaries stood with their seconds facing each other. Time was short, there was little talk of apology or retraction. The seconds handed them the pistols; at a signal from the Pole, both were to fire.

The signal was given. De Terry's bullet whistled over Jacob's head; Jacob's shot struck his opponent in the heart. He spun around a couple of times like a top and fell dead on the ground.

In the evening Jacob waited in his tent for the inevitable consequences of this occurrence. He was resigned to the point of lethargy; to himself he seemed gripped by a strong current against which it would be absurd to struggle.

Josinski entered hurriedly. "Good news!" he cried. "A patrol has found poor de Terry, but without his head. One of the Kabyle devils swarming around us has earned his piaster on your shot. In the camp it is said that de Terry ventured too far outside and has fallen at the hands of the enemy, and we escape a court martial."

A ray of joy flitted over Jacob's face. Fortune is a sorceress; even when one has given up everything, she can enchant with a smile.

Chapter 5

"YOU CERTAINLY LEAD a happy reclusive life here," said Josinski, paying Jacob a visit at the little outpost under his command.

Jacob replied with a smile.

"I can well understand that living among the officers might be too painful for you," Josinski went on. "I was quite afraid that you would deal with that, for in that case you would have had to duel with half of them, and have the other half as seconds. Don't get angry that I bring up that story; for my part, I am convinced that you are undaunted in danger. That time you faced de Terry's bullet, one would have believed that your whole life you have been practicing at facing pistol bullets, and courage is certainly needed to request such a post as you have here."

"Now you are judging me too kindly, my dear Josinski. It is not courage I have demonstrated, if by courage I am to understand the strong feelilng which is evoked by interest in a matter, and which for its sake causes us to defy danger. I am indifferent and apathetic. It is said that those suffering from seasickness lie stretched out and numbed by the illness and could, with the greatest indifference, hear that the ship is on the point of perishing; that's the way I feel."

"It would undoubtedly be the same with me, if there were no hope or almost a certainty that sometimes flashes through one's breast like a stab and drives the blood briskly through the veins. . . . Anyway, one cannot say that you live too comfortably here," Josinski interrupted himself, looking around at the barracks. "What kind of books are those you have there?"

"They are some that by chance ended up among my things when I left my fatherland, and that have really been my consolation. I would wish that you could understand them; they are stories about Icelandic heroes, and they are written in a peculiar way. Only actions are reported; the feelings which moved in the people concerned one must infer oneself, and one can never be tired of thinking about this."

"Tell me a little about it," requested Josinski. "In this way we will study Scandinavian literature in the African desert and spend the hot noon hour in a pleasant way. I am not a Frenchman; you don't need to be afraid that I will immediately use your story for a painstaking treatise on the character of the Old Icelanders."

Jacob laughed and said, "I will with pleasure fulfill your request, although I fear that the best thing—the Nordic fragrance—will evaporate in the translation. Perhaps it will go best if I close the book and tell the story from memory. At this moment there are three different episodes in my memory; I will begin with the story of a child. A man was named Thorsten and he lived in enmity with his neighbor Steinar, an evil, but very courageous, man. One time Thorsten with his ten-year-old son Grim and a small company of men had gone out into the district, and near a wood Steinar attacked him with a considerably superior force. Thorsten said to his son, 'You run into the wood until the battle is over', whereupon he and his men engaged Steinar. After the battle, the story now tells, they looked for Grim in the wood, and found the boy seriously wounded, but at his side lay Steinar's son, dead."

"Isn't it the same with you as with me?" asked Jacob. "One is seized by a mysterious horror, one is almost afraid to cast a glance into the wood and be a witness to the two boys' deadly, bitter struggle."

"Yes, that is really true; oh, do go on; this little sample makes me eager for more."

"One of the best heroes in Iceland was Gunnar, who lived on the farm Hlidarende . . . No, as I tell of him, my memory is too strongly filled; I can't make any selection. I will teach you Danish. You must read yourself about the moving friendship between Gunnar and the wise Njal, about the enmity between their wives Bergthora and Halgerda, about the calm irony with which the men alternately give each other monetary compensation for the manslaughter which the quick-tempered wives incite between their households, about Gunnar's glorious deeds and about his last battle, when his wife refuses to cut a lock of her hair for a bowstring and thereby save his life, because he slapped her two years previously."

"These stories are probably general popular reading in Denmark?" asked the Pole.

"No, not as far as I know," replied Jacob. "Now I will after all tell you how Njal died. His warlike sons, who all lived with him, have killed a chieftain, and in revenge they attack the farmstead, surround it, and set fire to it. It is toward evening when the building is in flames on all sides. Flose, the leader of the arsonists, steps up to the door and offers to let Njal out. Njal replies that he does not want to survive his sons, since he will not be able to avenge them. 'Come out, lady!' says Flose to Bergthora, 'for I don't want to burn you to death for anything.' She replies, 'I was married young to Njal, and have promised him that we would share good and bad with each other.' Then they both left the door and went back inside the house. Bergthora now wants them to carry her grandson out of the burning building, but the boy begs, 'It seems to me better,' he says, 'to die with you and Njal than to survive you.' Now Njal goes to bed with his wife and his grandson, orders the house servant to spread a fresh ox hide over the bed so that their corpses will be found undamaged, and lies down to die. But what makes the story most appealing and tragic is the feeling of guilt resting on all of them and contributing to the fact that they don't even really try to escape death, even if they all could be saved."

After a little pause, Josinski said, "This high contempt for death is one of the characteristics which the uncivilized races have over us. In that respect the Arabs resemble your Icelanders; I had an example of that when I was riding over here. I had gotten a little ahead of my troop, and, looking up by chance, I see, behind a ruined wall—presumably the remains of a mosque—a Bedouin who with the greatest deliberation is taking aim at me. But this deliberation was my salvation; I threw myself over onto my horse's side, so that I was hanging onto the saddle only with one leg, and scarcely had I done that when a bullet whistled over my horse's head. Now he was all mine. I drew my pistol and rode toward him, but when I get close to him, he coldbloodedly crosses his arms and stares at me with his coal-black eyes. I could not kill him; I left that to the soldiers who rushed up."

"Did they kill him then?"

"Yes. I think you're sorry!"

"Ah, no, although I cannot deny that I feel a kind of sympathy for this people. Right is on their side, and they defend it with wild, splendid courage. And then there is something romantic in them—they seem to belong to the earth less than we do; they fly lightly over it, and have not bound themselves to it with stone walls and plants. And nevertheless, when one sees their proud, strong figures, they seem to be more warmly loved by Mother Earth than we are. To see an Arab in his white, flowing robes alongside a French soldier with his red, short trousers and his ridiculous shako! To see Colonel Yussuf alongside a French colleague! He seems created by the Lord as a model for warriors; courage glows from his whole being, so that one has the feeling that bullets have to turn aside for him. I can never look at him without feeling a kind of pain at the fact that he has abandoned his people; how its heart must bleed when it sees him among the Christian troops! That's the reason that I am so apathetic and indifferent," Jacob went on, "I would like—there is nothing I would like more—to distinguish myself and have honors bestowed on me. But against this people I cannot fight; I seem like a mercenary to myself; I murder, if not exactly for money, then still for reward, for it is murder, even in pitched battle, if one is not killing in a just cause or at least for one's convictions."

"Just don't go over to the Bedouins!" said Josinski jokingly.

"Oh, no! We Europeans are chained to each other by civilization. I love the French—at a distance; I love them on account of the thought that the Lord seems to have had when he created this people."

"Yes, it is strange," Josinski burst out. "These people, who individually are so egoistic, frivolous, and vain, as a nation feel sympathy with all nations and are ready to sacrifice their life for them. I hate each individual soldier, but when I see a regiment march out, my heart beats with pride."

"The mass always makes that impression. One does not love one's individual fellow citizen, but one loves the entire people, nevertheless."

"Much could be said against that! I for my part love every individual Pole I meet; he is a small piece of my fatherland. The other day in Algiers I picked up a button from the street; it was a button from a Polish uniform, and it seemed a pity to me that it should be lying in the dirt."

"That's because your fatherland is suffering; a son of wealthy, proud England cannot endure seeing an Englishman abroad. But it is no wonder, either, that you cherish such a religious love for your fatherland, for Poland. That feeling is indeed shared by almost all Europeans. That struggle for a noble nation's independence and for human justice and honor we have all understood; under that flag the mind would not be divided, the heart would not bleed when one fell upon the enemy's ranks. And I for my part have perhaps especially learned to feel for Poland."

Josinski had risen and said with blazing eyes, "What if that flag were now again unfurled? What if Poland again summoned her sons and all who love her?"

"Yes, *if* that happened!" said Jacob.

"It has happened! Listen to the news: Poland has revolted!"

"Hurrah!" shouted Jacob. . . . "Yes, it is in Danish that I am shouting! Hurrah! Thank God!"

Josinski brushed his hand over his eyes and said, "We two are cheering alone here in the desert, but I am sure that you are right in what you said just now, and that at this moment half of Europe is cheering. Well, then, will you go with me to fight for Poland?"

"Yes, Josinski, I'll go with you. . . ."

"Why do you stop? Is there some doubt rising within you?"

"No, it was only a thought that there could possibly come letters here from my home."

"Write them that they in the future should address their letters to Warsaw instead of Algiers. Or are there other things . . . ?"

"No, it was only a passing thought. At this moment the colors of home are paling; my personal sorrows are becoming small and insignificant at the thought of Poland."

"Then do as I am doing and submit your resignation! There is no time to lose. But we have to get away, even if we must desert. If only no Arab is lying in wait along the way. . . . My friend! Don't believe ill of me if you see that from now on here in Algeria I am afraid for my life."

Chapter 6

I
THE ASSAULT

"I'm as hungry as a Kalmuck!" said a young officer who on that dark evening was accompanying Jacob through the small town. "After the good Captain Dalgetty's example, I have been tightening my belt on the march, but the more I tighten it, the more ravenous I get. Perhaps you have been so fortunate as to get good quarters; if so, I will invite myself as a guest. . . . Oh, so it's here! No, thanks! In that case, I'd rather go further to forage for myself."

Jacob entered the hut, which more resembled one of the mounds of earth in which farmers keep their potatoes in winter than a human habitation. Within the bare mud walls nothing presented itself other than three half-naked children lying on a little damp straw and staring anxiously at the new arrival.

The corporal came in and said, "This is a poor lodging, Lieutenant, and the board is not much better. But here is some bread and schnapps, if the lieutenant will make do with it. Tomorrow the Russians will have to offer breakfast, and I think it will be hot."

"Thank you, my dear Soltau. But where are the people who live here? Is there no mother for these children?"

"God knows; I haven't seen any."

"Where is the man who owns the hut?"

"He has probably moved into a doghouse! I chased him out to make room for the lieutenant."

Jacob said to himself, "Perhaps this is a Pole my father has fed at his table."

"Soltau, I prefer to go out into the fresh air; let the man come into his house."

"He will undoubtedly creep in when he sees the lieutenant and me go out; the lieutenant need not worry."

"Tell me, Soltau," said Jacob, when they were out in the open, "how can you be so pitiless as to chase a person out in this cold away from the little children? On other occasions I have seen you gentle and humane toward your comrades on the march."

"Pitiless, Lieutenant! Toward such a creature! If he could get a guilder for cutting all our throats, he would do it. If our sentinels weren't so watchful, there would already be a dozen Jews on the way to betray us to the Russians."

"But there are Jews who serve in the army as good Poles."

"Under arms—that's a different matter! Whoever kills Russians is my comrade, even if he were a Turk! An old soldier like me does not check baptism certificates. But if we didn't have these peddler-Jews in Poland, there would be that many fewer traitors."

"But then why don't you hang the damned spies as a scare and a warning!"

"We hang a couple every day, but they multiply like rats."

"Is it really only the Jews who are traitors?"

"No, God forbid, Lieutenant! Every such filthy peasant is a traitor; he hardly knows that a land called Poland exists. But every traitor we call a Jew."

"That's another matter!" cried Jacob, laughing. "In that case, lend me your bottle."

At that moment a shot rang out outside the town; in the dark night they could see the flash.

When they arrived at the spot where the shot had been fired, they found several cavalrymen gathered around a man lying writhing on the ground; they were threatening him and talking heatedly.

"What has happened? What's going on here?"

"Wait a moment, Lieutenant," said the corporal, bending over the man. "Just as I thought! Our host! On the way to Stoczek, aren't you, you miserable son of a cur, you damned Jewish traitor!"

The man lying on the ground wailed, "I am no Jew, I am no Jew, I am a Christian like you, I am your brother—*all man*

Schlemasol![1]—Oh, oh—My name is Michael Wucziewicz, the holy archangel Michael is my guardian angel, blessed be his name —*Mamzir ben hanido*[2] . . . oh, oh!" The Hebrew words he uttered in an undertone, so that to an uninitiated ear they sounded like whining.

"Ah, nonsense! What were you going to do in Stoczek? Confess, dog!"

"I only wanted to get some eggs for the distinguished gentleman who is quartered on me—*so sollt Ihr chaio hoben.*[3] Oh, oh!"

"Oh, you wanted to get eggs! Oh, is there no one who has a piece of rope?"

"I'll confess!" screamed the Pole, "I will tell you how many Russians there are in Stoczek, I know where General Geismar is. . . . Just let me live! Oi, *Schema Jisroel!*[4] Oh, oh, oh!"

"Hand me the rope!"

Jacob, who could hardly keep from laughing, partly at the cavalrymen who did not notice the curses, partly at the Pole who did not think anyone understood him, now intervened. "Take him to the colonel; maybe he can give important information. No, take the rope off his neck; you have already shot him—that's enough."

"That shot won't do him much harm, Lieutenant! He is only scratched a little; he fell from pure fear. But as you command; let's take him to the colonel."

Soon afterward the officers were summoned to the colonel and received orders to lead the troops quietly and cautiously against Stoczek.

"At two o'clock the general is coming here to Filipowko," he said in parting. "If only we could lead him as a guest into a conquered town!"

The officers hastened to their posts.

---

[1] "All my misfortune on you!"

[2] "The filthy son of a whore!"

[3] "So it certainly will go well with you!"

[4] Literally, "Hear, o Israel!" Here it means "Oh, God, it's all up!"

In the harsh, dark winter night the column noiselessly approached the enemy-occupied town.

Outside the outermost house lay a Russian sentinel frozen to death, a schnapps bottle at his side. His comrades were revelling noisily inside the house; their rifles stood stacked along the wall. With lowered bayonets the Polish soldiers forced their way into the house and overcame them without noise. Cut off and surrounded, the Russians were everywhere overwhelmed; only a couple of hundred men succeeded in grouping and in reaching a large barn, which they stubbornly defended until the Poles set fire to the building.

The colonel came riding up, his face expressing concern. "It's no good work that's been done here!" he said. "This fire can bring Geismar's entire corps down on our necks before the night is over. Have our guardposts pushed as far out in front as possible, so that the Russians won't overrun us like we did them."

At daybreak they heard noise and jubilation from the direction of Filipowko; it was Dwernicki's cavalry corps arriving; at the same time, on the other side of the town, the head of the Russian columns came into view, advancing to retake it.

It was that 18th of February; the first pitched battle for Poland's independence was fought.

Like an enormous snake the line of Russian columns wound toward the Poles and in the advance crushed the little troop holding the thicket and the hill on the other side of Stoczek. The artillery advanced onto the hill and opened fire; the infantry and the cavalry marched forward on both sides.

General Dwernicki halted in front of a squadron of lancers and observed the Russians. After a short deliberation he turned to his officers and issued orders to them.

The squadrons formed a line behind Dwernicki. He rode up to the front, halted a moment and surveyed the closed ranks, glittering with lances. Then he stretched out his hand and shouted, as he turned his snorting horse toward the enemy, "Poles! Lances at the ready! Forward!"

The trumpets screamed, and the earth rumbled as the cavalry swept forward.

Poland's eagle spread its wings and drank Russian blood.

II
LETTER FROM JACOB TO LEVY

Imagine a camp. In the middle are some tumble-down peasant houses—they represent palaces; in them live the general and his staff. Around these: dirty-grey tents (for only the heavens' clouds are our washwomen) and huts built of branches and earth. Among them swarm soldiers and horses; from countless holes in the ground rises smoke, for we cook like the small tent proprietors in "Dyrehaven" amusement park; Russian prisoners are led through the tent lanes, a spy is hanged on a dead tree, etc.

Then imagine that various small troops are sent out to forage, and that one of them is commanded by Lieutenant von Bendixen. They encounter an enemy troop; the corporal asks Mr. von Bendixen whether they should attack—yes, here there are people who ask my advice, just as in Copenhagen I used to ask yours! Such a foraging expedition is to blame for your getting this letter. We had come near a rather large (by Polish standards) farm, and were happily riding toward it, when we discovered that Russians were already occupying it. My corporal rides over to me and asks, "Does the lieutenant command us to turn back or attack them? " That was only a formality; I could see in the old man's face that he was considering no other possibility than an assault. Besides, the Russians had already spotted us and were riding at us—so that it was not exactly a great heroic act on my part that I ordered a charge. Now began one of those skirmishes which are the most interesting—for a spectator, that is. Jews are quite right when they say, "*Für'n Zuschauer ist kein Spiel zu gross* [For a spectator, no game is too big]." So we attack, and after a moment I find myself between two Russian cavalrymen. The thrust of one, which was very well-intentioned, I parried and riposted, so that His Majesty the Absolute Ruler now has one less Russian to absolutely rule over; but at the same moment the other one slashed me over the wrist, so that I dropped the reins. Now I could not wheel my horse around, and my head quietly prepared itself to be split; I think I wanted to think about all of you at home, but everything went around in my head. However, just as my opponent raises his arm, he receives a pistol shot in the breast. At the first moment he looked as though he had been surprised by something or other, at the next, he pitched off his horse. The Russians were then put to flight, and after we had killed a couple of dozen men and ourselves had lost a dozen, we were lords over as much straw as one can buy in Copenhagen for five rix-dollars. This we took home in triumph, and everybody praised our heroic exploit. I calculate that my share of the booty amounts to as much straw as a little Copenhagen family buys for their beds on moving day, and for this I have been promoted to first lieutenant. However, I must remain at home in the camp for a while. And so for that reason I can grind out a long letter.

You can undoubtedly notice that I now feel differently than when I wrote you from Algiers. You could, I am sure, read between the lines remorse and regret that I had left home—it almost could not be otherwise, for that was my thought day and night. I felt that my mind might have been a stagnant pool just as well in Denmark as abroad, and there I would not have been plagued by painful remorse, by torturous longing, by suffocating, consuming uncertainty. If I was tormented by ill will and contempt in my fiancée's family there, in Algiers I was subjected to similar persecution among the French officers, and I could not even enjoy the little consolation that I would have had at home in a good bed and with a good meal.

Here it is different! A completely new life has opened up for me. Here it is as if I had become involved in all of humanity; I am allowed to take part in a struggle for a great and just cause, and I am judged according to my deeds. To be sure, I am fighting with my visor down, like Ivanhoe at the great tournament, but when I do raise my visor and they see the disinherited, exiled race's countenance, they will certainly not deny me the battle prize. . . . However, it must after all be strange for you to read newspaper reports from Poland: it's me in the lines; I am a part of the great battles you marvel over.

The only thing I might have against life here is the fact that one almost ceases to live as oneself and becomes a part of the mass, without a will of one's own. But then there are other moments when life is like an ocean and one imagines oneself a swimmer who sees no barrier to his aspirations; all his powers frolic in the wildest jubilation, the soul almost flies into a frenzy of ecstasy over its freedom.

And then, too, I have the firm belief that I will not die here. In the first battle in which I took part I suddenly saw the *kever ovos*[5] in Copenhagen quite clearly. Since that time I am convinced that my grave will be dug there, and since they will scarcely embalm me and send me there if I fall here, it is absolutely necessary that I must get myself home alive.

When I come home then, I will, I'm sure, also be worthy of *her*. Oh, I have not forgotten her! When it is still around me, especially at night, their little parlor suddenly appears before me, and I see her sitting there, and it is as if my body is being drawn home, and I am almost beside myself, I cannot comprehend how I could leave. There are times when it seems to me that, even if she were not true to me, I could console myself with Poland's happiness, with having taken part in the great struggle; but at other times, when my comrades are looking to the future with anxious eyes, I console myself secretly with the thought of her, although at the next moment I regret that I allow myself that egoistic consolation. But nevertheless I am happy; I have two beautiful hopes to rejoice at, and the poor Poles have only one: the hope for their poor fatherland.

My dear Levy, I am often seized by an ominous foreboding on account of your long silence. She obviously ought to write to me; she is innocent—I believe that! I know that! But it would be unmanly of me if I wrote time after time, like a beggar. However, I console myself with the thought that her letters most likely have not reached me—God grant that it is true!

So, here is the surgeon! He will insist that my arm be amputated. He is a tall, thin German who really is a barber, but who here functions as a *doctor medicinae & chirurgiae*, and he has a grudge against me because I know more about the wound than he does. He says that since I am such a good surgeon, I should have stayed at home—yes, if only I had had him there to amputate the parson's wife, no matter how badly he might have

---

[5] Cemetery.

done it! Well, she will undoubtedly grow to have respect for a first lieutenant in the Polish national army! And just let me get a letter from Thora—if I am then not a captain within twenty-four hours, you may call me . . . a Russian. If I then come home as a captain, in the resplendent uniform (if I manage to get one made, that is to say), won't I then blot out the Jew Bendixen, so that nobody sees him?

III

A DARK CLOUD

Several months later the army was positioned in an entrenched camp on the Austrian border. Dwernicki had granted his soldiers several days' rest, after having long been hounded by a superior Russian force. An oppressive stillness reigned in the camp; only the commanding officer's mind moved with its former restlessness, calculating precisely its position, like the seaman guiding his ship through breakers and storm.

In front of the tent two officers were pacing back and forth in deep conversation—Jacob and Josinski.

Jacob was saying, "How glad I am to see you again, Josinski! What a stroke of luck that you were the one selected to bring us dispatches! And you have been promoted to major—I congratulate you with all my heart!"

"I cannot rejoice over my own good fortune when I think of my fatherland," said Josinski sadly.

"Your fatherland . . . Poland? What danger has come up? Haven't you repulsed the enemy from Warsaw in the great battles on the right side of the river, while we have swept the left side as clean as a living-room floor? Isn't all of Poland in revolt all the way from the Russian border to Austrian Galicia and Prussian Poland? Aren't there thousands of peasants here in Volhynia, ready to join forces with us? Just because we are a little squeezed here by the superior force, must one immediately lose courage? I'm sure old Dwernicki will hit upon a way out!"

"Oh, you don't know, my dear Bendixen, how matters stand! What does it help that we have been victorious at Grochow, at Wavre, and at Dembe, or that we have routed the Emperor's Guard and chopped down both his 'Lions of Warna' and his 'invincible' cuirassiers? What does all that beautiful enthusiasm help, that I was so happy about—like when we were pursuing the enemy after the battle of Dembe, and suddenly saw that there were Poles already after him; it was the inhabitants of Dobre who had marched out under the command of their mayor—that regiments made up almost of children rout the Russian veterans—that the Russians retreat as soon as they see the fourth regiment of the line advance with fixed bayonets— what's the use, what has that helped us? Skrzynecki stands still after his victory, so that one might think he had been defeated. Instead of throwing himself at the scattered, beaten, terrified Russians, cutting them down, taking them prisoner, clearing all Poland—instead of this, he is holding himself inexplicably at rest and permitting them to regroup and giving the emperor time to reinforce them with new masses. It almost looks as though he has become frightened himself, because he has been so daring as to strike the colossus so that it totters. Now he is allowing Dwernicki here to be pursued and cut up; Poland will lose six thousand of its best fighters because Skrzynecki is not stirring with his large army, which is burning with eagerness for battle. Oh, sometimes I am on the point of going raving mad from impatience! It is a good thing for me that I was sent away; for I could have killed Skrzynecki, my general. . . ."

"But is the situation here so desperate?"

"With thirty thousand Russians between us and our brothers! In a position which to be sure is almost impregnable, but with the Austrian border at our backs. Yet again the Poles are relying on Austria, although for this they have twice had to pay so dearly! Suppose that the Austrians open their borders to Rüdiger and let him attack us from the rear, maybe even help him! Persecuted Poland can expect anything."

Josinski was summoned to the general, and Jacob walked thoughtfully to his tent.

The 27th of April 1831 was the day the Russian general Rüdiger entered neutral territory and fell upon Dwernicki from the rear—when Dwernicki placed his trust in the Austrians, who disarmed his army and handed its weapons and the cannons it had victoriously conquered over to the Russians.

It was eleven o'clock in the morning, the attack had begun, the Russian cavalry had crossed the border, and the little Polish army was hard-pressed from all sides. Then Dwernicki decided on a sudden turn to fight his way through to neutral territory. Several squadrons were ordered to make a desperate assault to engage the enemy and cover the retreat.

There was a moment's stillness during the preparations; the squadrons assembled facing the advancing enemy masses. At such a moment thoughts move with supernatural speed; memories from the past, notions of the future flash by with blinding speed, but still very clear and definite.

"As a child I read omens," said Jacob to himself as the threatening majesty of the scene appeared before him. "From the snuff of a candle I prophesied playthings for myself, from the costume of a passer-by I foretold my happiness as I was going to Thora's father; now I will prophesy the lesser from the greater: if all goes well today, then I'll receive a letter—"

Trumpets sounded, spurs bored into horses' sides, the cavalrymen raised the Polish war cry one more time, and like a hailstorm they threw themselves at the Russians. The first ranks were overthrown, killed, ridden down; the entire mass bent like a grainfield under a storm.

From the other side were heard Russian commands; a tightly massed cavalry band trotted forward, clattering, and fell upon the Poles. The ranks disintegrated; a confused, desperate hand-to-hand combat began; the little Polish army swirled about as if caught in a maelstrom.

Jacob saw an enemy lance bore into Soltau's breast; one more time the Pole raised himself in his saddle, his eyes seeking the Russian with an expression of mortal enmity, but before his blow could fall he sank from his horse under countless thrusts.

Now Jacob saw nothing more. Curses, groans, saber thrusts, pistol shots resounded around him; mechanically he parried and returned thrusts, until he found himself beside Josinski in the Russians' rear and, following Josinski's example, spurred his horse into a wild gallop.

The horses dropped, but there was no Russian to be seen. They were saved, they were in Poland, while their surviving comrades would have to listen to Poland's struggle from Austrian prisons.

IV
MICHAEL WUCZIEWICZ

In constant peril, they marched on in a land overrun by Russians. Sometimes they found shelter with Polish peasants, who shared with them the few provisions which the plundering enemy had left; at other times they had to spend days and nights in the woods and in impassable regions, without other food than roots which they dug up out of the ground.

One night when they had bedded down on the damp ground and were vainly trying to fall asleep, Josinski said, "If this were another struggle and other enemies, I would let myself be taken prisoner. The bravest man surrenders to hunger. But to the Russians I will never surrender alive. I am only sorry for you."

"You shouldn't worry about me, Josinski!" answered Jacob. "I am enduring the sufferings and deprivations that I must undergo here with a kind of joy. I regard the whole thing as a decree of fate, as a purgatory through which I must pass in order to atone for former times of my life, and in order for me to become worthy of happiness. If only you didn't have to share the purgatory with me!"

"You are certainly a strangely good comrade," said Josinski, pressing his hand.

"It is actually nothing but egoism," said Jacob. "I have hopes of compensation for the sufferings we are both undergoing. Sometimes, when I lose myself in thoughts about my own situation, the mad delusion comes over me that everything that is happening here in Poland is happening only for my sake, so that I could come out and become a human being and avoid becoming moth-eaten. With the help of my medical skills, I see myself in a position to inform you that the brain sometimes hatches out such visions and delusions when it is weakened by too much fasting."

"Your joking tone almost dispels my hunger—listen, it is really cowardly to lie here and torment ourselves! Let's get out of the woods where we can. If we encounter Russians, then we will fall with weapons in hand—then it's at least over instantly."

"As you like, Josinski. Fate is perhaps speaking out of your mouth, as out of the Pythian priestess when she, fasting, sat on the tripod."

They went through the wood, and when they reached the edge, they could survey the region for some distance around. The moon was low and a part of the wood cast its shadow toward a solitary hut. At a distance of several hundred paces to the left lay a village, where they could see soldiers walking around; a little to the right, in the full moonlight, marched a Russian patrol.

Jacob clutched Josinski's arm. "I know this place! Here you must entrust yourself to my guidance!"

They stole through the shadows and opened the door to the hut, at the same moment that the patrol approached the place in the wood that they had just left.

Both involuntarily cast a grateful glance toward heaven.

When their gaze at the next moment traveled from the gentle, dawning sky to the interior of the hut, Josinski laid his hand on his saber.

The room was almost dark. In a corner, on a low, rough table, stood a little lamp casting its weak, uncertain light over a man sitting in a half-upright, bent-over position, as if ready to spring. His eyes flashed through the semi-darkness, playing upon the arrivals alternately, as if he were weighing which he should fly at first. His black caftan was rent at the breast, and at his side were visible some strange pieces of food: two eggs and a loaf sprinkled with ashes.

Jacob stayed Josinski's hand and stepped forward into the room, pronouncing the Jewish greeting "*Scholom aleichem!*"[6]

The Pole gave a start; his eyes protruded from their sockets to pierce the darkness and see Jacob's face. Then he cried, "Who comes here disguised in a Polish military uniform, to a loyal Russian? You are traitors! You must die!"

---

[6] "Peace be with you!"

"I am a Jew like you. Stand up, son of the Jewish nation, and help your brother!"

"Go away, traitor! I am not a Jew! My name is Michael Wucziewicz! The holy archangel Michael is my guardian angel."

"Will you take this word on your tongue while you are sitting *schivvo*,[7] perhaps over a beloved child; while the lamp of death burns and *mal'ch hamoves*[8] perhaps still hovers over your house? Why don't you at least add *mamzir ben hanido*! like when you were lying here outside?"

The Pole had leaped up; he laid his hands on Jacob's shoulders, staring him in the face, and cried, "Answer me! *Welch Sedre geiht Schabbas?*"[9]

"*Eikef!*"[10] replied Jacob after some reflection, while the Pole looked at him with tense expectation.

"Enough, you are a Jew! *Boruch habo bescheim Adonoi!*[11] Praise be to the God of Israel! A son of His people steps over my threshold and calls me brother! I have lain before the door of the *Schul*, and no one would tread on me; I have bared my back, and no one would beat me;[12] God's holy book has been closed to me; my children were buried, and I could not say *Kaddish* over them! I have been a *kelef mezoro*.[13] Say what you demand of me, *Du gebenschter bar Jisroel!*"[14]

"First, something to eat!"

---

[7] The terrible ceremony of the Jews, lasting seven days; mourning over a deceased. The clothing is torn, the mourner must not undertake any work, nor sit among other people, nor say "good day" or "good-by," etc.

[8] The King of Death, the angel of death.

[9] "Which portion of the Law are the Jews reading on Saturday?"

[10] The Seder (section) beginning with the word *Eikef, Ekef*.

[11] "Blessed be he who comes in the Lord's name."

[12] That is, when he, after being baptized (see the following), wanted to do penance and be taken back among Jews, and the latter did not dare to accept the penance.

[13] A mangy dog.

[14] "You blessed son of Israel."

"*Rachmin Schadai!*"[15] cried the Pole, bringing out some bread. "I wish to God that I had something better to offer you! Is he also a Jew?" he asked, when Jacob shared the bread with Josinski.

"No, but I want to ask you to guide him along with me to Warsaw."

The Pole's face darkened, and he said, "A *goy* has come in during my *Schivvo!* I will cast him out so that his fate can be fulfilled and he can become a *kelef mesz*."[16]

"Then I will go with him!" cried Jacob, placing himself in the Pole's way. "If he must die, then I will die with him! May the blood be on your head!"

"But with what oath shall I bind his tongue, that he will not betray what he will learn?" said the Pole in an abject tone.

"He will give his word of honor."

"A pretty *maschkon!*[17] No, will you assure me by His name, which is not uttered, by the *Jehudim Melech*,[18] that I can trust this *goy?*"

"I will!"

"So be it!" said the Pole with a sigh, going to a concealed trapdoor and from a recess pulling forth two human corpses. "Help me take the clothes off these!" he said.

"Russians!" they both cried, when they saw the uniforms by the light of the lamp.

"Yes, Russians!" screamed the Pole with almost insane gestures. "Yes, I am making war, too! On my own! My children, my three innocent little ones, the Russians impaled when they came back after you had defeated them at Stoczek. But they pay gold, and I serve them! Ha, ha, ha! I serve them!"

"But the Poles also pay gold, don't they?" said Josinski.

"Ha, ha, ha! I serve the Poles, too! The *starost* [governor] wanted my wife. He forced me to be baptized—his servants

---

[15] "Merciful God!"

[16] A dead dog.

[17] Security.

[18] King of the Jews.

dragged me to the church. *Der Gallach*[19] gave me the name of
Michael Wucziewicz, and the holy archangel Michael became
my guardian angel. And when I was baptized, the *starost* said
that now I could not be married to a Jewish wife, and so he took
my wife. She is at the castle with the *starost*, and my children
are killed by the Russians! Ha, ha, ha! Blessed be this war!"

He sprang over to the low chair beside the lamp of death and
the ashes-sprinkled bread, sat down in a crumpled position, and
mumbled Hebrew prayers, moving his body violently back and
forth.

After a long time had passed, Jacob said gently to him, "*Seid
mochel, Rabbi!*[20] It is written: *Oneis potur miklum.*[21] The day is
dawning."

The Pole stared at him as if he did not know him, but he
pulled himself together, stood up, and ordered them to put on the
Russian uniforms. When this was done, he asked if one of them
knew Russian, and when Josinski answered in the affirmative,
he instructed him to tell any Russians who might come during
his absence that Michael had been summoned to the general. "I
am now going to the general"; he added, "I will be back soon."

"To the Russian general?" cried Josinski.

"Am I supposed to go with you without a pass?"

When he was gone, Josinski said, "Maybe he is going to get
the Russians."

"Oh, no, don't worry! Let's rest a while; I am tired."

It was almost daylight when the Pole returned; he shared
some provisions with them, and when the meal was over, he
ordered them to follow him. But at the moment that they stood
in the doorway and the weak light of morning fell on Josinski's
face, the Pole suddenly sprang at him and shouted, "No, no! He
must not leave this place alive before he has knelt before me and I
have placed my foot on his neck."

Josinski turned with a smile to Jacob.

---

[19] The Christian priest.

[20] "Forgive, Master!"

[21] "In distress one may transgress the ceremonies," or "Distress breaks all laws."

"That he will not do!" said Jacob. "He is a Polish warrior."

"Then he must die!" screamed the Pole.

"*Rabbi!* You will not permit my blood to be spilled. But I will loyally go with my comrade. You must save him!"

"What am I to do!" wailed the Pole. "I have laid my hand on my murdered children, and I have sworn *chajei roschi*[22] that no Christian who comes in my power shall step over my threshold before I have trodden him into the dust."

"It is written: When it is a question of a brother's life, one is *mattur*."[23]

"Then God will forgive me," said the Pole hesitantly, going to the door.

"Stop!" cried Jacob, seizing him by the arm. "Evil thoughts may come on the way, and you might kill him. Don't leave here until you have given him *sholom*."[24]

The Pole struggled briefly with himself, then extended his hand to Josinski and said, "*Sholom!*" and with a heavy sigh went ahead of them out of the hut.

After they had walked silently for a long time, Jacob turned with an embarrassed expression to Josinski and said, "Josinski, now you have gotten to know what I would gladly have hidden— that I am a Jew."

"That I have known already for a long time," answered Josinski.

"How could you know that?" cried Jacob in surprise.

"I suspected it already in Algeria, and later I found out for certain by precisely the care with which you tried to hide your interest in Jews. But what does it matter!" he continued, seizing Jacob's hand. "The whole difference between us is that I believe that the Messiah has already come, and you, on the other hand, that he is to come—I would be happy if I myself could believe that Poland's Messiah will come. I am eager to learn something about how matters stand, and still I dread what I will learn."

---

[22] "By the life of my head."

[23] Released from his word.

[24] Peace.

He hastened his steps to overtake the Pole who was striding on ahead, and said to him, "My friend, what news is there from Warsaw and the Polish commander-in-chief?"

The Pole said nothing, and Josinski repeated his question; but when the Pole continued on his way without replying, Josinksi turned to Jacob and said, "I think he hates me because he has been forced to save me; you speak to him."

Jacob addressed the Pole: "Why won't you answer my friend's question?"

"Answer him? Why doesn't he call me by my name? 'My friend'! His friend! I am not his friend! If someone speaks to me, my name is Rabbi Chivo."

"Rabbi Chivo! Will you tell me whether you know where the Polish commander-in-chief's position is now?"

"Yes, at Prague."

"At Prague!" cried Jacob and Josinski at the same time. "Has he then been defeated?"

"Yes, at Ostrolenka."

"My God! My God!" said Josinski. "Ask him whether he knows anything about the uprising in Podolia, Lithuania, Volhynia."

"Put down, dispersed!" the Pole replied to Jacob's question.

Josinski clasped his hands and sighed convulsively. But within Jacob there arose a burning indignation over the malice with which the Pole spoke of Poland's misfortune; he seized Josinski's arm and let the Pole go on ahead.

"Ask him what kind of general he went to, in the village," said Josinski a little later, and to indulge his friend Jacob forced himself to approach Rabbi Chivo once again.

"It was the commander-in-chief," replied the latter.

"The commander-in-chief! Diebitsch himself?"

"Diebitsch? He died of the plague! It was Paschkewitz Eriwansky! . . . Listen," he went on, pulling Jacob close, "what do you want in Warsaw? I tell you, misfortune is hovering over the whole city. Go over to the Russians! The Russians' eagle is strong, and its talons are gilded."

Jacob turned from him without answering.

"Try to find out more from him," whispered Josinski.

But the Pole knew no more or would say nothing. Several times he looked in Jacob's direction as if he had something on his mind, but each time he turned away again with a shake of his head.

V

BENJAMIN. THE FALL OF WARSAW

Several days after his return, Jacob was summoned to a meeting with the chief of police.

"I have had you summoned," said the latter, "only so that you can furnish an explanation concerning a man who has been arrested as a spy. He maintains that he knows you and has traveled here only to seek you. We thought for a time that he knew you were dead, and for that reason offered this evasion. But since you have now returned, you may as well go and see the fellow before he is hanged."

"What is the man's name?" asked Jacob.

"It's a Jew; he calls himself Benjamin."

"Oh, General! He is innocent!" cried Jacob, jumping to his feet. "For God's sake let me hurry so as not to be too late."

Jacob flew to the prison.

In a damp room Benjamin was lying on straw, pale and emaciated, his teeth chattering in a fever.

"My poor, dear Benjamin!" cried Jacob, throwing himself over him, pressing him to his breast, and kissing him. "You, here! In this dreadful place! Poor, poor Benjamin!"

Benjamin looked at him with a wan smile, clutched his hand, and kissed it.

The prison guard motioned Jacob aside and whispered to him, "Don't touch him; he surely has cholera."

"Not touch him!" cried Jacob with tears in his eyes, "He must come home with me! I will immediately make arrangements so that he can be released."

In the evening, when Benjamin had awakened from a short sleep and in a weak voice was asking Jacob innumerable questions and himself interrupting him to tell of his trip and his imprisonment, Jacob said, "Don't you have with you any letter or message at all for me, Benjamin? Didn't you save anything at all when they robbed you?"

Amid his pain, Benjamin smiled slyly and asked Jacob to take one of his shoes and cut it open. "I hid a letter there from your friend Levy. He said that I must take good care of it. It was a true *masol*[25] that I thought of hiding it so well. *Die wurden gut ge-uhst!*"[26]

With trembling hands Jacob cut the shoe open and extracted a letter. It read as follows:

> The peaceable Levy sends the warrior Bendixen his greeting.
>
> You are really not worth a reasonable person's writing to you, for it is, after all, unknown whether you will receive the letter alive. However, for the moment I will assume that you are alive, and inform you what I put up with and endure for your sake.
>
> For a long time I prayed every evening: Dear God, don't let Jacob Bendixen be shot today by an Arab, Bedouin, Kabyle, or the like. Yes, I did that and felt really relieved thereby. But now I receive a letter from which it appears that already in December of last year you were going to leave Algeria for Poland, and while I was making you safe from the Kabyles, etc., you were exposed to Cossack lances. Now you have perhaps proceeded to Java, Abyssinia, or Guinea, and are being shot at by poisoned arrows, while I work and slave to keep the Cossacks away from you. I won't put up with it any longer. If I am to deliver up prayers for you, then give me your whole itinerary with date and hour for each place, so that I can keep an eye on you or at least know where I should enquire after you if you have sometime, as it says in the newspaper, absented yourself from your residence and have not subsequently announced yourself.
>
> I am writing this with a man who undoubtedly will ferret you out wherever you are. He came up to my place and said that he had come a long way, to wit, from Funen, to learn where you were, and now he was going to go the rest of the way to find you. I said to him, "Benjamin! Will

---

[25] A real stroke of luck.

[26] "They were well fooled (i.e., the robbers)."

you also go crazy? But that is *Chat gaddjo!*[27] Don't you think that the vagabond can be killed without your seeing it?" He replied, "*Losz mir menucho!*"[28] When I told him you were in Poland, he was happy: "Rabbi Nathan Fürth lives there! He ate dinner one *Schabbas* at Rabbi Philip's; he has probably taken care of the lad." But when Benjamin learned that he had to travel by sea, and I was out with him to negotiate to get him on board with a Danzig skipper, he almost lost the desire; he looked at the water and asked if he couldn't travel by land. But when I told him that he would in any case have to cross some water and that the land trip would be protracted, he mumbled, "*In Gottes Nomen!*" and went home and packed. He bought an orange for you, and I think he speculated about taking a piece of kosher meat along, for he said, "The poor lad was accustomed to having the best in his father's house; it must be difficult for him to eat military food."

What do you think—if you had stayed home and had lived quietly and calmly with this Benjamin and me and a couple of other good friends, gotten yourself a card game from time to time, on Saturdays eaten your *Scholunt*, even if it had been cooked on a pig[29]—do you think that Thora Fangel would have married Lieutenant Engberg any more quickly for that?

Now listen, Bendixen, these words are, to be sure, the principal matter in this letter, and I have the obligation to give you an accurate report. It is a bitter spoonful you must now take—think a little about the hand that is giving it to you.

Some time after you had left, Wholesaler Fangel came up to visit me. I will reproduce our conversation for you as accurately as possible. He said that he had asked his son if you had any reliable friend here in town, and his son had named me, and had been so courteous as to

---

[27] A merry Jewish song about a cat that ran after the kid and ate it, the stick beat the dog, the fire burned the stick, the water put out the fire, the ox drank the water, the butcher slew the ox, the angel of death slew the butcher; but then the Lord came and slew the angel of death.

[28] "Leave me alone."

[29] *Scholunt* is the Jewish Sabbath dish. Most love this dish; of anybody who has it prepared without observing the rest of the religious customs, the other Jews say mockingly that he sets (cooks) it on a pig.

recommend my character. That's what one gets from not getting mixed up with women and engagements. "Well," he said, "I wish to speak with you as men of honor can speak with each other: we have received a letter from Bendixen."

I suppose I showed my surprise, for he immediately added, "You probably don't know that; here it is—I ask you to read it."

Yes, indeed, it was in fact from you.

"It is an affectionate and upright letter," said the old wholesaler, "and it has raised questions which under the present circumstances urgently demand a quite different seriousness than before. He writes: 'Don't you really believe that there is a common divinity in which we can live?' I have until now believed that, because I am no friend of the clergy, and because I have regarded Bendixen as an honorable and uncorrupted character, with whom my child could be happy. I still believe everything good about him, but. . . ."

Oy weih![30] I thought, now there has come a "but."

". . . But how are they to be able to live happily together with his over-sensitive nature, with the sympathies he has, and which he cannot stand to be touched? He speaks of childhood differences; but what if they now got married and had children and these children's upbringing were different from his? And if the two people are to live together, how then is their life together to be truly good and intimate, when his memories go one way and hers another, and there is enmity where they meet? God knows I would let her go to France with her husband, but in France will he and she not think and feel differently than here at home? Their memories will only become stronger, and yearning will then make her just as sensitive, as far as her past is concerned, as he already is now. I cannot help it, but I think I can see them sitting, one winter evening, around the fire and turning their backs on each other, both disheartened, even unhappy. Will you read the closing of his letter? He blesses my Thora, and may God reward him for his love, but even the blessing seems to have a completely different significance for him than for us. Don't take it amiss, Mr. Levy, but it seems to

---

[30] Alas!

me that these words don't have power until they are spoken in Hebrew. What do you say, Mr. Levy?"

"Wholesaler," I answered, "I was against the love affair and the engagement from the very first, naturally not because I had anything to say against your daughter, but because I did not think that anything good could come of that kind of relationship. When it happened, I tried to have as good an effect as possible; but when the misunderstanding happened anyway, I wished for a quick break. But now I hesitate again, for now Bendixen has made a great effort, he is hopping about out in the world and I dare say is shaking a great deal of dust off himself, and he takes this very much to heart, and it is a matter of his salvation, and if your daughter will some day go with him to France . . ."

"Yes, if she will! If she would! But will she? When we got the letter, there was a lot of weeping at home. I have a sister-in-law who is no friend of Bendixen's, and even she was quite moved for a moment, but indeed said immediately afterward: 'All's well that ends well.' I told my daughter that she should think it over well, and that I didn't want to hear her answer until three days later but that then it was to be definite. On the day it was to be settled, they went to communion, and when my Thora came home and I asked her, she cried, and I didn't get a sensible word out of her. I gave her the choice, and she didn't choose. But now, a week later, her aunt brings me her engagement ring—here it is . . . Will you accept this ring?"

I was somewhat surprised at the speedy solution of the problem, although I should have thought of it at once. But I collected myself; I was after all your second, and I have, to be sure, read about how seconds ought to behave in a duel. I bowed very courteously and coldly and accepted the ring. You can be quite at ease; they did not notice any emotion on our part.

When the old wholesaler was finished with his diplomatic mission, I could see by his face that his heart was heavy, and that he would like to say some kind words. But he would have regretted this weakness when he had gone out the door, and therefore I helped him to a nice, polite parting.

And now to make a long story short, her wedding to Lieutenant Engberg is taking place just now.

Yes, my friend, you can now come home without worrying. I do think that you are reasonable and won't disgrace me, after I have helped so much with your education and watched over your dignity while you are away, by going and making yourself ridiculous and, for example, shooting yourself. Bear in mind that it is no act of heroism, when one has so many guns to choose among. If you are bound and determined to do away with yourself, I only ask that you have so much regard for my good name and reputation as your friend, advisor, and *pro tempore* agent that you do it with propriety. Let some time pass, so that people can see that you have not done it rashly and later regretted it; if you then deliberately and advisedly proceed to the deed, fix for a moment your thoughts on the green room at the maternity hospital, where Gröndal and I are sitting contentedly, smoking our pipes while you are taking your own life; see also for a moment in your thoughts your mother's and your father's graves which are standing forsaken on *Johrzeit*,[31] and then you can, in God's name, go to hell!

I get really angry while I think that you might behave like a child. If I were only with you for a moment, I would give you such a scolding! It is best that this letter rests a little while I stuff a pipe and let my anger settle.

What happened with the marriage I don't really know; the wholesaler was not completely frank with me, and I could not demand that of him, either. Since you left, Wilhelm Fangel has been absolutely *broiges*[32]—that's what I get from associating with you. König told me that his sister heard that a serving girl had eavesdropped and heard the row between you and Engberg. There was gossip, the wholesaler heard something about it, and the match was called off. Right after a broken engagement a young girl is easier to get into a new engagement, than if some time passes. That is now my theory.

This is damned unpleasant, I know very well. You have, I suppose, been there fighting before Warsaw as if it were a holy city containing your Dulcinea, and now you see that you have been fighting like a Don Qui—yes, there's probably no point in my writing out the name

---

[31] The anniversary of a relative's funeral, when one goes out and prays at the grave.

[32] Sullen, angry.

completely. But now the worst is over, the operation has taken place, the wound will heal quickly if it is properly treated. To distract yourself you can, of course, travel a little around in peaceable countries; that is the best medicine against love. From what I have seen of love, damned if it is to be compared with anything other than the disease called, in colloquial speech, hiccups. If the patient's attention can be distracted from hiccupping, it will pass.

Take a little pleasure trip and then come home and show them that you are not too downhearted. Benjamin said immediately, when I told him the story, "That's good! Rabbi Hirsch in Middelfart has a daughter; she has a lot of money, and she is not married." Come home, Jacob Bendixen! Will you give the parson's wife the satisfaction of being able to say that she has gotten you killed or maimed? Put on a sarcastic face the first time you meet them on the street, or in a friendly manner go over and congratulate them—do what you like, but just be reasonable and let the Pole beat the Russian or the Russian beat the Pole—what the hell does that concern you, really? Even if the Russians take Warsaw, you can still very well become *Doctor medicinae & chirugiae* and in time get a tremendous practice.

Now that's all I know. If this dosage does not help, then you are not worth wasting a prescription on. In that case, I remain with unutterable contempt

Your former friend
Martin Levy,
Cand. chir. & med.

Jacob had risen; he leaned his forehead against the window and stared out with an unthinking gaze. It was toward the close of summer. The evening was dark, but the skies clear; the stars looked down from the sky like still, serious eyes; the houses stretched like living beings toward the sky, as if yearning to draw breath.

A red glow blazed up suddenly, coloring the roofs of the neighboring houses, wild screams resounded in the adjacent streets: "Down with the traitors!" and there ensued howls and jubilation; loud hoofbeats like advancing cavalry, shouted attack orders, shots, piteous screams; a sudden stillness and thereafter again wild, howling din. In final desperation the deceived Poles were tearing each other to pieces.

Everything went past Jacob's consciousness like misty images.

Finally it became absolutely still.

He came to himself hearing his own name uttered moaningly in the room. When he approached Benjamin's bed, he saw that the latter was blue in the face and was fumbling about with his hands. "*Seid Ihr do?*" moaned the dying man. "I want to say something . . . It is Jacob, a son of Rabbi Pfeives . . . *soll't ich ihn nit kennen? . . . My wife has borne a son . . . Masoltov, sog' ich . . . Jette, sie wor so schön . . . Do ist der Mal'ch hamoves!*[33] *Do kommt Er! . . . Weih, weih! Wo sind die guten Jehudim, die do sogen die Widdo?*[34] . . . *Oschamti, bogadti, gosalti, tofalti scheiker*[35] . . . *Do ist sie, do ist Jette! . . . Ja Jette!*[36] . . . *Jainkef! Ben Rabbi Pfeives!*[37] *Eur' Mutter stirbt vor Eimo*[38] *für Euch . . . Sie meimisen*[39] *Euch . . . Oh, Schema Jisroel! . . .*"

Benjamin was dead.

Jacob sank down before the corpse. He tried to weep, but his burning eyes remained dry . . .

"The Russians are here!" shouted an officer, bursting into the room.

Jacob started up, seized his weapons, and hurried to Wola.

"There is no danger yet!" said Josinski with blazing eyes, when he, busily bustling about, met Jacob. "In a few hours it will break loose. Put your ear against the breastwork, and you can hear the cannons rumbling far off. But they will attack these

---

[33] "There is the angel of death."

[34] "Alas, alas! Where are the holy Jews who recite to the dying the confession?"

[35] Words of the confession: "I have sinned, I have acted faithlessly, I have stolen, I have lied."

[36] "Yes, Jette."

[37] "Jacob, son of Rabbi Philip!"

[38] Fear.

[39] "They will kill you."

fortifications and these defenders in vain! And when they are exhausted by the battle and want to withdraw, tomorrow will come the twenty thousand fresh Polish troops under Ramorino, who will cut them to pieces. Now we have them! Now Poland will be victorious!"

Josinski went off after having given him a warm handshake. Jacob said to himself, "It would have been a pity to tell him that I have received a warning order. Let him keep his hope a few hours more."

He leaned against the breastwork and looked up at the sky, where the stars, one after another, paled and disappeared; in the east began a pale reddish glow, while the rest of the sky seemed to become darker, and strange round mist shapes floated in the air.

"You, God, up there!" he said, turning toward the red streak and stretching out his hand. "You, Lord over humans—if You exist! Now I tell You that if I get out of here alive, I will murder a person. Now I have told You!"

He felt a hand on his arm, and when he turned he saw Rabbi Chivo.

"*Kol Jisroel achim!*"[40] said the Pole with solemn earnestness.

"And what about it?" said Jacob.

"Go, away, brother, from this place! I tell you: He whom they call Ramorino is not coming. He is sent five days' march away. He will not come before Warsaw is taken."

"Rabbi Chivo!" said Jacob, "You have saved my life; now I will save yours—go!"

"Tomorrow it will be too late," said the Pole pleadingly, "I will seek you and find only your corpse. I tell you: This city must fall. It is like a sawed-through tree; they give a signal, and it topples. Go over to the Russians, if you must have war above everything!"

"Go away, Rabbi Chivo!" shouted Jacob, grasping his saber.

---

[40] "All Israel's children are brothers."

"Now, now, *kreisch nur nit!*"[41] said the Pole anxiously. "*Kommt heraus: ein Jed!*[42] But he was after all with me in *Schivven*," he muttered as he moved off.

A cannon shot gave the signal that the sixth of September had dawned over Warsaw.

Hundreds of fiery maws emit their thunder; works which men have erected as solidly as if for eternal monuments crash into rubble, but on the ruins stand the Polish defenders.

The enemy pushes closer; long salvos of rifle shots ring out; still closer to each other the mortal enemies advance, fighting with the terrible bayonet.

Once more the Polish eagle rises victorious; the Russians give way.

A bullet had struck Jacob's breast; he lay on the bloody ground and was a half-unconscious witness to the raging battle.

There was a lull in the fighting, and an order came for still more Poles to leave Wola and proceed to other points of the fortification. Josinski's regiment was among those who in obedience to the fatherland's trusted commanders followed the order and abandoned their brothers, whom they would never see again.

The thought that Josinski would leave him pierced Jacob's breast with such pain that he lost consciousness.

It seemed to him after a while that he saw Rabbi Chivo bending over him, with his head resting on his breast. Then he suddenly heard Soltau and the cavalrymen shouting, "You damned Jewish traitor! Is there somebody who has a rope?"—"I am no Jew!" wailed the Pole. "He is no Jew!" said Josinski's voice. "I beg your pardon, Jew!" said Lieutenant Engberg, running him through with a sword. "*Oy, Schema Jisroel!*" screamed Rabbi Chivo, clutching his breast, from which the blood gushed. Out of the wound flew Rabbi Chivo's soul like a horrible black serpent; it wound itself around him and swept him with dizzying speed through a limitless, dark space. Suddenly he crashed with a roar

---

41 "Only don't scream"; "Don't make noise."

42 I.e., "There you see what reward you have for doing a good deed to a Jew!" If it had been a Christian, the Pole would have said, "*Kommt heraus: ein Goi.*"

like that of a hundred cannons against a wall and at that he fell into a dreamless sleep. Only once did he seem to awaken and see Josinski weeping; then there was again a stabbing in his breast until he sank back unconscious.

Chapter 7

IN THE PRUSSIAN BORDER PROVINCE, on the Neisse, lies a village surrounded by low mountains. At one end of the village the mountains recede, forming a semicircle around a fruitful valley through which flows the river. Scattered isolated houses lie before the village in the entrance to the valley; if one looks down from the mountains toward the village, they, with their friendly surroundings, look like playing children who have run out ahead of the flock of adults.

In one of these houses, which belonged to a family of Polish descent, Josinski and Jacob had found refuge. As soon as Jacob's wound permitted, Josinski, in secret and surrounded by dangers, had set out with him to cross the closely watched border. But the trip and the inner anxiety had repeatedly cast Jacob back on his sick bed, and the year's most beautiful time had passed for the two friends in distress and suffering.

It was now late in the summer, and the time for their parting was approaching. The nearer it came, the more taciturn and almost gruff Josinski became; he seemed almost to be angry at Jacob because he was having to part from him.

The last evening, when their luggage lay packed on the table, among the weapons and travelling coats, every now and then he would go out to take a walk around, but each time he quickly returned and sat down silently by the window.

Finally he said, "You are also sitting the whole evening without saying a word; one would think we were two old women about to part."

"Josinski, I am thinking of the many hours we have spent together; who knows whether we will ever meet again."

"You can go with me, after all!"

"But you know very well what is drawing me home. Why don't you rather give in to me and go with me to Denmark? It is not yet too late to change your plan."

"What should I do in Denmark without any goal or aim?—No, I see very well that our paths are no longer the same; we have to part."

After a long silence, Josinski began again, "How well the place fits the time. Behind these dimly lit mountains everything lies in mysterious darkness, like the future. Among the dark masses only the brook moves, springing down over boulders, almost like a living being; now it is hidden in the dark, now it plays in the moon's ghostly light, as if a thought suddenly seized it, to be forgotten at the next moment. It is the never-slumbering memory of my fatherland."

He went on, "One doesn't know how strong he is. A year ago in Warsaw, when Poland still had a people, an army, and victory smiled on our arms, the mere thought of such a time as has come now would have seemed to me fatal. Now it is here, real, alive, and still I live, I eat and drink quite well, as if nothing had happened that might weaken the appetite.—Look, just now the brook sprang high up in the moonlight; it was like one of the shooting, stabbing thoughts of revenge."

"Revenge," said Jacob thoughtfully, "yes, if only by taking revenge one could alter what has already taken place, if only by killing a man one could also kill his deeds!"

Josinski turned and looked at him. "You did not have such second thoughts when you were lying in a fever mumbling the name of the man who stole your bride with such fervor that blood streamed out of the wound in your breast."

"That was perhaps precisely with the dreadful feeling that I cannot avenge myself and yet cannot give up revenge. It was the desperate longing that unconsciously felt how powerless it was. Yes, in the first moment! Then I could have hurled myself at him like a wild animal! But now later when I have imagined that he was in my power, and I went through all the possible ways in which I could cause him pain and myself become happy, I had to give them up one after the other, and had nothing left than the consolation that vengeance belongs to God."

"Being religious suits you well!" said Josinski sarcastically as he abruptly left the room.

Jacob remained sitting silently; after a time passed he went over to the table and picked up Josinski's saber as if to look at it. He bent closer and closer over it and finally pressed a kiss on it, so fleetingly and secretly as if he feared that someone might see it.

A little later Josinski came back; he seized Jacob's hand and said with tears in his eyes, "Forgive me, my dear Bendixen, that I am so fierce and unfriendly toward you. Just now I feel so depressed, I am bitter toward myself and the entire world. Before, when I went out, I am sure I said a word that wounded."

"Oh, no, Josinski! I will be frank with you; I confess that you were right. This religiousness is actually a hypocrisy that I carry on with the deity. I don't even know whether such a power exists, but it is after all possible, and I am afraid of offending it so that it becomes angry and robs me of the only thing and the last thing that I ask for in this world."

"My poor friend! Do you truly believe that by doing this you will get the deity to perform the miracle that she is still true to you?"

"I don't know, Josinski, but it does seem so natural to me . . . I cannot stand the thought that it might not be like that! You ought to have known her, you ought to have seen this lovely being! . . . I will love God and the whole world, if only she has kept her love for me; I will press any Christian to my breast and call him brother because she is a Christian girl. I gladden my soul by telling myself fairy tales about her, about how I come home and see her again. I have seen her standing at the altar with him; the minister opened the Holy Book and recited the prayers; she stood trembling; the minister asked, 'Will you take this man as your husband?' She moved her lips—then I suddenly stepped forward, and with a cry she threw herself into my arms—but this fairy tale is too unreasonable! . . . I have seen their home. She was sitting at his side at the tea table; he was reading in a newspaper and yawning; she was pale and thoughtful and was toying with a teaspoon. Then the maid came and announced that a foreign officer was outside and wanted to speak with the lieutenant. He went into his study, I stepped out to meet him and challenged him—now I was an officer! Then she dashed in and cried, 'Spare him, spare my child's father! If you want satisfaction, you shall have it. Here, in the presence of my husband, I tell you, my beloved, that I have loved only you and will love you eternally.' . . . Then I went away and offered up my life for a beautiful and holy Christian cause. Perhaps the Lord will then permit me to begin my life all over in another place; for I certainly see that it has here gotten off to a wrong start."

"This evening we will be merry!" cried Josinski. "I will make a festive bowl! Then we will drink until my horse is brought to the door. I will sing one more time the Polish song, and you will sing of happy love . . . maybe our hearts will break then, and we won't have to part."

"I cannot die yet," muttered Jacob.

They sat silent for a while. Josinski began again, "It is so difficult for me to part from you, Bendixen. With you I seem to lose for the first time my fatherland. I remember that as a child when I was sent from my father's estate in to the military school in Warsaw, I didn't begin to cry until the carriage drove home and left me behind, alone. And then it is as if I am also tormented by pangs of conscience because you have sacrificed a great part of your fortune, perhaps your entire fortune, for Poland's sake. It is the duty of the son to pay his deceased father's debts, so that at least he can lie with honor in his grave, but you know that I possess nothing."

"My dear Josinski, it is painful for me to hear you talk like that. Why will you also regard me as a foreigner? Besides, I am not poor; at home I still have means—my father was rich. It is not the worry about livelihood, either, that is the most difficult thing for us two."

"Now the day is dawning," said Josinski, turning to the window. "Now we can count the minutes we have left. I would gladly hold fast onto them, and yet I would wish that they were over.—Do one thing for me, my friend: let us ride together away from this place. On the way we will suddenly turn our horses each to one side; we will not turn around for several hours afterward; then it will be over."

Chapter 8

THE STEAMSHIP DROPPED ANCHOR, and boats came alongside to land the passengers.

On the steps of the customs house the one was met by wife and children, to the other a friend called a cheery welcome, a third was greeted by his servant, who with bustling care proceeded to seek out his baggage—only one walked through the crowd without being noticed and wandered in feverish excitement through the streets.

Now and then a weak ray of gladness flew through his soul at seeing again the familiar places, but at once his mind gave a start as if from fear of abandoning himself to happy feelings.

He stole past the Fangel house—now he saw it again! The blinds were pulled down, and he said with relief, "I thought so; they are at the country house. She is there, too. This evening!"

He turned about to visit Levy's residence, and he smiled as he imagined the latter's happy surprise.

Levy, he was told at the hospital, had long ago moved away and now lived at his old landlady's.

"Goodness, is it you, Doctor!" cried the old woman. "I didn't recognize you, you know, before you spoke. Please, come in and sit down. Why, how you have changed! You really look as though you have gotten ten years older, yes, indeed you do. Yes, young men," she added, admonishingly threatening him with her finger, "they live, when they go abroad, especially in Paris, where there are so many bad women, yes, indeed, there are."

"Tell me, my dear madam, where is Levy?"

"He has gone out for a walk, yes, indeed he has; I think he went with Mr. König. He came and got him, and you surely know how young men are. But he is such a nice man, the doctor, you must believe that. So I am truly sorry that he now must go abroad. . . ."

"Will Levy go abroad?"

"Yes, indeed he will that; he will go to Sweden to study cholera. Yes, young men! They find it easy to travel out into the world! There is nobody to look after them. . . . Will you go already, Doctor? Come back this evening, then Mr. Levy will definitely be home, quite definitely, he is such a nice man."

"No, I must go to the country this evening; but please tell him that I am staying at the *Hôtel du Nord.*"

"Ah, to the country! To visit good friends! Yes, that will indeed do you good! Yes, indeed, I will certainly tell Mr. Levy . . . Good-by, Doctor! Yes, now we will surely see you again from time to time. Bye-bye!"

"Maybe it is a good thing that I didn't meet him," he thought as he went out of the street door.—"And now!"—he put his hand on his heart as if to subdue the violent, anxious beating.

It was an evening in September. Over the sound the full moon rose, dark red, from behind a black layer of clouds; but little by little it became brighter, until it shone in its clear, yellow light and as it rose it drove a stratum of white clouds before it in an arc. The soft light shone upon the sea and the undulating beach and the fields, where the grain lay in swath or was placed in stacks. A deep stillness reigned over the whole countryside, no gust of wind moved the leaves of the trees, and from the beach there was only a faint sound of the water, like soft, shuffling footsteps.

The remote spot in the garden where Jacob was standing was reached at intermittent intervals by the sound of violins and flutes from the brightly lit country house.

"There's music; they are happy!" he said as he stood in trembling expectation. "Oh, now I remember, today is her birthday!—She used to come here often," he went on, "here I will wait for her, this evening and every evening, until chance or fate brings her here.—At this moment she is perhaps dancing—once she danced with me!—If I now quite calmly were to come in the door and say 'Good evening!' to them. . . ."

There was a rustling on the path; someone was coming—it was Thora.

She approached slowly and thoughtfully the spot where he was standing.—Then he was again close to her! He could have fallen on his knees and worshipped her. Lost in contemplation, he did not move; it was as if he wanted to postpone the rapture of meeting until the last moment.

She came past in an opening in the trees; the light of the full moon fell on her face. Her cheeks were very red, and her staring gaze had that glassy expression from before. He could not explain to himself the sinister feeling which this glassy-eyed stare aroused in him, and he hesitated to step forward.

Suddenly there was the sound of footsteps. Thora turned toward the sound, and a young man appeared and put his arm around her waist and led her into the arbor.

They sat down; he embraced and kissed her.

She whispered, "Where is my husband?"

"He was completely drunk when I left him."

She shivered and tore herself out of his arms. After a little, she stroked the hair from his forehead, looked him fixedly in the face, and said, "Grabow! There will come a time when you abandon me, and you will then despise me; but I don't respect you, either—you should know that."

"Now don't be childish!" he said, putting his arms around her.

Her eyes again took on that glistening, glassy expression, and their lips met in a long kiss.

"Sh!" said Thora, starting up. "I thought I heard a moan . . . it was a terrible moan."

"Ah, it was probably the wind moving the leaves! Don't worry about that!"

"No, it was somebody!—Listen, now there was a rustling behind us, down in the ditch!"

"It was probably some dirt rolling down."

"No, it was somebody! Go out and look."

When he came back, he said, "There was a man sitting and resting at the edge of the ditch, but when I came out he left. It looked like an old man. You see now that there was nothing. . . ."

Chapter 9

"BENDIXEN IS HERE!" cried Levy to Gröndal as they met early in the morning in the street.

"Oh, that's the reason you are going in a gallop. When did he arrive?"

"Yesterday afternoon he was at home asking for me.—Are you going with me up to see him? He is staying over in the hotel."

"Yes, if I can rely on him being well shaved; for we're probably supposed to kiss each other?"

"No, I had just thought of acting as though he had not been away at all. He will certainly look odd when we come in quite cooly and say hello instead of throwing ourselves around his neck."

"Sure! That's à la Wessel. I'll go along."

"Afterwards we can hold a little drinking party for him at the hospital to make up for the coolness."

"Oh, yes; you have good ideas today."

"I'm looking forward to the expressions on his face that I'll make him put on. It's a good thing that I have you along, otherwise we would probably start talking immediately about the story with Thora Fangel—I'm sure you remember, he was engaged to her."

"Yes, who has not been a fool in his younger days!"

"You talk like a book.—Let's try to get hold of the hotel clerk.—No, wait, here it is on the registration board . . . Bendixen—number 54. Good, arrange your face in the proper expression. Are you ready?"

"Listen, Levy, now that it occurs to me: I really liked Bendixen when he was here at home. Let's go in and shake his hand decently and even give him a good kiss, if it cannot be otherwise. We can, after all, dry our mouths afterward."

"Now I think, God forgive me, that you are getting soft-hearted."

"Before you think so basely of me, I will go in and put on an expression as if I were going to devour him. Knock!"

Without waiting for a "Come in," Levy opened the door and went in, with Gröndal following.

Jacob was lying fully dressed across the bed asleep; on the table stood a wax candle burned down into the candlestick, with the dying flame licking up the long snuff.

"Where the devil can he have been last night?" said Levy.

"He's lying in camp, don't you see that? He is imagining that he is still in Poland—now I know that we can surprise him without resistance! You hold his hands, and I'll hold his legs."

"No, it is cowardly to surprise one's enemy asleep; better let him sleep it off. Listen, you run out to the hospital and arrange a morning drinking party, and I'll wait until he wakes up."

"If only we could take him out there and wake him up in the middle of the party, with the clinking of glasses and bottles, he could, by the gods, be made to think that he had never been away at all!"

"Gröndal, you are getting poetic; you are making a fairy tale out of *Thousand and One Nights*."

"Am I?" said Gröndal, "Then good-by."

When he had gone, Levy rolled the blinds up and put out the candle. He sat for a while by the bed, looking at Jacob's pale, sunken features; suddenly Jacob began to groan, and Levy called out, "Bendixen! Bendixen!" softly at first, then more and more loudly, until he took Jacob by the arm and shook him.

"Who's there?" cried Jacob, starting up.

"A good friend! A Pole on his father's side!"

"Levy!" shouted Jacob, springing out of bed, "Is it you?"

"Who should it be otherwise? Who else but me would stand an hour by the clock shaking his rediscovered friend?"

"Was it a dream?" said Jacob, rubbing his eyes.

"Which one? That I was shaking you? If so, it was a damned lifelike dream."

"Yes, it was indeed a damned lifelike dream."

Levy was silent, looking at him.

"Levy!" said Jacob, seizing both his hands. "So we meet again!—Now I have nothing else in the world but you!"

"No? Then where do you have yourself? Did you leave yourself behind in Poland?"

"No, but now there is no other person I care about."

"Can I depend on that? Not even. . . ."

"Don't mention her name! Don't let me hear that name!"

"Bravo! That's the way you should talk! But you didn't need to scream so loudly; but the intent is good. This very day you can get the slip that you are discharged."

"Oh, yes, now I am cured!" said Jacob, beginning to walk up and down.

Levy followed him and said, looking at him askance, "Yes, let's just have ourselves a little exercise. Peripatetic philosophy is not to be despised, either. Well, since you are so healthy, what do you plan to do with yourself among the children of man for the benefit of them and you?"

"I had for a moment thought of going out into the street with a knife in each hand and stabbing people to death as long as I could move."

"Heavens! It was a good thing I came before you went out."

"But then I thought that then they would overpower me and institute proceedings against me and take me out to the prison, and then the whole town would go out to see the Jew beheaded."

"That's quite correct. You have, I see, used the campaign in Poland to study Danish law and justice."

"Or, on the other hand, of setting fire to the house and the town, on all sides; but then they would probably sentence me to slavery or put me in Bistrup insane asylum."

"You argue absolutely sensibly. By the way, what had the poor houses done to you?"

"But you heard that that is merely fantasy; I will let the houses stand."

"All right, that is very good, and you shall have thanks for it; but it nevertheless seems to me that there is a little fever in that fantasy. . . . Listen, that's right: you did tell my landlady that you were going to the country—haven't you been out there and caught cold last evening?"

"No, that was only a dream."

"What?"

"That I saw her."

"Did you also dream that you spoke with her?"

"No, something prevented me."

"Ah, you dreamed that her husband prevented you?"

"Yes, her husband, ha, ha, ha!"

"You laugh so heartily. Was he so funny when the two of you talked?"

"I didn't talk to him."

"Where is Benjamin? People of that kind," added Levy in an undertone, "know by instinct what is happening to the person they take a liking to."

"Benjamin? He is dead."

"Dead! Benjamin?—What did he die of?"

"Of cholera."

"Hm . . . well, I will say a *Boruch dajon emmes*![1] He has earned it.—Tell me now in brief, Bendixen: have you spoken with any of the Fangels?"

"No!"

"Good, then you should in the future be careful not to dream that you see them. People might believe you dreamed about the possibility of Engberg's needing a friend of the family."

"Ha, ha! It would certainly be wrong if people believed that."

"What belief do you yourself profess? Is your heart not oppressed by any doubt?"

"No, by heaven, I don't doubt. I am absolutely sensible."

"That's very good. Then come on, let's go out to the hospital; it can't hurt you in any case to become even more sensible."

"Levy! Seven years ago you brought me out there for the first time—what did it lead to? No, let me stay away from people; I hate them!"

"What evil have the earth's thousand million people done to you then? They must have shown themselves very ungrateful for

---

[1] Formula of blessing when someone is dead.

your benefactions, since you will no longer let your countenance
shine over them."

"Listen to me, Levy: my love for the Christians is over. If I
could eradicate them altogether, I would do it; but they are too
strong for me. Let me at least stay out of their way; let me have
to hear no more that the vilest fellow is better than I am, when
he merely uses the word 'kike'. I will try to keep control over
myself; I will live quietly and calmly and associate with nobody
but you."

"I thank you very much for the honor you have intended for
my insignificant person, but tomorrow I'm leaving for Sweden
and I'll be away for quite a while."

"Can't I go with you?"

"Not very well; when I am at the Swedish hospitals, I can't
take care of my duties as a nurse."

"Ah, I can then just as well stand on my own two feet."

"Yes, you have even learned to walk. You are a grown man;
you are even thinking of taking a knife in each hand and
stabbing people to death."

"I was carried away; I am ashamed, Levy."

"Yes, when you are in respectable company. Now come along."

"Levy, let me rather stay home!"

"You can just try out the goods out there; maybe you'll get
the taste for Danish punch again. Come along!"

"I might meet Wilhelm Fangel out there."

"Gröndal is arranging the party, and he will naturally not
send for Fangel. And even if he did, it is not for one who has
fought with Diebitsch Sabalkansky and Paskewitsch Erivansky
to be afraid of Wilhelm Fangel. Now come on and let's go!"

"Welcome, great man, here!"
sang the medical students, standing in their dressing gowns in a
double row inside the door, each with a full glass in his hand.
Levy, with a deep bow, led Jacob into the room, and when the
fanfare was sung to the end, Gröndal stepped forward and said, "I
have the floor. As director of this celebration, I call for three
cheers for the hero Bendixen, who has taught the Russians what
kind of fellows the people from the royal Danish maternity

hospital are for killing. For this man to whom the hospital owes a great deal I call for a thundering cheer. But you must not shout loudly, for there is a sick woman lying downstairs. Drain your glasses, and that is just as good as the best cheer, and as far as Bendixen is concerned, to make up for it he will be crowned with a wreath."

The door opened, and a medical student, clad in a midwifery student's dress, entered with a wreath of linden twigs and went up to Bendixen.

"That is Victoria," said Gröndal, "and the wreath is a laurel wreath. With a graceful movement the goddess will place the wreath on his head. Denmark is a grateful land."

With the effort to make the wreath fit, the goddess tore the withered leaves off, and when it finally was firmly in place it looked like a crown of thorns, which gave Jacob's pale and thin face a dying expression.

"You look too proud to me, with your laurels!" said Levy, taking it off.

"Dinner is served, gentlemen!" shouted Gröndal. "What is the hero Bendixen without food!"

Jacob had his place at the head of the table; behind him was hung a collection of the largest surgical instruments, representing a trophy of war.

"Bendixen!" somebody shouted, when there reigned a moment of quiet during the meal. "Tell us something of your deeds. The Polish women are good—black hair and red cheeks—aren't they?"

"Gentlemen!" said Levy, getting to his feet. "Our highly revered president has given me the floor. A long time will pass before you hear this voice again, for I am going away. Do not weep, my friends; we will meet again, if not here, then on the other side. Like the Indian warriors, it will console me in the hour of parting, if I can take with me the certainty that my wigwam will not stand deserted. I propose to you therefore that you permit Bendixen to take my place; the pipe which I have smoked he shall also smoke; the glass I have emptied he shall also empty; if he gets drunk out here, you will give him bed and coffee in the morning; you shall watch over his morals and virtue, as if it were my own person—do not permit any of the midwifery students to seduce him! Will you promise me that?"

"We promise!" they all shouted, raising their glasses.

"Then I am serene; then my memory will not die. Let us empty our glasses!"

"Damned if that's not my fun-loving Holstein cousin!" someone shouted. "I hear his spurs in the corridor . . . Come in!"

"Hello, Lieutenant Grabow! Welcome! Come and have a drink with us!" resounded from all sides.

"Thanks, but I'm damned if I have any great desire to drink now; I caroused last night."

"Is that any reason? In that case, you could never drink during the daytime! Will you have wine or cold punch?"

"Then first let me have some herring salad, if you have any."

"It's a constant dish here at the hospital! Take a seat on the bed beside Bendixen. He is a prodigal son who has come home. Bendixen, this is Grabow; I will say nothing else to recommend him. I am sure you will be good friends."

Bendixen looked closely at Grabow, almost more closely than politeness permitted.

He had one of those carefree, irresponsible, cheerful faces which one likes, almost against one's will. One now and then meets such a person and instinctively feels a kind of envy, for Fortune seems to have written on his forehead: I want everybody to love this naughty boy.

"Make a little room for him, Bendixen; I'm sure you two warriors can get on well together in the same bed."

"I have made room for the lieutenant," said Jacob, moving over still more.

"No, now he will end up sitting under the trophy!" cried Gröndal. "Bendixen shall not be pushed away from it—I, as the master of ceremonies and president, must see to that."

"I was not pushed away; I gave way voluntarily," said Jacob.

"I am very grateful for your courtesy," said Grabow, sitting down.

"You are not in good humor today, Lieutenant!" remarked one of the medical students.

"Oh, I was cleaned out last night."

"Did you pay?" asked his cousin.

"Yes, as long as I had anything—have you ever heard otherwise? And then I lost a lot more on my word of honor. But I'm almost convinced that one of the other players cheated. The other was so drunk that one could have pricked him on the eyelid, but he was devilishly lucky—although I didn't begrudge it to him."

"With whom were you playing?"

"Well, naturally I can't say that now after the fact. But what is the occasion of the morning drinking party here?"

"It's for Bendixen, who has come home from long journeys."

"Bendixen!" cried König, "Now you probably won't take your exam? You will live off your money and become a Maecenas for your old comrades, won't you?"

"Yes, that could well be," answered Jacob.

"How many patrons do you want?" asked Gröndal. "You are courting the Old Man in order to get the battalion surgeon's post."

"Ah, my love is not requited; Banner is getting the post."

"That's—; I almost said something I shouldn't! But he is still a junior medical student and has worse grades than you?"

"Yes, but he is from an older and better family."

"I wonder who will get the post in Vejle?"

While those around them carried on a lively conversation concerning professional matters, Lieutenant Grabow turned politely to Jacob and began a conversation. He possessed to a high degree the gift of being able to carry on a conversation almost alone. Jacob drank one glass of wine after the other and laughed loudly at several of the lieutenant's stories.

Levy bent toward them and asked, "Pardon me, but have you two met before? You look as though you were going to kiss each other."

Jacob put down the knife that he had been playing with.

Grabow replied, "Mr. Bendixen likes cavalry life just as I do. People with the same taste get acquainted quickly."

"Yes, we have the same taste," said Jacob, laughing.

"Bendixen and Grabow resemble each other, damned if they don't," said the man sitting next to Jacob. "Isn't that true, you others?"

Now that their attention had been called to it, they found that there really was a striking resemblance between the faces, in spite of differences in features.

"Yes, we might perhaps be mistaken for each other," said Jacob, bursting into song.

"I didn't exactly mean that," answered the other, "for, without flattering, Grabow is the handsomer; but that's right, Bendixen, sing a song. Let's hear a Polish song; you do have them at first hand."

"No, that won't do," said Gröndal, "she is in damned bad shape downstairs. Let's leave the table."

When Levy, Grabow, and Jacob stood outside the street entrance, Levy said, "I must go out to the customs house and speak with the captain, and then I must make the rounds saying good-by. Will you be at home in a couple of hours, Bendixen?"

"Yes, I am going straight home."

"If you are going up by way of the square, then we could walk together," said Grabow.

When they had walked a little way, Grabow began, "It is quite strange that we have known each other only a couple of hours, and it already seems to me as if we were old friends. Listen, you could give me good advice on how I am to get out of a damned pinch."

"Do you think I am the right person to turn to?" asked Jacob with a smile.

"Yes, why not? We can at least try. You see, I lost, as you probably heard before, all my cash last night. That's all the same, as far as that goes, for I can surely get through until the end of the month. But I have had my portrait painted, a kind of little miniature portrait, and I'm supposed to get it today, and the damned artists don't give credit."

"Then leave your portrait lying there until the end of the month; you can, after all, look at yourself in the mirror until then."

"Ha, ha, ha! That was damned well said. No, you see, it is intended for a present to a lady."

"Can't the lady wait till the end of the month?"

"Yes, indeed, my dear friend! But you see it was her birthday yesterday, and she was supposed to have it already yesterday, but it wasn't ready then. So I promised her last night that she would get it today."

"Oh! Yes!—Yes, that is a different matter, to be sure."

"Yes, and she is a cute little woman, besides."

"Ah, she's married!"

"Yes, but I knew her from before, over in Holstein, when I was stationed there. When I came over here recently, it was very pleasant to renew an old acquaintance."

"Then you perhaps already at that time had a little *liaison* with her, eh?"

"Heavens no! Not then.—But give me some good advice now; I *must* and *will* raise 100 rix-dollars today."

"Does the portrait cost that much?"

"No, not quite that much, but 100 rix-dollars is a nice round sum—where am I to get it?"

"There are enough people in town who lend money."

"God knows there are! But those people don't lend money without security, attachment of one's pay, accepted bill of exchange, and the like. Do you think such a fellow would have any feeling for the fact that I must send the lady of my heart my portrait? No, listen, you know what, you lend me the money, Bendixen!"

"Me? Ha, ha, ha! What a peculiar idea!"

"Why? I think it's quite in order."

"Quite in order? . . . Oh, yes! . . . That would be beautifully done . . . That deserved a reward!"

"You can set the terms yourself! I will sign without a murmur!"

"All right, Lieutenant!" said Jacob, slapping Grabow on the back. "You shall have it! On reasonable terms!"

"Hurrah!—Can I come with you and get the money?"

"No, I won't have any until a couple of days from now."

"Just like the other Jews," muttered Grabow under his breath. "But, my dear Bendixen, you know I need it today. You can, after all, just as well let me have it at once."

"On my honor, I don't have it today; I must first make arrangements for it."

"Oh, can't you easily let me have it at once?"

"Listen, Lieutenant, in two days I will do you and the lady of your heart that little service. If you want to come then, you can. Good-by!"

"The day after tomorrow, then?" the lieutenant called after him.

"Yes, the day after tomorrow."

Chapter 10

"WELL, HAVE YOU BROKEN UP some of the bonds?" asked Grabow.

"Yes, now I have the money for your portrait."

"Do I get it? It seems to me that you look as if you had changed your mind."

"That only depends on whether you accept my conditions."

"You can set the interest yourself; I won't haggle."

"Don't worry about the interest; it is something else that I require."

"What is it then? If I can do you a service, I will do it, so help me!"

"It depends on this: I want to send a little note with the portrait."

"What? Maybe a *billet d'amour?*"

"But you have not even told me the lady's name."

"That's also true . . . but you will perhaps tell her that you have lent me the money?"

"Why should I do that? What an unreasonable idea!"

"No, you do look too honest for such things."

"You can certainly know that I will not write anything which you would have occasion to avenge. It is a notion that I had."

"Yes, but it is certainly a damned strange notion—besides, the lady is not feeling really well right now."

"Did she catch cold?"

"How do you hit on that?"

"Oh, that is the usual thing when people aren't well."

"Ha, ha! Yes, you are certainly right there. But, as I said, she is not well, and it is difficult to get anything to her."

"If you can get the portrait to her, I'm sure my note can get in."

"Hm, yes; but damned if I really feel like doing that."

"Then you don't get the money."

"That's really putting a knife to my throat—well, all right; but then do me a service in return."

"What would that be?"

"There is a *kammerjunker* of my acquaintance—lend him 50 rix-dollars."

"Will that close the deal?"

"There is my hand!"

"Good, now I'll write the note."

Jacob went over the the table and wrote:

> There really was someone at the arbor last Wednesday and it was I.
>
> *Jacob Bendixen*

"Well," said Grabow, "that was short; it can't be dangerous. Give me the note, and I will certainly take care of it."

"No, just a moment! Now you can write here the tender epistle that is presumably to accompany your beloved features; then we'll put my note inside. Then we'll go over and get your portrait, and then in my presence you will send a messenger off with both parts at once. You can easily make sure that I don't hear to whom it is going."

"That is damnably thoughtful. But you can just as well leave the note to me; I will, on my honor, take care of it."

"Hm, yes.—But what misgivings can you have against my arrangement, if you really intend to take care of the note?"

"Then it seems I must be frank with you: the portrait costs only 25 rix-dollars."

"I won't deduct the rest—here is the money."

"You are a damned fine fellow! Let's go to work; however I will talk my way out of it later!"

A week later, when Jacob could no longer endure having no news from the world, he went out to the hospital.

Gröndal and some of the other medical students were sitting in a quiet and serious conversation and smoking their pipes.

When Bendixen came in, it looked as though they took little notice of him, but continued their conversation with lowered voices.

A little later one of the students went out and came back with a pair of old trousers. He went over to Bendixen and asked him, "Bendixen, how much will you lend me on these trousers?"

"What is the meaning of this?" asked Jacob, turning blazing red.

"Oh, don't pretend to be so holy! We know the whole business with Grabow and the *kammerjunker*. That went fast—you probably studied the art in Poland!"

"You will get the hospital's business," said another, "We will remember you for the sake of old acquaintance."

The flush on Jacob's face had given way to a deathly pallor; he crossed his arms over his chest and said, "What has Grabow told?"

"Oh, nothing at all remarkable!" said a student who had spoken first, stretching himself in his chair and putting his hands in his pockets. "A scene from daily life. A lieutenant is embarrassed for money and complains to Mr. Moses. Mr. Moses says that he can probably help him, but money is expensive in our times. That doesn't matter, says the lieutenant, just let me have it. Yes, I don't have it myself, says Mr. Moses, but I can get it in a couple of days. The lieutenant goes around saying delightedly that Mr. Moses is a helpful man. But a couple of days later Mr. Moses pours a whole pail of cold water on the lieutenant's enthusiasm, and the lieutenant says that the money is the costliest that he has ever received."

Jacob said, "Did Grabow tell under what terms he got the money?"

"Heavens, no, he was discreet! He said that it was a matter of honor to remain silent. . . ."

"Bendixen!" interrupted another, "Actually, that is damned well done. Two good customers at once, and so fast! But you have always had the reputation of having a good head."

Now Gröndal rose and said, "Listen, Bendixen, that pipe that Levy has smoked you will not get to smoke, and from his glass you will not get to drink. Otherwise, for Levy's sake we will not throw you out, so that you can, if you like, come and eat your meals here at the hospital."

Jacob turned silently from him and left.

"A man has been here asking for you several times," said his landlady when he came home. "He looked as though he had something important on his mind."

"Didn't he give his name?"

"No, but it was probably an officer; he will surely come back immediately. I said that Mr. Bendixen would soon come home."

"Good!" said Jacob, going to his door.

"Mr. Bendixen," said his landlady, "are you ill? You are so pale, and the whites of your eyes are quite red. Shall I not make you a good hot cup of coffee?"

"No, thanks," said Jacob, going into his room.

Shortly afterward Grabow arrived.

"Now she is dead!" he cried.

"Who?" asked Jacob, holding on to the table.

"The lady to whom you sent your note!"

"Well, what can I do about that?" said Jacob, fumbling his way to a chair.

"What you can do about it? What was in the note you sent her? She was lying there constantly screaming at the note and asking where it had come from."

"Was she in bed? Was she ill, then?"

"Yes, she had caught an inflammatory fever."

"Well, is it so strange that sick people are delirious?"

"Hm, yes . . . I must say, you are so calm that I must believe you. Damned if I didn't almost think you had written the note on poisoned paper."

"Ha, ha, ha! What accusations one can hit upon!"

"Yes, she is dead now, and it is a pity, for she was a pretty little woman.—Listen, if you should ever meet Lieutenant Engberg, don't let on, because it was his wife—now it's all right to say that, since she is dead."

"No, I won't," said Jacob.

"Listen, Bendixen, now I am coming again to you as a savior; lend me twenty rix-dollars or so—I should after all attend the funeral in style."

"Grabow! If you could sell yourself to me with skin and hair, then I would let you have the money."

"It is certainly true that I have no solid security to offer except my own person, but I can get my life insured."

Jacob raised his head and looked at him; then he said, "Oh, that's not necessary."

"Then lend me the money."

Jacob continued to stare at him without replying.

"Do me the service," Grabow persisted. "I don't know how you can be so hard. Such a rich guy like you really has power over us Christians."

"Do I?" cried Jacob, springing up. "Do I? . . . Then write down the IOU! I will dictate!"

Chapter 11

ONE WINTER MORNING the Jews' closed black hearse pulled up in front of a little house on a side street in central Copenhagen. A corpse was carried out, followed by a crowd of poor Jews, who, after the coffin was placed in the vehicle, fought for places in the coaches standing at the disposal of the funeral procession.

Some of the coaches were invaded from both sides at once so that there was a frightful crush inside, with much screaming and wailing. Other coaches were assaulted from only one side, and sometimes it happened that a person jumped in one door so hastily that he flew out the opposite one. In short, it was an old-fashioned Jewish funeral.

Behind the funeral procession walked the more distinguished pious Jews and those of the poor who had been unable to gain possession of coach seats. A mob of riffraff pursued the hearse, howling, whooping, and throwing stones; policemen dashed around in the crowd dealing out blows to those who were throwing stones and to those who were not throwing stones.

In one of the coaches sat seven elderly Jews, who, after reciprocally pushing and cursing each other, gradually calmed down. They began to look around inside the coach to find out with whom it was that they were together.

"*Bei mein Leben*—Mosche Ringstedt!" cried one, stretching out both arms—insofar as there was room—toward another who was sitting at some distance from him, in a corner, "*Wo kommst Du her?*"

"Ephraim Gedaljo, *so wohr Gott lebt!*" cried the one addressed as he struggled to free a hand to extend to his newly recognized friend.

"*Wenn kamst Du?*" asked Ephraim.

"Gestern Obend. Wie lebt Dein' Fra' und Kinder?"

"Sie essen und trinken gut, unbeschrien.[1] Worum kamst Du nit Freitog Obend? Schabbas hättest Du'n Bonensupp'[2] bei mir essen sollen—koscher,[3] bei mein Leben! Nebbisch, musz't so rasen bei Wintertog!"[4]

"Nu, nu, ich gedenke gute Masmatten[5] zu thun, dorum ras' ich. Das letzt' Hemd musz man verkafen um'n Kohtzin zu werren."[6]

"Erst gestern Obend bist Du gekommen? Und schon hier?"

"Na, 'n armer Mann musz Alles mitnehmen. 'S wird 'n gut Zedoko geben."[7]

"Und Wie![8] Der wor reich, und do sind kane arme jorschim,[9] die 'nem armen Mann 's bischen Verdienst schief ansehen."

"Was wor er eigenlich? Ich kenne ihn gor nit! Er hiesz Jainkef Bendit, nit wohr?"

"Was wor er? Woher? Ich wa'sz nit! Do wird 'n gut Zedoko geben—dorum bin ich mitgegangen!"

"I have him known!" said one of the others who wanted to be more distinguished than the first two and therefore spoke Danish.

All the six others turned to the speaker, as quickly as the space permitted.

"Who is he?" Mosche Ringsted quietly asked his neighbor.

"That's Schaie Jisroel. He has more money than you and I!"

"He was a pious man!" began Schaie Jisroel, and raised his eyes reverently toward the coach ceiling.

---

[1] An almost untranslatable word; literally "not summoned," i.e., "knock on wood."

[2] I.e., Scholunt.

[3] Pure, sumptuous.

[4] "You, poor soul, have to travel like this on winter days."

[5] Business, trade.

[6] A Jewish saying: "You have to sell your last shirt to become a rich man."

[7] "Generous funeral alms will be distributed." (At the grave, alms in proportion to the deceased's fortune are distributed to the poor.)

[8] "And how!" i.e., "You can bet on that!"

[9] Heirs.

"Pious?" one of the others interrupted him, "I never heard him named among the Chadissim."[10]

"Oh, he had his own ways. But he went regularly to *Schul*, and on Yom Kippur he stayed there, just as well as the most pious, the whole day. He had his seat next to me, so I know," he added with authority.

Since no one dared to contradict him, he continued, "He was a pious man! He gave more voluntary gifts to the Jewish Free School than the whole *Kohl*[11] together. He was in all the *Chrevras*,[12] and whenever he discovered a Jewish boy apprenticed to a Christian, he immediately saw to it that he was taken in by a Jewish master. As soon as a boy was put into those damned college classes that make the best Jew into a *Goy*, he was right there and got the boy put behind a counter. *Zichrono livrocho!*"[13]

"What *Geschäft* was he in?" asked Mosche Ringstedt.

Here Schaie Jisroel's face darkened, and he said, "What *Geschäft* was he in? Better ask, what *Geschäft* did he ruin? He ruined the *Geschäft*, my *Masmatten*. They ought to give *me Zedoko!* Just yesterday the fat *kammerjunker* came to me. Yes, he says, you'll probably demand a lien on my salary or a security, my good Mr. Israel.— Demand? I say, I don't *demand* a lien or a security, *Herr Kammerjunker*.—Will you lend me money without that, then? he asks.—If the *kammerjunker* wants to borrow money, I say laughing, then that's another matter.—Oh, he says, Bendixen was a completely different man; but now he's upped and died on us. He was a *Schentelman*, my good Mr. Israel. If in a pinch a man didn't have either a salary lien or a security, he could offer his word of honor, and he accepted it, as if he understood about words of honor. You don't, Mr. Israel.—No, God forbid, *Herr Kammerjunker!* I said; any other solid security, only not a word of honor. For ages I've had so many words of honor outstanding from lieutenants that I could equip a whole army.—

---

[10] Outstandingly holy men.

[11] Congregation.

[12] Charitable organizations.

[13] "Blessed be his memory."

Then the *kammerjunker* laughed and pawned a pair of new epaulettes that he had probably just got from the goldsmith and paid for with his word of honor."

"*Schentelman?*" Mosche Ringstedt asked his neighbor. "What is that, a *Schentelman?*"

"How do I know?" replied the man consulted. "It's probably somebody who charges a hundred percent."

"All the rest of the scum," Schaie Jisroel continued, "he referred to me. That *Masmatten* is good; a man actually earns more by lending three marks on a coat or a shirt than by lending 100 rix-dollars on the salaries of the high and mighty. But there is so damned much weeping and wailing, and it's easy to leave yourself open to *risches*. He was open to it, too, *ohne* that, just because he *didn't* want to lend them. If a poor woman stood in front of his door and begged no matter how much to borrow one mark on a scarf, and even if it was worth five rix-dollars, he wouldn't let her in. Then *kemech* said that he was a miser, a blood-sucker, and a kike . . . kike—they love to say that. Next door to me lives a Christian who charges 200 percent, they call him a kike, too."

"To hell with the kikes!" someone screamed outside, and a rock sailed through the coach window.

"*Ole mi jat!*"[14] cried Mosche Ringstedt as he shrank back in the coach. In the avenues outside the gates the policemen raced after the boys.

After a period of anxious silence, curiosity awoke again in the passengers, and Mosche Ringstedt asked, with an expression as if his mouth were watering, "Did he really do such good *Masmatten?*"

"*Avaddo!*[15] He had more than he could manage. I was supposed to have gone into partnership with him."

"You, Schaie Jisroel?" somebody asked expectantly.

---

[14] A garbled pronunciation of "Olom at"—"In eternity." Here is implied a curse on whoever threw the rock, or else Mosche Ringstedt meant to vow that he would never again go to such a funeral.

[15] "Certainly" or "You bet your life!"

Schaie Jisroel didn't answer immediately, in order to enjoy the curiosity of his listeners, then went on, "Last Yom Kippur we were standing together in *Schul*, like always. Then Doctor Levy came in and stood right in front of us. . . ."

"Doctor Levy?" Mosche Ringsted broke in, "Is he a son of Leibche Levy, who was married to a daughter of Mendel Kohn?"

"No," answered Ephraim Gedaljo, "He is a son of Leib Schächter."

"Och, of little Leibche Schächter? I knew him! And his son is a doctor? Is he a good one? Does he have much to do?"

"*Und wie!* He has just come home from Sweden, there they made a lot over him!"

"That's a real *naches*[16] to hear! So what about him, Mr. Israel?"

"If you can just let me tell and save your questions," said Schaie Jisroel crossly, "Well, he came in and stood right in front of us. He stared at Bendixen, and then I also looked at him. *Nebbisch,*[17] he was quite pale, he surely couldn't stand the fasting. Then the doctor said, How's it going, Bendixen? A lot to do?—Bendixen answered, I'm nearly drowning!—Then the doctor said, Do you have more to do than you can manage? You ought to go into partnership with your colleague, Mr. Schaie Jisroel.—I winked at the doctor to show that I was agreeable.—Yes, said Bendixen.—I took his arm and said, Now, now, we can discuss that tomorrow; I'll come up to see you.—Then he turned to me and stared at me, and all of a sudden, thud! *do liegt er!* and the doctor had to take him home. From that day on he wasn't able to carry on his *Geschäft* any longer, but got weaker and weaker, until he died—I was that close to it!"

"What did he die of?" asked Mosche Ringstedt.

"They say, of an old wound," answered Schaie Jisroel. "He had been in the war when he was young."

"When he was young? I didn't think he was an old man," said one of the others.

---

[16] Joy.

[17] "The poor devil."

"Well, I'm just saying that; he looked older than he was."

"In the war?" said Ephraim Gedaljo. "Well, there he *oser*[18] ate *koscher* and kept *Schabbas*."

"He wasn't pious in his younger days. He is even supposed to have been engaged to a *Schikse*.[19] But then the Lord's spirit came over him, and he left her and became an orthodox Jew. Do you know Reisches Aron, Ephraim Gedaljo? Well, he sat with him along with Doctor Levy, the last days he was sick. The last night he didn't utter a word. When death came, he sat up and stared around and called out for the Law of Moses, the blessed Torah."

"Didn't he say his *Schema Jisroel?*" asked the persistent doubter.

"No, but he called out, as I'm telling you, for the Law of Moses, the *gebenschte* Torah, and that is just as good! He was a pious man. *Gebenscht sei sein Neschommo!*"[20]

They arrived at the cemetery, and the coach discharged its burden.

While the corpse, in accordance with the Law, was washed in warm and cold water in the mortuary, Uncle Marcus and his two sons sat with the funeral *Chevro*[21] and sang *Tehillim*[22] in a subdued voice; the other members of the procession strolled back and forth on the paths and in the courtyard.

When the corpse was wrapped in the Thallis and laid in the flat, rough coffin, Uncle Marcus and his two sons were summoned. They got up weeping and went out to put stockings on the deceased and ask him for *mechilo*.[23]

The lid was placed on the coffin, and the call went out, "*Zu Halvaio!*"[24]

---

[18] An exclamation of negation. Here it can be translated approximately with "For damned sure . . . not."

[19] Christian girl.

[20] "Blessed be his soul."

[21] Organization, society.

[22] The Psalms of David.

[23] For forgiveness for the wrong they might have done him while he was alive.

[24] To the pallbearers.

The pallbearers lifted the bier onto their shoulders and started moving out to the cemetery, while the *gabbe*[25] circulated in the crowd and rattled the poorbox, calling out, "*Zedoko tatzil mimoves!*"[26]

At the entrance to the cemetery between the low, frosted trees the bier was set down on the ground, a circle was formed, and the prayer *Hazur tomim poalo*[27] was softly and monotonously recited, and then, quietly praying, they lifted it again onto their shoulders and carried it to the grave, reciting the prayer *Yoseif beseiser elyon*.[28]

Around the little mound of earth and the grave they again formed a circle. Amid profound silence the lid was pushed aside and a little bag of earth was placed under the deceased's head. The lid was screwed down and the coffin was lowered into the grave.

Outside there were bellows of "Bloodsucker! Kike!" and rocks were hurled, followed by howls under the police clubs. A rock sailed in and reached the grave, landing on the coffin, which resounded with a hollow sound; it was as if the corpse were moaning.

A closed padlock was thrown into the grave as a sign that at this funeral all further mortality should be locked up, and then Uncle Marcus stepped forward and cast the three first spadefuls of earth; after him came his two sons, then the rest of those present. As soon as one had tossed in earth, he went out of the cemetery and washed his hands in the courtyard.

When everybody was gone, one single figure remained standing at the grave; it was Levy.

He looked for a time after the departing crowd, and when he was alone, he folded his hands and offered a silent prayer. Then he took a little earth from the grave and concealed it in his breast.

---

25 The president of the funeral society.

26 "Charity is salvation from death!"

27 "The acts of the Creator are above reproach."

28 "He who is throned in the shadow of eternity."

When he started to go, he turned around once more; for a long time he looked out over the town, toward the woods where he had seen the deceased in youth's joy of life, and said,

"He once believed in eternal poetry and eternal life!"

Author's Afterword

FROM TIME IMMEMORIAL, writers have had the reputation for being *genus irritabile* and averse to acknowledging faults in their works. If this is true, it does not come merely from egoism or vanity, for even with the best will to judge himself impartially, a poet or writer can have great difficulty in placing himself outside his work immediately or shortly after its publication. Moreover, a work that has been composed with love and solicitude contains the intellectual maturity which the writer possessed at the time of its composition, and some time must obviously elapse before he can look back on it with greater maturity.

A *Jew* was written in the years 1843–45. Whether I was satisfied with the book when it came out or not, is, I am sure, immaterial to the public, and I therefore observe only that I now believe I have seen the faults from which the composition suffered. The question has then been what I should do with regard to the second edition. The justification for publishing the book again lies in the fact that a book dealer wanted to publish it after it had been sold out almost since its appearance. But on the one hand I could not have it printed with all the faults and defects which I saw clearly; on the other hand I hardly had the right to rework it completely, inserting new action and new characters in the old names, and making the first edition a used frame for a new painting.

I have tried to solve the problem by undertaking changes which are seemingly insignificant; they consist in the letter which is inserted at the end of Part 2, Chapter 15, and in the answer to it, by which Levy's letter to Jacob has been enlarged, in Part 3, Chapter 6, V. They are insignificant in volume, and, moreover, I believe that any reader will read them as something naturally belonging here, which was only forgotten in the first edition. But without altering or expanding the story, these additions call attention to the principal religious question and contribute to answering it, even if not exhaustively, and the tragic ending which the whole action acquires is thereby somewhat better motivated.

Without regard to how the defect is now remedied, and indeed without regard to the more or less poetic treatment—the composition of characters and situations—one might think that the Jewish material, which is the basis of the book, has become out of date. This will, to a certain extent, be correct, insofar as one is referring to the civic changes that have taken place in recent years.[1] But if one means that opinion, public sentiment, atmosphere, and instincts have changed in the same way, I think I may decidedly deny it. Nor has Jewish life ceased within the circle embraced by the awareness of the readers; the law granting political equality—only three years old—has not yet been able to have its full effect, and the question will remain: what relationship to themselves and to their faith will those come to have, who take advantage of the civic freedom and equality; and in what conflicts will those find themselves, who are brought up in the true, quiet Jewish family life, in accordance with tradition, and thereafter come into contact with the Christian world? Both sorts still exist in many different nuances, just as they did seven years ago.

In the last chapter I have somewhat softened what in the first edition was presented too sharply and cuttingly, but in this connection I am bound to say that even if I could have reworked the entire book and added a lengthy exposition of the religious conflict, along with this I would still have kept essentially the present conclusion. The reason for this is that I believe that it contains a profound, if bitter, truth. I can supply no proof for this, since I think that judgment in this matter can be

---

[1] Concerning this I could have wished to add something in the two English translations of the first edition which have appeared. But since I did not initiate nor contribute to these translations, nor did I have the opportunity of reading them before their publication, I could hardly write an introduction, although at the last minute this possibility was offered to me.

pronounced only by those "who have their blood in it," and they
would be regarded by others as partial. Nor could the proof be
adduced at the moment, unless I of necessity mixed into the
matter a great deal from daily life, from that life which is
written in the sand, obliterated, and rewritten. I only call
attention to the fact that the last part of the catastrophe, which
in its entirety is inevitable in one way or another, now comes in
the way that Grabow, making Jacob's acquaintance and hearing
that he is rich, instinctively notes that side of Jacob's nature
and life which seems to him to be related to the sordid. He wants
to borrow money from Jacob, and, completely misunderstanding
Jacob's words, eventually thinks that he can do this by offering
good "terms." And when the matter proceeds and Jacob has
appearances against him, these appearances are quickly
interpreted as the truth by others—far more quickly and easily
than if he possessed a certificate of baptism. What must now
happen, when misfortune weighs him down and the world has
turned away from him? Jacob is by nature too ethnically Jewish
and also in part too weak, in part too sensitive to be able to rise
above society; he withdraws within the synagogue's narrow walls,
to his affectionate late family's home, and since he takes refuge
there only out of bitterness and anger, he cannot attain there the
love and peace which is undeniably to be found in this secluded
life. He makes it a fortress from which he fights; he wants to do
good to his own, but to do good by helping them away from the
Christian whom he himself has loved. During this short
attempt to lead this life, which is hateful to his nature, he
suffocates; he perishes from lack of air in the enclosed space into
which he believes himself thrust by the world. This could be
developed more in all its details, but it would have then become
more painful without gaining in an esthetic regard.

Besides the changes cited, consisting of additions, here and
there abridgments have been undertaken; notably, an entire
section with its historic description of Polish conditions has been
cut out.

In a number of details concerning Jewish legends and
customs, the present edition is more accurate than the first. For
example, in Part 1, Chapter 4, in the story of Joseph's brothers in

Egypt, I have used a written tradition instead of an oral one, and although the changes consist only of a few lines, it seems to me that the description has taken on a new, almost dramatic life.

In the same place in the first edition there was added an inaccurate note with reference to the words "the next evening of the festival." The correct explanation is this: the Jews' holy days are determined according to the new moon. In the old days, while the Temple was standing, they observed most painstakingly from an observatory the moment when the new moon occurred, and at the same moment they lit a beacon on one of the mountain peaks near Jerusalem. Beacon upon beacon shone then over the Holy Land, informing, within a few minutes, all Jews that it was the new moon. Since the Sadducees were in constant conflict with the Sanhedrin—when they had not themselves, through a revolution, installed its members—they once had the idea of playing a trick on it and lit the beacon prematurely. History or legend does not discuss specifically the more detailed consequences of this quite characteristic event. After the destruction of Jerusalem, the Jews had to make do with their lunar calendar, but since this cannot always be absolutely accurate with regard to that moment when the new moon occurs—between the 29th and the 30th day—the days are celebrated doubly, to avoid any mistake. Exceptions are fast-days and sabbaths.

In the long note in Part 1, Chapter 7, a few words are added concerning the care which is taken, in the reading out of the Torah, to avoid reminding any of the readers of either a misfortune or a mistake. A historical anecdote can be added to this. When King Agrippa (who became mortally ill in the theater in Caesarea) was once present in the Temple, it so happened that precisely those words in the Torah were read out, in which it is forbidden for a foreigner to rule over the Jews. He burst into tears—for he was of the Idumaean Herodes family—but the whole assemblage called to him, "Don't worry, Agrippa, you are our brother!"

1 June 1852

KENNETH H. OBER

Translator's Afterword

WHEN THE DANISH WRITER and journalist Meïr Goldschmidt (1819–1887) published his first novel in Copenhagen in 1845, it created a sensation. It realistically depicted, for the first time, the life of a cultured and enlightened Jew from birth to death. The European reading public was accustomed to Jews being portrayed in literature either as comic figures or, less frequently, as hopelessly idealized cardboard ones. Now the Jewish character was being presented "from the inside," and it was the first time that readers in general had been allowed an intimate look at Jewish household ceremony and synagogue ritual. This "exposé" was resented by many Jews, who still vividly remembered the organized anti-Jewish riots and pogroms which had spread across Europe in 1819, the year of Goldschmidt's birth. Most of the Jewish population would have preferred to remain inconspicuous and unnoticed. Probably expressing their thought, the Danish Jewish critic Georg Brandes (1842–1927) wrote in 1869, "Goldschmidt should not, as I once heard a witty Jew express it, constantly serve up his grandmother with sharp sauce."

The novel established its author not only in Denmark, where a second edition appeared in 1852 and a third in 1899, but abroad as well. Translations appeared in German, Yiddish, and Russian, and two translations were printed in England in the same year, 1852. Unfortunately, neither translation was adequate, and both have long been unavailable. One was done by Mary Howitt, that indefatigable amateur translator of Scandinavian literature who is probably virtually singlehandedly responsible for the fact that Hans Christian Andersen, another of her victims, has only recently begun to be properly understood in the English-speaking world. The other translator, Anne S. Bushby, had also had a stab at translating H. C. Andersen, with no better results. Neither lady seems actually to have been very competent in the Danish language; Mrs. Howitt's title page bore the admission "adapted from the Danish"—a phrase quietly dropped when her translation was reprinted in 1864. (Incidentally, Mrs. Howitt once accused H. C. Andersen of not knowing Danish well!) Since the translations by no means do justice to the original, it is just as well that they are long out of print and unavailable, even in research libraries. A new translation has long been needed of this unquestioned classic of European literature.

The novel, in demonstrating the destructive effects of the nineteenth-century European environment on an idealistic Jewish personality, broke new ground in several respects. European readers were by the mid-nineteenth century accustomed to Byronic heroes, but Goldschmidt's novel presented them with their first Jewish hero with Byronic overtones. But more importantly, this was the readers' first acquaintance with Jewish customs and rituals, presented authentically in the language of the Danish Jews themselves. Goldschmidt found it necessary to provide extensive footnotes to translate the Yiddish and Hebrew expressions and to explain the ceremonies and customs presented.

Although many of these expressions and customs are widely recognized and understood by present-day non-Jewish readers, the footnotes are, of course, retained in this translation for their historical and literary value. Danish scholars (e.g., Anja Nathan) have demonstrated that Goldschmidt's descriptions of Jewish life and culture in Denmark at the time are correct and accurate. Even during Goldschmidt's time, assimilation and acceptance of the Jews in Denmark were proceeding rapidly, and there was soon to be no "Jewish problem" in Denmark (witness the Danes' organized rescue of almost the entire Jewish population from the Nazis during the occupation). But Goldschmidt himself had had to feel the corrosive effects of anti-Semiticism constantly, for example from Grundtvig and even from Kierkegaard. Especially insidious was what the Danes call the "little anti-Semitism," which is, obviously, still very much with us.

A new, accurate translation of Goldschmidt's novel is long overdue. It is a literary masterpiece that deserves the international audience that such a translation will provide; it is also a masterpiece of historical writing. Not only does it preserve in realistic colors a picture of the Jewish culture of nineteenth-century Denmark as it has never been painted before or since, but the destructive effects of anti-Semitism depicted there—destructive for Jew and Christian alike—constitute one more warning that still needs to be heard.

Goldschmidt related that once in a conversation with a close Christian friend, he had for the first time unburdened himself of his accumulated sorrow, resentment, and bitterness over the oppressed condition of Jews, even in the relatively tolerant Denmark of the time. The friend had simply not been conscious of the restrictions placed on the Jews, and had said, as they were parting, "With feelings like those, one writes a novel." Goldschmidt went home and wrote the final chapter of the book the same night. This final chapter distills and concentrates the author's bitter message.

This translation was made from the second edition, which was revised by the author and which appeared in 1852. The footnotes are those of the author. Translator's comments are enclosed in square brackets.

Kenneth H. Ober

Some Titles in the Series
JAMES J. WILHELM
General Editor

1. Lars Ahlin, *Cinnamoncandy*.
   Translated from Swedish by Hanna Kalter Weiss.

2. *Anthology of Belgian Symbolist Poets*.
   Translated from French by Donald F. Friedman.

3. Ariosto, *Five Cantos*.
   Translated from Italian by Leslie Z. Morgan.

4. *Kassia: The Legend, the Woman, and Her Work*.
   Translated from Greek by Antonia Tripolitis.

5. Antonio de Castro Alves, *The Major Abolitionist Poems of
   Castro Alves*. Translated from Portuguese by Amy A. Peterson.

6. Li Cunbao, *The Wreath at the Foot of the Mountain*.
   Translated from Chinese by Chen Hanming and
   James O. Belcher.

7. Meïr Goldschmidt, *A Jew*.
   Translated from Danish by Kenneth Ober.

8. Árpád Göncz, *Plays and Other Writings of Árpád Göncz*.
   Translated from Hungarian by Katharina and
   Christopher Wilson.

9. Ramón Hernández, *Invitation to Die*.
Translated from Spanish by Marion Freeman.

10. Edvard Hoem, *The Ferry Crossing*.
Translated from New Norwegian by
Frankie Denton Shackelford.

11. Henrik Ibsen, *"Catiline" and "The Burial Mound."*
Translated from Dano-Norwegian by Thomas Van Laan.

12. Banabhatta, *Kadambari: A Classic Sanskrit Story of Magical Transformations*. Translated from Sanskrit by
Gwendolyn Layne.

13. *Selected Poems of Lina Kostenko*.
Translated from Ukranian by Michael Naydan.

14. Baptista Mantuanus, *Adulescentia: The Eclogues of Mantuan*.
Translated from Latin by Lee Piepho.

15. *The Mourning Songs of Greek Women*.
Translated from Greek by Konstantinos Lardas.

16. *Ono no Komachi: Poems, Stories, and Noh Plays*.
Translated from Japanese by Roy E., Nicholas J.,
and Helen Rebecca Teele.

17. Adam Small, *Kanna–He Is Coming Home*.
Translated from Afrikaans by Carrol Lasker.

18. Federigo Tozzi, *Ghisola*.
Translated from Italian by Charles Klopp.

19. *The Burden of Sufferance: Women Poets in Russia*.
Translated from Russian by Albert Cook and Pamela Perkins.

20. Chantal Chawaf, *Mother Love, Mother Earth*.
Translated from French by Monique Nagem.